2000

Free, Perfect, and Now

Connecting to the Three Insatiable Customer Demands: A CEO's True Story

Robert Rodin

with Curtis Hartman

A Touchstone Book
Published by Simon & Schuster
NEW YORK   LONDON   TORONTO   SYDNEY   SINGAPORE

To Gordon Marshall, who created a great company; to Dick Bentley, Nida Backaitis, and my colleagues at Marshall Industries, who made it grow; and to my wife, Debbie, without whose support the story would never have been told.

TOUCHSTONE
Rockefeller Center
1230 Avenue of the Americas
New York, NY 10020

First Touchstone Edition 2000

TOUCHSTONE and colophon are registered trademarks of
Simon & Schuster, Inc.

Designed by Karolina Harris

Manufactured in the United States of America

10 9 8 7 6 5 4 3 2 1

The Library of Congress has cataloged the Simon & Schuster edition as follows:

Rodin, Robert.
    Free, perfect, and now : connecting to the three insatiable customer demands :
a CEO's true story / Robert Rodin with Curtis Hartman.
        p.   cm.
    1. Customer services—United States.   2. Consumer satisfaction—United
States.   3. Customer relations—United States.   I. Hartman, Curtis.   II. Title.
HF5415.5.R63   1999
658.8'12—dc21   98-47849
                                                                                                    CIP

ISBN 0-684-85022-2
    0-684-86312-X (Pbk)

Contents

Introduction

Picture yourself for a moment, sitting at a desk, flipping through the latest issue of your industry trade paper. What would be the headline that would make your blood run cold? How about a report that Microsoft was about to enter your industry? Or that your biggest competitor was now open for business around the clock? What if some upstart .com IPO with a multibillion-dollar market cap were targeting your customers, promising new e-commerce capabilities and lower costs? Or a newly merged communications powerhouse had found a way to marry its infrastructure with your interface and content?

No wonder so many managers today are so apprehensive about the future. It is too easy to imagine the worst—and too common to find that reality exceeds it. We live in an age of anxiety, no matter what business we're in, where only the paranoid survive, as Andy Grove so famously put it. There are no safe havens anymore, no protected markets or regions. There is no way to predict exactly from where the next competitive threat will come, only that it will come. Soon.

A year ago, as I was finishing the hardcover edition of this book, I worried that some of what I'd written might seem too "out there" to mainstream managers. Terms like *24/7, bandwidth,* and *convergence* were considered arcane. People were still debating if, how, and how soon network technology would change the way business worked. Inside my own industry I'd been labeled "Captain Internet," dismissed as an alarmist for my insistence that companies would either have to make radical changes or risk competitive obsolescence.

What a difference a year can make. Today—with Internet usage projected to grow more than one thousand times over the next five years; with IPOs exploding and venture funding pouring into virtually every vertical market; with thousands upon thousands of new companies launching new ideas, technologies, and organizational models around the world; with new alliances and new competitors with new solutions for enterprise resource planning and customer relationship management—the debate is over. Everything is being transformed. Now. Totally. The question today instead is how soon the distinction between e-business and conventional commerce will disappear completely.

I didn't write *Free, Perfect, and Now* to offer a glimpse into a crystal ball, however. I wrote it to help leaders at all organizational levels prepare for a future that remains turbulent and unpredictable. Told in the context of a real company in a real world, it is about understanding the vector and velocity of change, recognizing the larger trends in the marketplace, and discovering how to ride them, individually and as part of a team. It explores how to break down barriers and build connections, creating organic structures to help people and technology work together dynamically, aligned with the voice of the customer and the forces of marketplace change. Those issues remain as critical today as when I first started writing.

The job of a leader is to be ahead of the curve, to look beyond conventional expectations and outside individual experience. Curiosity is the best driver, knowledge the most valuable capital. We are accountable to the future, not just one part of the puzzle, responsible for our own competitiveness in a continually shifting context. Nothing can, or should, get rid of the anxiety that pressure produces. But that anxiety, if harnessed, can ignite an exhilarating journey of discovery, learning, and growth, as you'll see in the chapters that follow.

The year 1999 brought change for Marshall Industries as well. We've been profiled in a Harvard Business School case study and dissected in MIT classrooms. We were named the number-one business-to-business Web site in the world for two consecutive years by *Advertising Age* magazine, the number-one most comprehensive business-to-business site by *Business 2.0* magazine, and the number-one information-technology innovator by *Information Week* magazine.

We've changed organizationally, too, aligning ourselves with the larger forces of industry consolidation, supplier policy, and compressed margins. By merging with Avnet, one of our two largest competitors, we've expanded our boundaries once again, combining Marshall's collaborative culture and innovative technology design with Avnet's global infrastructure and product coverage, creating a new competitive solution that made sense for customers, suppliers, and employees alike, and delivering a 121-percent premium to Marshall's shareholders. For all of those changes, though, the challenges we face remain the same as they were when I started this book. They are the same challenges you face, with the same risks and opportunities.

The future is today—not the next five years, but the next five minutes. Your customers will keep demanding more, cheaper, faster, better, pushing you toward the impossible competitive ideal: free, perfect, and now.

Will you invent tomorrow's marketplace, or will you become its victim?

1
The Customer Connection:

Addressing the Problem

"Why Do They Call It an Idiot Light?"

Do you lie awake at night, as I do, worrying that someone will come along tomorrow and eat your lunch?

In the electronic '90s, knowledge is king, the Web never sleeps, and competitive challenge increases exponentially. It's easy to feel overwhelmed. Dizzied by the frenetic pace of change and confused by overwhelming choices, too many managers react with too little too late—then sit back and watch as their companies or their careers slowly wither.

Could this be you?

Absolutely.

Does it have to be you?

Absolutely not—if you can open your eyes to the three new imperatives of customer-focused organizational design: *free, perfect, and now.*

Whether we work in the glass towers of the *Fortune* 500 or a garage startup in Silicon Valley, all of us in business wrestle with the same intractable dilemmas. How do we compete in a networked world of mass customization, shrinking margins, and global competition? Yesterday change came gradually; today it comes in a flood. How can we ensure that our organizations offer substantial value to our customers now—and in the future? No one knows what the world will look like in five years or even five minutes. How can we prepare for a tomorrow that we can't predict?

I don't have an easy answer to either of these questions. If there were a pill you could take to stay ahead of the curve, I would have taken it myself long ago. What I have instead is a story of management on trial; a tale of transformation, of great risk for great reward, and of the hard lessons we have learned about inventing a new future.

As it happens, it is my own story, and that of Marshall Industries, the electronics distributor I lead, but the challenges we faced at Marshall are those confronting every organization anywhere in the world today. I'm not a consultant pretending that change is a matter of five steps and a pep talk: I've lived inside its gut-wrenching turmoil. Six years ago we bet our company on a radical experiment, tearing our healthy $500 million business down to bedrock. We threw out all of our old motivational tools, taking 1,100 managers off management-by-objectives (MBOs) plans and incentives as well as abolishing commissions for our 600 salespeople. We changed every operating system at the same time. Then we set out to reinvent ourselves. From those sleepless nights and desperate choices, I've brought back a new perspective and a new prescription, tested in a bare-knuckle business: a better way to think about designing an organization to master the currents of change.

It starts, like everything else in business, with customers. No matter what business you're in, your customers all want the same three things: They want it *free,* they want it *perfect,* and they want it *now.*

Impossible, you say? What do *you* want when you buy? Don't you think your customers want the same things?

Impossible or not doesn't matter in the end, because these three things are what the market searches for regardless. I guarantee you that as you read this, somewhere, around the corner or around the world, someone is figuring out how to sell your product or service cheaper, faster, or better than you've yet imagined. Recognizing that, your survival depends on your ability to create an organization that can chase those same elusive goals, only even faster—or risk losing your customers to the competitor who does.

Look at how drastically your own day-to-day activities have changed, from the way you book your airline ticket to how you get your money from an ATM to shopping for car prices on the Internet. Five years ago, who had a cellular phone or a fax machine at home? Now they're everywhere, changing the way all of us connect and communicate. The business landscape has changed even more dramatically. Today, the world competes in ways we couldn't have imagined a few years ago, driven by six powerful forces: networked technology, globalization, demographics, the compression of product life cycles, mass customization, and the growing importance of supply-chain management.

"Only Connect"

Marshall Industries is a fifty-two-year-old, $1.7 billion electronics distributor, traded on the New York Stock Exchange. But we're as different today from the old seat-of-the-pants middleman as the Internet is from a cow path. Think of us as a high-speed junction box, a connection between two sets of incredibly demanding constituencies. On the one side, we have some 150 suppliers, such as Toshiba, Texas Instruments, and Hitachi, all depending on us to get their products to market. On the other, we have over sixty thousand customers, including IBM, Hewlett-Packard, and WebTV, who rely on us to get them what they need. We're in the middle, thirty-seven locations and 1,600 people, 600 of them salespeople.

It can get pretty intense inside all that. Suppliers and customers measure the life cycles of successful products in months. They live or die on their time-to-market and time-to-volume, and turn to us for help with increasingly complex inventory, manufacturing, and quality-control problems.

And Marshall delivers. We still move boxes—we ship over ten thousand cartons through our robotic warehouse each day—but we also sell our ability to move information, the real-time business intelligence our customers need most, available twenty-four hours a day, seven days a week by phone or fax or over one of our twenty-four Internet sites. We still deliver parts—over 250,000 different items, ranging from semiconductors and disk drives to liquid-crystal displays and programmable logic devices—but we also sell our ability to create made-to-order solutions, our collective thinking power to anticipate the customer's business problems and to design processes to solve them.

"Virtual distribution," we call it, and it has turned our conventionally successful $500 million company into a $1.7 billion iconoclast in under six years. No less an authority than Bill Gates has decreed that in the wired world, the middleman is obsolete, but we're proving him wrong. We are becoming our customers' connection to the future, connecting people to people, people to technology, answers to questions, solutions to problems, and order to chaos.

Virtual distribution didn't spring fully formed from my head one bright spring morning. The initial vision of value-added service through a seamless and frictionless connection with each customer's infrastructure was largely mine. But the reality, however, was developed through thousands of conversations over the last six years, involving everyone in the company talking day to day with their customers and one another, taking thousands of small steps up the learning curve.

Every day, suppliers and customers make instantaneous choices about which distributor to use. The challenge is to nurture relationships that become more meaningful as they progress. We have to be able to provide sophisticated answers to problems that customers may not even know they have. Like a furniture designer trying to create an ergonomic chair, we've tried to design our interface to fit customer needs, letting their voices tell us how our processes should look and feel. Everyone at Marshall asks the same one-on-one question: How can I serve you better? How can we more quickly achieve the goals of free, perfect, and now? We are discovering what virtual distribution can mean, together, through the answers we find.

Of course we're open twenty-four hours a day—customers around the globe want service around the clock.

Of course we're open-book, open-architecture, open-door—knowledge is power, and it needs to be spread, not hoarded.

Of course we're continually accelerating our investment in research and development—technology lets us break down the walls between us and them, and helps to build the trust that deepens partnerships.

Our customers wanted a connection that was faster, cheaper, and easier to use, so we learned how to give it to them. We'd wasted time, energy, and money moving paper through a system of evaluation, sign off, or approval. Every data-collection point provided an opportunity for error. Now we move that information electronically, making it available to everyone who needs it whenever they need it, simply with the click of a mouse. Marshall's customers can monitor an individual order until the parts arrive at their assembly line; they can check backlog and inventory status electronically; they can measure their materials usage against modeled demand projections. Suppliers can watch what's moving in their markets, by part number or region, in dollars or units, then tailor their production, pricing, and forecasting against Marshall's numbers. Engineers can review the latest specifications sheets and technical information for any piece on Marshall's line card; they can order a standard sample or order a sample specifically tested for their design, whenever and from wherever they want.

We didn't just increase the quantity of information we share, though. We improved its quality too, by designing our software to analyze such competitive problems as order planning, supply managing, demand modeling, and strategic forecasting. When a customer talks with a Marshall employee, there is no need to waste time with transactional basics; they can both see the same numbers and share the same real-time picture of opportunities and trends. Thus, they can take on specific individual headaches together and tailor solutions that optimally take advantage of each company's skills. We have become supply-chain managers, connecting our business partners to the expertise and support they need to stay competitive, leading a growing global alliance that is spreading through Western Europe, the former Eastern bloc, Israel, South America, and Asia.

We don't always get it right, of course. Virtual distribution remains a work in progress. We've made some good strategic decisions and executed some of them well, but we've made some bad decisions, too, and executed them terribly. It's not the specific decisions that matter, however; no single new process or tool makes the big difference. What matters is the overall design process itself, using a method of asking questions that nurtures continuous innovation and teamwork, builds customer focus and employee involvement, and delivers ever newer ways to add value for the customer.

Every manager wants customer-focused employees and teamwork, of course, but few actually design the system necessary to create them. Instead, managers often get up on the soapbox at a meeting and announce, "We're going to be more competitive this quarter. We're going to be more flexible. We're going to improve quality and increase teamwork."

If you're just trying to make a halftime pitch, that may be a fine message, but as a strategy it won't get you any real traction. What exactly should "more competitive" mean to your organization? How can you know if you have the processes and structures in place to increase competitiveness? How do you measure it next quarter? But strategy, too, is meaningless without an operational definition. Teamwork, for example, might mean sales, marketing, and credit working together on a new project to develop a support system for the new requirements of an emerging customer. Yet even an operational definition is insufficient: we need a method to make teamwork or competitiveness happen, a way to coordinate people, material, methods, equipment, and environment, aligning them all in support of the same goal.

Business today is like a marathon race in which the runners don't know the course layout, the number of hills, or even who all of the competitors are going to be. In such a race, you don't just put on your sneakers and go out and compete—it takes discipline and commitment, a concrete plan and a complete training regimen. Moreover, it doesn't help much to have someone barking, "Run faster, run faster," from the sidelines, or offering a bonus for cutting the time on the next mile. Instead, success comes from putting all the elements—the right shoes, diet, technique, outlook, strategy, and inspiration—together properly.

Management by method works the same way. Building a discipline, it asks the marathoner's question—What does it take to compete?—and tries to assemble all the necessary elements. It's a "fourth-generation language," in computerspeak, after management by doing, management by directing, and management by objective. Management by objectives focuses on each part of the organization as if it were independent, through numbers, then tries to coordinate the results. Management by method gets results by focusing on the system as a whole. It teaches everyone to recognize the competitive pressures and trends facing the organization, then gives them the tools they need to respond and the training, technology, and responsibility to act as if it were their names on the door.

Asking the design questions that can move an organization forward is primarily the responsibility of senior management—CEOs, executive vice presidents, CFOs, CIOs, and board members. Only they have the authority and resources to launch the strategic and structural initiatives called for, and only they have the clout to see them through. But, at the same time, men and women at every level of an organization can reinvent the way they do their individual jobs in much the same way on a smaller scale, developing the same discipline, tools, and design skills. Don't just measure yourself against competitors or industry benchmark: try to look around corners, anticipating your future challengers, aiming at the ultimate goal—free, perfect, and now—and searching for the quantum leaps that make you more competitive as you move forward. If you're not learning new things every day about how the forces of change are redefining value in the marketplace, how can you possibly compete with someone who is?

Acting on this learning is not always easy, though. No one likes change, except, perhaps, a wet baby. By the time most managers reach senior leadership, they have a successful track record, a style of inquiry and problem solving, years of experience and a history of success. So they stick with what they know. But in an era of radical change, the style and tools that made you successful in the past may not work anymore. How valuable are ten years of experience if the experience is the same, repeated year after year?

It may well be, in fact, that our whole hyper-competitive global-electronic era, seemingly so ubiquitous, is still only a rambunctious pre-adolescent. Consider these items: In 1996, Americans sent over 100 million e-mails a day; within the next five years, that number is expected to exceed 5 billion. Three years ago, who knew the meaning of "www.anything"? Today, great corporations thrash about in the electronic jungle, chasing one false scent after another. Supposedly wired investors have launched scores of purportedly pioneering technocompanies, only to watch them crash and burn. And yet, consider this too: More than half the people in the world have never made a telephone call, let alone used a computer.

Do you see the risks? Tomorrow's competitor may be invisible to you today, sitting behind a terminal in Riga or Cincinnati or Shanghai. Do you see the opportunities? The only thing more breathtaking than the planet's astonishing new information infrastructure is the potential market for it: billions and billions of untapped customers in billions and billions of the earth's off-line crannies. Are you prepared to compete?

What Could the Dinosaurs Have Done?

By any conventional measure, Marshall was thriving when I assumed the president's office six years ago. Founded in 1947, the company had grown into one of the industry's top five, building a reputation along the way as a savvy and scrappy competitor. Yet we felt as if we were running on a treadmill. And while the numbers were good, our customers kept asking for ever lower prices, fewer defects, better real-time service. I was afraid—terrified, to be honest—that we wouldn't be able to deliver.

We seemed stuck in place. No matter what we tried, we were still out of step with our fast-paced customers and their dizzily changing needs. We talked about searching for excellence and customer-focused service, but I couldn't see what we did differently from everybody else that would win us a place in the evolving market. We moved boxes with the best of them, but we didn't do anything that made customers say, "Thank God for Marshall."

I was afraid that we were becoming a dinosaur: big, slow, and destined for extinction. However, unlike the dinosaurs, we knew we had to change. The part we didn't know was what we had to change into or what we would have to do to get there.

We couldn't shut down a $500 million operation for a month or two to consider our choices. We had to design on the fly, and fast, our urgency fueled by shared anxiety. As a first step, we dumped our old competitive model centered on MBOs and pay for performance, dispensing with all the commissions, contests, and individual bonuses that constituted our industry's standard motivators. In their place, we agreed that everyone would be paid the same way, on salary, and share a companywide bonus pool based on our common success. Then we moved to our operating system, replacing—over one tense weekend—the 700 different computer programs with which we conduct our 750,000 daily transactions.

Our product lines and the parts we carried stayed the same, but we changed how we sold them, refocusing our mission on customer partnerships, which would be win/win and results driven. We developed a new selling process that lets us turn one-shot customers into lifetime partners, weaning our sales staff from the temptation to compete on price, teaching them to sell Marshall's ability to add value by solving problems. Then we jumped into electronic commerce, becoming the first in our industry on the Internet.

There's no confusing Marshall with some ultra-cool Web startup in Seattle or Brooklyn. But "coolness" aside, we've built a Web site that generates real sales and profits; in fact, it's been named the number-one business-to-business Web site in the world two years running by *Advertising Age's Netmarketing* magazine. Marshall on the Internet (www.marshall.com) is a virtual catalogue and more. Not only does the Net provide 450,000 part numbers, 300,000 data sheets, and up-to-date inventory and pricing information, but it also features a daily broadcast of industry news, on-line chat, and a real-time individually customized headline service. The Internet also lets us communicate new products to the world faster than anybody else in the industry. To support this, we offer translation into twenty-four languages and currencies, available from the European or the Asian/Pacific server. As of late 1998, the Web sites average more than 2 million hits a week and draw visitors from seventy-five countries.

Our Web sites help us generate considerable sales, and this is indeed invaluable. But it turns out that the actual sales transaction is the least important part of what our Web sites do. What really counts for customers is what happens before and after the sale, all via Marshall on the Internet. If you're an engineer designing a new piece of hardware, for example, you can visit our Electronic Design Center to download sample code, test it on a virtual chip, and analyze the chip's performance. If you like what you see, you can order shipments through MarshallNet, the company's secure connection with suppliers and customers, each of whom sees a Web site modified to their own specific needs. So, if you need training in a new technology, there's no need to send another team of engineers to another shabby hotel—NetSeminar, a Web site connected to our digital studio, allows suppliers to train customers with video, audio, and real-time chat capabilities. Each site like NetSeminar—and we connect to many—is a different way to augment the interface with customers.

We changed our technology, but none of these innovations could have worked if we hadn't changed how we managed people, too. Out went the old pyramid that put the CEO at the top. We replaced that model with one that placed customers atop a flat matrix. The job of the front line is no longer keeping managers happy; the manager's job is to keep customers happy. Middle managers no longer simply pass along instructions and monitor performance; their job now is to train, teach, lead, and coach those on the front lines, helping them develop the skills to do their jobs better. We gave the CEO a new title, chief quality officer, and an expanded range of responsibility. The job isn't to shout out orders anymore—

"sell, sell, sell!"—or even to set strategy. Now the job is to lead, but also to build quality at the same time: banish the bottlenecks, improve the communication, and keep everyone's eyes focused on the same target.

None of this came easily. Skeptics called our flipped-over organizational structure a public-relations gimmick. Competitors dismissed our Internet presence as a waste of money. Our pay plan was denounced with a signed editorial in the industry press. On a few days we felt as if we could leap tall buildings in a single bound, though on many more we felt that all we could do was pound our heads against the wall. But every step and misstep has taken us closer to our three seemingly impossible goals.

It's not free yet—but changing our incentives and metrics has focused us all on the numbers that matter most, our customers' bottom lines. It's not perfect—but changing our technology has put us at the center of the supply chain, firmly in the information business, and allowed us to develop ever more sophisticated solutions to problems that our customers hadn't even anticipated. And it's not now—but changing the work we do and the way in which we do it has made us simultaneously more responsive and proactive, better equipped to learn from our mistakes and act on what we learn.

No one depends on customer service more than a distributor, particularly in an age of disintermediation. We don't make anything of our own; we sell only what our suppliers give us, parts that our customers can buy at the same prices from some two hundred other companies. In other ways, though, our business is like any other, large or small, in any other industry today. We worry, like everyone else, about bringing value to the changing marketplace, about sitting uncomfortably between increasingly demanding customers and suppliers, about trying to marry content with delivery, about our ability to adapt to the future, both individually and organizationally.

Free, Perfect, and Now speaks to those concerns. It is for senior executives worried about competitive differentiation, revenue growth, and share price. It describes new ways to make old buzzwords—words like "continuous improvement," "empowerment," and "customer satisfaction"—real again. It is for middle managers worried about performance, either individually or as part of a team, showing ways to become an effective change agent no matter where you stand in an organization. It is for business professionals of all ages and levels worried about development and growth, illustrating how to build the portfolio of skills that will keep your market value high well into the next century.

Most of all, *Free, Perfect, and Now* is meant to be a book of solutions, a handbook to help leaders at every level build the skills that turn ideas into results. Each chapter explains how to design a different element of the company of the future, step by step, from strategic planning and mission design to technology investments and market connections to leadership, employee buy-in, innovation, and global alliances. Chapters end with Manager's Workbooks, toolboxes detailing the key rules of competition in the electronic marketspace or the way to design a more effective compensation system.

One word of caution, though. *Free, Perfect, and Now* is not for the faint of heart. I'm going to show you a path to radical change, but it's not for the quick-fix, feel-good crowd.

It's not enough anymore to "reengineer a process," add a "quality circle," create a new team, or mouth the catchphrase of the month. Changing your organization isn't like changing your socks. You need to question everything: assumptions, values, and strategy; tactics, processes, and methods; hardware, software, and people. Each company—and each manager—must determine what will work best for them.

You can't invent a future with magic bullets or buzzwords. Radical changes start at the heart and spread outward, turning the world upside down and inside out. Who you are must change, as well as what you do. But you can't do it alone. No one is as smart as everyone. You need the hearts and minds of everyone in your organization, married to the powers of technology, all focused on the same target.

While you can't predict the future, you can prepare for it. And that, as we're learning at Marshall, can become a way to invent it.

2

You Don't Know What You Don't Know:

Learning Where to Look

Where Is the Future Found?

If you could step back and look at the world from a distance, you could see the future. It's out there today, waiting to change your competitive life.

If you had been in Albuquerque twenty-five years ago when a hobby kit called the Altair 8800 fired the imagination of Gates and Allen, Wozniak, Jobs, and Bunnell, you might have predicted Intel Inside, the rise and fall of Apple, or the fall and rise of IBM. Thirty-five years ago, if you had visited the Washington, D.C., lab where J. C. R. Licklider was blue-skying about an "interactive intergalactic computer network"—later dubbed "ARPANet" —you might have predicted America Online or Amazon.com or the rise of electronic commerce. One hundred fourteen years ago in the Duryea Motor Wagon Company garage outside Springfield, Massachusetts, you could even have seen the death of the proverbial buggy whip industry, although few in the business saw it at the time.

The problem is that, in reality, the future can be hard

to recognize. It's not evenly distributed; it's hidden in corners. While there is no shortage of clues, they are buried beneath a crush of information. Radical adaptation to shifting customer demand is the first law of business survival today, but how can you learn what you need to know in order to anticipate those shifts?

Most managers, unfortunately, search in the wrong places. We need an early warning about the new technologies, new competitors, and new ideas that could take our market position away. Too often, however, we focus our attention inside our organizations and end up self-absorbed, out of touch with our customers' changing problems and priorities. Our design needs to respond to the forces of change driving the evolution of the marketplace. But if that's not what we concentrate on, that's not what we'll see.

American corporations have long been the best in the world at monitoring and analyzing internal performance data, measuring with ever-greater precision such details as what each salesperson ships in any given quarter or the penny profitability of each P&L center. Those numbers, though, may not be the best indices of what is happening in the marketplace, for while our companies and our careers are judged, quite rightly, on cash flow and return on investment, profitability and market share, those may not tell us what we most need to know. They won't show us the opportunistic individual customers who are deserting us one by one until their numbers show a mass defection. By then it's too late. That's when the idiot light comes on.

Why did IBM and Digital lose $25 million in market value between 1984 and 1994, while Microsoft and Intel gained $70 million? It's not because Bill Gates and Andy Grove were smarter than John Akers and Ken Olsen, but because Gates and Grove recognized and capitalized on the changes in customers' values. In an open-architecture world where anyone could build a computer, confused and cautious consumers wanted something to trust. Taking advantage of this, Gates and Grove sought to provide the operating system that ran the machine and the chip that gave it its speed. They built Windows and "Intel Inside" into the brand names that control the critical pressure points of their industry supply chain today. Why did USX (formerly U.S. Steel) and Bethlehem close plant after plant over the last twenty years while minimill Nucor opened eight new ones? It's not just because Nucor was better managed or had better technology, although it was and did, but because Nucor's management anticipated the regional market for low-cost construction metal and built the team, facilities, structures, and processes to serve it.

The pattern is the same in industry after industry: customers' changing values make the old model obsolete. The giant airlines, tied to hub-and-spoke service, plummet, while Southwest soars by offering customers the direct flight convenience and no-frills cost structure that they crave. Woolworth disappears while Wal-Mart thrives. Old-line retailers, such as Saks and Nordstrom, dismiss television's home-shopping networks as marginal, ignoring the early stirrings of an industry now grown to $3 billion in annual sales. The only way to anticipate those kinds of seismic shifts in your marketplace before it's too late is to focus outward and forward, looking at the world through the lens of your customers. What is worrying them? What factors are having impacts on their lives? Where are they trying to go? Then look at yourself in the mirror. Is your organization designed to listen to those voices? Is it responsive? Proactive?

If you want to adapt, you need to look around corners and watch for the social, organizational, or technological trends that could change the customer's value equation. Don't just read *Fortune* and *The Wall Street Journal*. Look at *Fast Company* and *Inc.*, *People* and *Wired*. Don't read just your industry journal; pick up something outside your discipline, such as *The Journal of Psychology* or *Lingua Franca*. Don't benchmark yourself just within your industry, because that breeds complacency. Your inventory turns may be better than your competitors', or your delivery more user-friendly, but it's the competitor that you don't know about who can blindside you. Your benchmarks must be the same as your customers' ultimate desires: free, perfect, and now. Watch how the growth-market innovators chase that evolving target; look at established leaders like Cisco Systems, FedEx, and Dell, as well as upstarts like Cayenne Software and Acses. How are they using technology to change the interface with the customer? What are they learning to do cheaper, faster, or better than anyone has ever done before? Could that technology change what your customers would pay for?

I'm not suggesting that anyone will ever replace human ingenuity or creativity with a sliver of silicon. But computers can be a turbocharger to put ingenuity and creativity to work faster and more efficiently. Moore's law still holds true: chip power doubles every eighteen months, while the cost of computation drops 30 percent a year. That changes how your content can be created, whether you sell steel, shoes, or career-investment services, and it changes how you have to be organized and operated to create it. It changes how your content is delivered, and how demand and share of mind are built.

What would your customers ask for if price were not a factor? Marshall's would ask for speed, coordination, and communication. They want time, today's only irreplaceable currency. Finding better and faster ways to use technology is how we give it to them.

You don't have to be a propellerhead whiz kid to anticipate new-technology adoption or even to understand how a chip works. You have to know only what chips networked together can do for you. Think application: the hole you need drilled, not the tool you're going to drill it with. Pay attention to the way new technology enhances the interface with your customers and how a change in capability can change your customers' definition of value.

Watch the heavy hitters, early adapters such as Scott McNealy of Sun, Jim Barksdale of Netscape, or Larry Ellison of Oracle. Win or lose, in addition to their significant power to determine which technologies will shape the future, they have proven ability to spot the next hot buttons for customers. Listen to the blue-sky thinkers, too, people such as Esther Dyson, editor of newsletter *Release.1;* Nicholas Negroponte, the Massachusetts Institute of Technology Media Lab guru; and John Perry Barlow, cofounder of the San Francisco–based Electronic Frontier Foundation. They may be wrong, or even wrongheaded, but they'll stretch your sense of the almost possible.

Follow the money, too. Where is Intel spending its annual multimillion-dollar research-and-development budget? When Andy Grove predicts "on-car computing"—personal computers built into automobile dashboards loaded with mapping and entertainment systems—he has the resources to make it happen. You don't need to be able to predict whether that bet will pay off; what matters is why he made it. What potential customer value is he trying to capture? What technology envelope is he trying to push? What is he trying to do that your customers wish you could do?

Bill Gates has even bigger feet, given Microsoft's $9 billion in cash and $166 billion market capitalization. Where does *he* want to go today? In 1997, Gates's $150 million deal with former rival Steve Jobs made headlines, but besides that, Gates also invested in sixteen other companies during the year, seven by acquisition and nine by partnership, alliance, or joint venture. These companies were in all kinds of fields, including e-mail, voice recognition, translation, on-line video, on-line telephony, on-line billing and receiving, high-speed data networking, Java programming, interactive media, Internet TV, and Web traffic analysis. These moves indicate two things. First, he's betting heavily on his Windows NT operating system and server software, trying to gain the same control of industrial-strength corporate networks that he has of the Windows desktop. And, at the same time, he wants to push Microsoft deeper into your home with his $425 million purchase of WebTV, which makes a set-top Internet box, and a $1 billion investment in Comcast, the cable company that creates high-speed network connections.

Love Gates or hate him, you have to pay attention. Microsoft remembers what companies like Borland and WordPerfect forgot: Past performance is no guarantee of future success. The government's antitrust suits may slow Microsoft's progress; competitors will attack its flanks. Gates may even be wrong about the road ahead. But he didn't become the nation's richest man and the leader of a marketing juggernaut with twice the market capitalization of General Motors by misreading where the opportunities lie. What is he seeing that you should be seeing? And what might he be missing?

The Clockspeed Imperatives

Academics, borrowing a term from computer designers, call the $860 billion electronics business a "fast clockspeed" industry. They study it much as geneticists study fruit flies, watching evolutionary trends play out as companies rise and fall in accelerated time. Today more than ever before, technologies become critically important more quickly and obsolete even more quickly. Product life cycles are shorter, competition hotter, margins tighter. The fastest and most nimble startup can soar from garage to initial public offering (IPO) in months while the mighty can fall with a single misstep.

Relentlessly opportunistic and continually new, high technology has always been an exhilarating, if demanding, industry for Marshall to serve—and an ideal place from which to watch as the major currents of change roar through a real-world marketplace.

The future of commerce is being invented here, in Silicon Valley and places like it around the world, at the junction of innovation and imperative. But the secret isn't in the silicon. Although technology remains the great enabler, the critical accomplishment is organizational, the way people and technology are bound together to get the maximum power from both. The necessary creativity isn't confined to any specific location, either, although the 1,350 square miles south of San Francisco is its commercial capital and prime exemplar. That creativity is as much a state of mind and a model as a geographical fact, a new way of thinking about a new economy, a frontier that has spread through Texas's "Silicon Gulch," New York's "Silicon Alley," Scotland's "Silicon Glen," and Israel's "Silicon Wadi." Think of it as a giant talent pool, flat, democratic, and intensely competitive, with everyone linked in a web of interlocking relationships, all driven by speed, pizza, and the rush of shipped product. The solutions that will transform the world's economy are tested here first.

Every business, in time, will have to react to the explosion of bandwidth, the acceleration of globalization, and the changing demographic. But that time has long since come to the new economy. Every business, high tech or low, will have to wrestle with the compression of the product life cycle, the rise of mass customization, and the growing importance of supply-chain management. But those challenges are immediate and critical here. In the high-tech world, they are seismic shifts that demand a nonlinear response.

Silicon Valley has changed since I first came west in 1983. Back then, we wrote in Word Star and calculated in 1-2-3. Fruit trees still grew around San Jose, and the traffic delays were shorter, at least in my memory. Trilogy and Go were the hot startups; Hewlett-Packard and Apple, Amdahl and Control Data were the established leaders. Big Blue, soon to be anointed Big Brother on Superbowl XVIII, was the big power, while Microsoft was an obscure operating-systems supplier barely out of the garage and still privately held. The face on magazine covers wasn't Andy Grove, then Intel's president under CEO Bob Noyce, but Nolan Bushnell, the pipe-smoking creator of Pong and Atari, poised to make a comeback with a talking bear.

Yet even in those days the valley was a fixture in the national imagination. It was the home of the new, the place where the silicon semiconductor was invented and the integrated circuit perfected; where a single research lab churned out in rapid succession the computer mouse, the graphical user interface (GUI), and the local-area network; where the classified ads read "Used Mac for Sale" and "hard-charging company founder, SF, 30s, seeks SM, same." Obsession ruled. Work was personal; computing was social. Rebellion against the status quo was the norm. "Two men in a garage" wasn't just a legend—it was a legacy that stretched back through Steve Wozniak and Steve Jobs in Cupertino in 1976 to Bill Hewlett and Dave Packard in Palo Alto in 1939, a promise that anyone with a hot idea or a cool new tool could start a company of his own and change the world . . . or at least get rich.

Fifteen years after I first saw it up close, that fervor is still intact. The pressures, however, have gotten more intense. The clockspeed is faster and the numbers bigger; the competitive bar is higher and the challenges more complex. In 1983, Eagle Computers's $355 million IPO was the talk of the valley. Today, Netscape's 1995 offering—a $2 billion valuation on a company with just $16 million in revenues, which earned twenty-four-year-old founder Marc An-

dreessen $60 million while reserving another $250 million for
Netscape's rank and file—is the benchmark. In 1983, the valley's
mantra came from Steve Jobs, who spoke of looking for "the
insanely great." Today it comes from Hunter S. Thompson:
"Faster, faster, faster, until the love of speed overcomes the fear of
death. . . ."

The valley has always lived with boom-and-bust cycles, but the
last four years have brought the most explosive and sustained
growth spurt in its history. Fueling this growth is the Internet. Information technology has become the nation's largest industry,
while the software segment grows more than twice as fast as the
overall economy. There are more startups than ever, and they're
growing faster and introducing more dazzling technologies with
more dizzying speed. There's more venture capital money available,
too, but that money is harder to get without a proven track record, a
tested management team, or a solid lock on competitive alliances.

The battles are harder as well. In 1996, for example, Andy Bech-
tolsheim, one of the original engineering geniuses behind Sun Microsystems, sold his startup, Granite Systems, to Cisco Systems, the
booming network manufacturer, for $220 million. Fifteen years ago,
he says, he might have made a different choice. "Then, you had
stodgy, traditional companies dominating some of these technologies and, as a result, it was relatively easier to compete against
them," he explains. "Now, any new startup will compete with startups from the 1970s and '80s, including Intel and Microsoft. The
window of opportunity created by ignorant or conservative companies has really shrunk."

Increasing the competitive pressure so dramatically creates more
than a change in intensity. It also creates a change in kind, bringing
unprecedented nonlinear challenges that require marrying people
and technology in radical solutions. Take staffing, for instance. People have known since the 1960s, when Peter Drucker first coined
the term, that success depends on the ability to attract, maintain,
and nurture "knowledge workers," but today the demand is higher,
the need more critical, and the shortage more severe than ever.
Netscape went from 2 employees to 350 to over 2,000 in the two

years leading up to its IPO. That's too many people to integrate into a team, even with the help of a better employee handbook or a second day of orientation. Last year Cisco Systems hired 1,200 people each quarter, but still left hundreds of spots unfilled. Wages are soaring across the valley, with starting programmers earning $75,000, yet almost 20,000 jobs went begging last year, reflecting a national crisis that is expected to produce a shortfall of 1 million programmers between now and 2007. That's not a problem that an organization can overcome by beefing up its human-resources department or increasing its recruiting budget.

People have talked about the decentralizing power of technology for years, too, but now geographical dispersion has become commonplace, producing another change in kind. Engineers create designs for major players such as Bay Networks, Newbridge, 3Com, or Intel from their home offices, on-line, with a high-speed connection to the Internet. Such wonders can't be managed and coordinated with the same old interface and tools. More important, from Marshall's point of view, they can't be marketed to in the same way either: their value equation has changed.

We see six major forces driving innovation for our fast-clockspeed customers. Individually, each is a nonlinear change that demands a radical response. But they don't operate individually. They combine and cascade, each accelerating the power and complexity of the others, inexorably creating a new business universe with new rules, new gravitational pulls, and new dependencies. Together they define the competitive battlefield of the new economy and shape the models of success that can show the rest of us our future.

Bandwidth

Remember 1996, when people worried that our fledgling "information superhighway" was on the edge of a terminal traffic snarl? Too many users, they said, and not enough capacity. The fastest telephone-line modems delivered data at 28,800 bits per second, when you could connect at all, with 56,600 on the drawing boards. One Valley CEO, since replaced, dismissed the Internet as a gimmick, comparing it to the CB-radio craze of the 1970s.

Today—when every telephone company and cable operator in the country is competing to add capacity; when DSL modems deliver 1.5 million bits per second; when electronic commerce is ubiquitous—those days seem quaint. Before the turn of the century, data traffic will exceed voice traffic on the nation's phone lines, as the network links everything—intranets and Ethernets, satellites and cell phones, smart cards and dumb chips—together effortlessly. Over the next five years, the number of computers in use will increase from 200 million to 500 million, while the volume of goods and services sold on-line will shoot from $8 billion to $327 billion. And like the chip, author George Gilder predicts, bandwidth will keep getting cheaper and faster at the same time, tripling in capacity every twelve months for the next twenty-five years as competition pushes the cost toward free.

So what? Data is like garbage, as one of my colleagues says—it's easy to gather, but harder to put to work effectively. If you don't know what you want to do with it, more is just more.

Electronic commerce should be the biggest beneficiary, as bandwidth explosion allows early innovators to create the tools necessary to build new revenue streams, improve customer service, and enhance productivity. For most companies, however, electronic commerce will remain a sinkhole. They'll chase the latest hot technology without knowing what they want it for, throwing good money after bad, when what they really need is to redefine their business model first. Success comes from an enterprisewide response to the new communications potential, one that integrates technology into a larger vision of a new customer connection, then translates that into a redesigned approach to everything from human-resource development to operations and customer service.

Consider this: Charles Schwab manages $50 billion in assets with more than 700,000 active accounts and maintains a 50 percent market share of the on-line brokerage industry, but it wasn't technology that made Schwab an electronic-commerce poster boy—it was a new concept for the business. Would-be competitors such as Smith Barney and Fidelity have an equally impressive array of telephones, computers, and customer data bases, but Schwab saw early on that financial products like mutual funds and IRAs were becoming a commodity, differentiated from one another only by the services that came with them, and that the network could make the old expenses of the local office unnecessary. Then he designed an infrastructure and an interface that let him withstand those seismic shifts in the value equation.

Global competition

Thirty-five years after Walter Wriston, then president of Citibank, forecast the instant and free flow of capital and customers around the globe, it has come to pass. In 1973, the market capitalization of the world's businesses has been estimated at $9.2 trillion, of which 66 percent was located in the United States. By 1996, global market capitalization had grown to $12.6 trillion, with 64 percent of that outside our borders. Today, companies in 158 countries are competing with American businesses to find inventive ways to bring to market products and services with more features and benefits or lower and lower costs. They're hungry, figuratively and literally—and they're one mouse click away from our customers.

Moreover, the fastest-growing pool of software-programming talent isn't in the United States. It's in India, where the number of programmers is swelling by 60 percent a year. Indian coding exports, up from $225 million five years ago to $1.6 billion in 1998, are expected to hit $3.6 billion by the year 2000. It's an example not lost on would-be competitors in Brazil, China, Russia, and the Philippines. The expansion of bandwidth means that anyone can do any business anywhere and anytime—and will. What does that do to the model?

Demographics

Like everyone else over twenty, I grew up comfortable with the traditional connections; I kept in touch with friends, family, and customers by phone; bought my groceries in a store; and visited customers in their offices. Our children, however, are growing up with cyberspace as part of the fabric of their daily lives. They shop for CDs from around the globe via the Web and do their homework with a search engine. As they come of age, we'll have to learn to sell to, inform, and entertain them how, when, and where they want, whether we seek them as employees or as customers.

A new generation gap is being created, a product of a mass-customized, networked, and globally connected planet. Unlike the gaps of the past, though, this gap isn't just about music or hairstyles; it is about definitions of value and competitiveness. We'll have to develop new methods to attract and hold the attention of the new generation and establish new ways of working together. Will they work in traditional headquarters? Will they be in major cities? Will they work from nine to five? Will they connect with computers, beepers, high-definition television (HDTV), text, voice, GUIs? How will we coordinate their efforts with our own?

How big are the numbers here? Of the 5.7 billion people alive today, 2.3 billion, or 41 percent, are still under the age of twenty. How will that change the business dynamic?

Compressed product life cycles

"Sometimes I think we'll see the day when you introduce a product in the morning and announce its end of life at the end of the day," Alan Shugart, chairman of disk-drive manufacturer Seagate Technology, laments. He's not the only beleaguered leader feeling the stress. Between 1992 and 1997, auto giant General Motors spent over $100 million on an information-technology reorganization aimed at cutting its product cycle time from forty-six months to twenty-four by the year 2000. Its rival Toyota, meanwhile, spent less and hit eighteen months last year. In 1997 alone, 25,000 new packaged goods, including over 12,000 food products, were introduced, most of which never found space on the shelf, while Hollywood released forty holiday-season films, fifteen during the last seven days of December, and took most off the screen in under two weeks.

We all want to get new products to market faster, whether we sell cars, coffee, or computer parts. That's where the margins are. Hitting the market quickly takes advantage of innovation's premium, and allows a company to move on to a new product before the competition can drive prices down. But you can't cut cycle time in half by telling your people to work harder or work faster, even if they could: you have to redefine how they work and how they work together. That's a communication and design challenge, not just a motivational or technological one. What data do you give them? Information is power, but power for whom and for what? There's enough bandwidth to give everyone everything. The questions are how they should use it, and what they should use it for.

Outsourcing can help cut time to market, but that exponentially increases management complexity. Plus, short life cycles for new products make it harder than ever to predict market demand. Forecast too high and you sit on worthless inventory; forecast too low and you risk shortages, losing potential sales and fueling customer dissatisfaction. How do you coordinate everyone so the right volume hits the market at the right time? You can't do it without first deciding to take down the walls that traditionally have separated companies from customers and suppliers.

For the fastest-clockspeed companies, the conventional definition of the product life cycle is becoming obsolete. Look at how Netscape launched its popular Navigator 3.0 Web browser, for example. Netscape used its home page to identify and define customer needs, test alternative solutions, and integrate acquired knowledge into design as a continual process. Then, in February 1996, six weeks after Navigator 2.0 hit the market, a beta version of the next-generation product was posted on the company's Web site. Beta 1, revised and updated, went up in late February, followed by Beta 2 in early March. Public releases of the software in progress followed every few weeks until August, the "official" release of Navigator 3.0 and the beginning of the design for Navigator 4.0. That's an attractive model for any business that wants to respond to changing customer value in real time, but it's a strategic choice, not a technology decision. It can't be duplicated without first designing the infrastructure and interface to integrate the voice of the customer into every corner of your business.

Build-to-order

It's not enough anymore just to make new things faster. Increasingly, market share goes to companies that can tailor their product or service to individual customer requirements, serving a demographic of one. But mass-customized, made-to-order, cut-to-fit solutions add still more complex forecasting and logistical challenges. Suppliers have to be chosen for speed and flexibility, then integrated into the operation to maximize efficiency and minimize cost. Managers must be adept with sharing crisp information about customer needs and the capacities available to meet them, and able to effectively marry content and delivery.

Look, for example, at how Dell computer makes the build-to-order process work and translates operational efficiency into low cost and ease of purchase. The company's connection with the customer's changing value equation is immediate and continuous: Dell doesn't build a box until someone asks for it. Sometimes customers carefully weigh their options with an engineer or project manager before choosing the configuration that best fits their needs, but more and more often they make buying decisions on-line. Meanwhile, Dell's inventory levels stay low, usually at just enough parts for no more than three hours of production. The supply chain, too, is kept short, and importantly, differentiated between providers of complex and commodity parts. The former, which may require customization, are sourced regionally to enhance Dell's dexterity, while the latter are sourced globally for cost. Orders to both are sent in real time through a single supplier logistics center, via a Dell extranet. On average, Dell then ships the customer's order within three and a half days of the original call.

Build-to-order has turned Dell into the envy of its industry. Its net income soared 91 percent to $518 million for fiscal 1997, on revenues that rose 41 percent to $7.8 billion. Competitors such as Compaq, IBM, Hewlett-Packard, and Packard Bell have all tried to duplicate the Dell model, with scant success so far. Finding comparable suppliers and technology was relatively easy, but because these companies all rely primarily on resellers to take their products to market, none could forge the same intimate customer connection that Dell has. And that is the fuel that powers Dell's success.

Supply-chain management

The high-tech battleground has been shifting away from manufacturing and toward pure research and development ever since the late '70s, when product assembly moved to Taiwan, Korea, and the Sacramento Valley in search of cheaper labor costs. Yet even as this happened, managing a supply chain was still relatively easy then: buy your parts at the best price, make a world-class product, and you'd be competitive. These days, it's different. Today's world-class products often represent a complex linkage of many skills—sometimes nothing more than a concept developed in-house, with engineering, forecasting, and production, along with distribution, sales and marketing, and customer service, all farmed out.

Companies no longer compete against their direct rivals alone. Instead, they compete as supply chain versus supply chain, with market share and margin going to the organization that can harness the best talents in the world and network them all together most effectively. Aiming for a global build-to-order customer base with a continually changing definition of delight is a risky business, and the window of opportunity keeps getting smaller. Point-of-sale scanners can capture the relevant market facts; electronic data exchange can speed those facts across the supply chain; automated warehouses and agile manufacturing can respond to them, but they can't create the vision necessary to put all that data to work.

So What?

Seem obvious to you? Who needs to hear again that business is globalizing, that product life cycles are shrinking, or that there's an Internet out there?

Perhaps *you* do—unless the design of your organization is continually searching for new ways to bring those "obvious" forces into consideration.

Give yourself a reality test: Imagine that you're a customer with a problem, impatient or frustrated, and willing to change suppliers tomorrow. Then call your office number after 6:30 P.M. Who answers the phone? What kind of service do you get?

If your company's critical capabilities aren't accessible to customers twenty-four hours a day, you aren't designed to meet the future. You may think that you understand that the world competes around the clock, but your system says that you don't believe it.

Voice mail isn't the solution. Customers don't want "push one for this and push two for that." They want gratification NOW, a real person to help them when they need help—and they'll take their business to whoever gives it to them.

If you think that having a home page counts, think again. Electronic commerce isn't about hits per month or even about sales dollars; it's about a new connection to the voice of the customer. And simply communicating in English alone may not be good enough anymore, either. If potential customers want to do business in Chinese, someone will do it for them, and in the process position themselves to do business with Hong Kong and Shanghai.

If anyone in your organization has to ask someone else for a price quote, you're not designed for the future. There is no more time to waste with handoffs; all of the predictable, mechanical steps of moment-to-moment business can go into the plumbing. Open information architecture can be designed to give all your employees what they need when they need it, with no one to ask and no one to tell. This creates customized efficiency that builds staff training and organizational learning into the customer interface itself.

If you're not ready to give up the old management style, you're not designed for the future. "Command and control is dead," *Forbes ASAP*'s Editor's Letter insists. "The chip and the Net have killed it." Vertical integration is dead, too: if you want everyone to play in your own sandbox with your rules, you won't be able to establish the network of entrepreneurial alliances necessary to build a successful supply chain.

Finally, and most of all, if you think that you are ready for tomorrow, you're not. There is no end to change, and no end to the questions that this quest for free, perfect, and now demands you ask. Who in the world is figuring out how to serve customers at a lower cost? Closer to perfect for your customers' changing values? Faster?

We ask ourselves those questions every day at Marshall. Our survival depends on our being able to answer them quickly and truthfully.

These should be heady days for us. "Virtual distribution" has been feted in the national press and lauded in a Harvard Business School case study. Some of our customers swear by us, at least for the moment, and we've spread our logo around the world. But so what? Despite Marshall's success, and our hopes for success in the future, I still lie awake at night, worrying that someone somewhere will find a way to eat our lunch. Change keeps accelerating, transforming our industry, and altering our customer's value equation faster than I'd ever thought possible.

So what if our stock price and profits go up? That's important, but it's not enough. Are we creating what we'll need in order to survive tomorrow? So what if our sales go up? Are we increasing customer satisfaction and loyalty? Are we looking at the new competitors, new technologies, and new ideas that could take our market away? Are we designed to respond to the powerful forces of change that are driving our customers' value equation?

We've reinvented our company. So what? Tomorrow we have to go out and reinvent ourselves again.

I can't predict what Marshall will look like in five years. Our competitive world is changing so drastically that no one knows what anything will look like so far in the future. In the industrial age, tomorrow was just a little bit different from today. In the electronic age, change isn't merely incremental anymore; it's exponential, and it happens yesterday. Survival depends on staying ahead of its rush, shooting its rapids as a kayaker shoots class 4 white waters. At Marshall, we're trying to prove that if you're strong, smart, and lucky—and you paddle hard enough to go faster than the water itself—you can slice your way through, creating your own path ahead of the force.

Manager's Workbook

The fight is won or lost far away from witnesses. It is won behind the lines in the gym and out on the road, long before I dance under those lights.

—MUHAMMAD ALI

Seven Survival Rules

It's not the enemy you can see that will eat your lunch: it's the enemy that doesn't even show up on your radar screen until it's too late to fashion a counterattack that you have to be ready for.

None of the old protections of time and space apply anymore. There's a new competitive universe being born, propelled by the explosion of bandwidth, with all new pulls and forces:

1. Time is the currency that counts

Faster is better than cheaper—and customers will pay a premium for it. With ever-shortening product life cycles, their success, and yours, depends on speed, and the coordination and communication that make speed possible.

2. Market share doesn't matter

Your customers are relentlessly opportunistic; they have to be. They'll desert you in a nanosecond if someone offers something better. What matters today is your share of each customer's total attention. To keep their business, you have to learn to anticipate their problems, then focus on developing individual solutions that make them more competitive.

3. You're only as good as your supply chain

You can't compete based on your talents alone anymore. Today, business is supply chain versus supply chain, competing in a global market of fickle and continually more-demanding build-to-order customers. Seamless and frictionless internal connections have always been the challenge of organizational design, but when that design has to stretch across multiple organizations, the challenges become radically more complex.

4. Get over yourself

Nobody ever saw the future by staring at his or her corporate navel. Internal analyses and measures are critical, but at best they can only tell you how you're doing today, not what you should be doing tomorrow. To see what's next, you need to look outside yourself. How are your customers' demands changing? How could new trends or new technologies change what they value?

5. Explore what others do

Read magazines and books about things outside your field; study companies whose products seem unrelated to yours. There isn't a business in America that couldn't learn something about marketing from Starbucks, about data management from the Ritz-Carlton, or about customer service from Dell. Sometimes, the best ideas aren't new, they're just hiding out in someone else's market. Don't limit yourself to solutions or ideas that you know how to implement. Think blue sky. Aim for free, perfect, and now. The idea is the hard part; implementation will follow, even if it is impossible to picture given the way your business works now.

6. Study the stars

Folks like Bill Gates and Andy Grove didn't get to be so successful by coming up with bad ideas. Draw up a list of "advisers" whose work you can watch and analyze. What does Gates see in WebTV? Why is Grove so interested in computer technology for cars? Tracking the what and why of people "in the know" will give you a heads-up on trends destined to change the way you compete. Look at what outsiders think, too. Investors like George Soros and Warren Buffet have made millions from investing in smart companies. Watch where they put their money. What are they betting on? Where do they think new value lies today?

7. No rest for the weary

There is no end to change, and competition will only accelerate. There are no guarantees of survival, no protections except your own ability to produce something new today—and embrace its obsolescence tomorrow, using it as motivation to inspire something better still.

Time Bombs

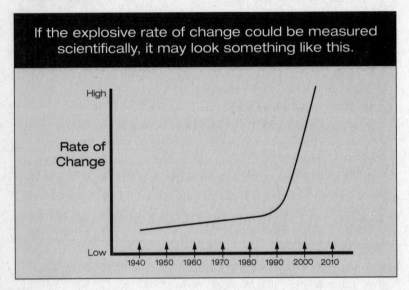

If the explosive rate of change could be measured scientifically, it may look something like this.

What does this admittedly unscientific graph illustrate? Pick your subject—the amount of data the Internet can carry, the importance of globalization, the compression of product life cycles, the demand for individually crafted solutions—and the trend is always the same, even if the decade markers are inexact. Change isn't linear anymore. It's a time bomb, accelerating unpredictably, explosively, and exponentially. The only management forecast that you can make is for ever-greater unpredictability.

Reality Test

It may be that your company already "gets it." Perhaps the talk of seamless customer connection and efficient and focused service that glitters from your annual report is bona fide. But even so, it's still easy, with all the pressures of day-to-day management responsibility, to miss where you fall short of your promises.

Information has to be summarized. You, as a manager, don't have the time to look at discrete transactions. However, unless you have personal experience with the way in which your organization connects with the outside world, you don't know what really lies behind your results.

So give your words a reality test. It won't take more than a day, and I guarantee that you'll see things that you'll feel compelled to change:

Experience your own service

No matter what you sell, you have no idea how your customers feel about your service or product until you order it, buy it, eat it, use it, or call for help with a problem. Staple yourself to an order—how many steps, handoffs, and opportunities for error do you pass through before the request is fulfilled? Call customer service and describe a problem. What do they say when you complain that you can't understand the manual, or that things just don't work?

Talk to your receptionist

What *really* happens when a customer connects with your switchboard? Just having an 800 number is no guarantee of an effective customer response. Where do the calls from customers with problems get routed? Do they get bounced around from extension to extension? Dropped into voice-mail "press one for this and two for that" hell? How often and how fast do they get answers and the information they need?

Talk to an accounting clerk

What do they see in their day-to-day work that doesn't show up in your finance report? They see little things that don't make sense all the time, from supply costs to travel expenses, but no one ever asks them about items like this. In particular, visit the midlevel folks in accounts payable: they know where the money is going, and may define a good manager, a good salesperson, or a good branch or division differently than you do.

Experience your competitor's service
How does it compare to yours? What happens when you order it, buy it, use it, or call with a complaint? What do they do faster, better, or cheaper than you? Does it matter? Do they see something about your customers that you don't?

3
Frustration by Design:

Why Bad Things Happen in Good Organizations

Management Frustration 101

By the end of the 1980s, I had spent seven years at Marshall and was newly promoted to vice president. I accepted frustration as one more cost of trying to manage people day by day. Like every organization, ours had its problems, but we had a strong entrepreneurial heritage, a profitable niche, and a hard-earned reputation for aggressive selling and strong personal service.

Marshall was a post–World War II creation, one of several thousand local, franchised distributorships launched by returning veterans who had been bitten by the electronics bug. One of them was Gordon Marshall. A ham radio operator as a kid and a decorated B-24 pilot in the war, the twenty-seven-year-old Marshall had wanted a job as a manufacturer's rep when he finished his business degree at the University of Southern California in 1946, but he got no offers. So, he set up a business of his own. Newly married and nearly broke, but relentlessly confident, he started with a basic idea: buy low, sell high, and serve the customer. He sold everything from poker chips to war surplus before he won his first electronics franchise, distributing precision potentiometers for a company named Heliopot.

Distribution was a ragtag business in those early years, a Wild West of pure selling driven by price and personal relationships, and Gordon struggled at first. But people liked the lanky, no-nonsense former flier, and he was lucky enough to ride a swelling stream of new products from the Korean War through the '50s, which pushed the company up near the $10 million plateau by the early '60s.

Gordon was smart, too. He was one of the first to see the promise of semiconductors, and his investment in them carried the company up to $100 million by the late '70s. Smarter still, he was the first to connect Japanese suppliers to American customers, and this would swell sales up to $500 million in 1990, making Marshall a midsized player in a newly consolidating industry.

Distribution was still an immature business in 1990. For everyone, it went day to day and deal by deal, but we prided ourselves on running the company by employing the best management thinking we could find. We had a Marshall motto, "Satisfaction through Service," and an explicit goal, "Number One in the Marketplace." We searched for excellence, we thought, by relying on a complex system of management by objectives (MBOs) that appealed to everyone's self-interest: people were ranked, reviewed, and rated according to individual or small-group performance—credit on days outstanding, division managers on their division's profits and losses, product marketers on sales versus forecast and inventory budgets, and sales staff on gross profit dollars. Internal competition—division versus division, region versus region, and product line versus product line—was keen as salespeople battled one another to win a nonstop round of promotions and contests, fifteen or twenty at a time, with TVs, VCRs, and cruises awarded to top performers.

The numbers were good; customer base and volume grew steadily. But I worried—constantly. The old days were dying. Personal relationships were still central to the business, but just taking orders and shipping crates wasn't good enough anymore. Suppliers and customers were asking for better performance, talking about Baldrige awards, mandated ISO9002 standards, and six-sigma quality, 3.4 defects per million from their distributors. Meanwhile, Marshall seemed stuck, unable to implement the necessary new processes and controls to consistently get the right parts to the right place at the right time, running faster and faster just to stay in place. I'd work a sixty-hour week, facing one minicrisis after another, but when I went home on Friday night the company never seemed any better for my efforts.

Month after month the problems were always the same. Everything was momentarily critical, but never life-threatening:

• Our salespeople would ship ahead of schedule to make a number or win a prize. Our customers, on the other hand, were insisting on delivery in a window of one day early to zero days late—but because of our incentives, our organization still shipped ahead.

• We shipped over 20 percent of our total sales in the last three days of each month. Our goal was to ship anything that wasn't nailed down. At month's end, we'd work past midnight to get everything out the door. I don't know how many of you have ever seen semiconductors. They are very small, and they have part numbers with ten to fifteen digits. Can you imagine a warehouse person picking those parts at 2:00 A.M. and getting them all correct?

• We held customer returns. We had to make sure that the returns coming in did not get counted against sales in the period for which we were trying to hit the numbers. So, if a customer returned items, sometimes our salespeople would put them in the trunks of their cars and keep them there for a few weeks until they could be counted as returns for the next period. In the meantime, if we needed that inventory for another customer, we'd have to buy unnecessary stock.

• We opened bad credit accounts. Any order was a good order as far as a salesperson paid on gross profit was concerned. Just book it.

• We found extraordinarily creative ways to charge expenses to one another's profit and loss statements. As long as it was on another division's P&L, it wasn't real money. Somehow, headquarters ended up picking up everyone's expenses.

• We argued constantly about corporate-cost allocation. Who was going to pay for the new computer system, the new warehouse, or the new training programs that we needed? Nobody wanted those costs to be allocated to his or her P&L.

• We would bring in our high-priced executive-management team every quarter to sit around the room for two days and argue about how they were going to allocate the bad-debt expense or the expense of new investments, when that time would have been better spent developing a strategy for the future.

• We had a motto in the company: SWAT—sell what is available today! Marshall sells leading-edge technology. In fact, some of the items we sell today were not even in production just ninety days ago. Under SWAT, though, we were encouraginging our sales force to sell the old technology, the easy stuff to sell. We were not directing our customers toward the wave of the future or helping our suppliers bring their new products to market.

• Our divisions hid inventory from one another. The semiconductor industry practices product allocation, and when we received our allocation, we would in turn distribute it to our divisions according to their needs. After that, our managers devised creative ways to hide the inventory they wanted to hold on to for their own customers, sometimes even sending it out of state in UPS trucks so that they could honestly tell other divisions they were out of stock. When their own customers needed the inventory, though, it would magically reappear.

• We stopped buying "high movers" when we hit our inventory budget, despite the fact that our customers purchased these items on a regular basis.

• Then, at the end of this monthly madness, we had to split commissions. As our customer base became national and then global, our salespeople had to coordinate purchases around the world. This increased the number of people involved, and all who touched a sale wanted their cut of the action. If a customer did design work in one area and purchasing in another, our divisions would argue about who would get the credit for the sale. To address this, we tried to construct an accounting infrastructure that would keep track of every time someone said hello to a customer.

Our solution to all the problems was usually to pump up the adrenaline. If sales were faltering, we would order up a pep rally or kick off another contest. When we saw regions or divisions fighting, we would make our most stirring appeals for cooperation. "We're a team," we'd plead. "We've got to work together. Pursue excellence. Fight and win." At themed yearly meetings we'd show a video of fighter jets and say, "You've got to be like an airplane pilot and kill the enemy." And we'd play rock music, and everybody would hug and get into a frenzy—and then nothing would happen.

Sound familiar? You reason and argue, cajole and threaten, and nothing much changes, no matter how good your intentions or how hard you work. It's a textbook example of Management Frustration 101.

Don't misunderstand me. Nobody was trying to mortgage the company. Marshall was a great place to work, filled with high-energy camaraderie, not *Glengarry Glen Ross* with better lighting. Still, the more our customers cranked up the performance pressure, the higher tensions and anxiety inside the company climbed. People kept pushing the system to the limit, trying to make things happen no matter what got in the way, but continually hitting the same walls. Quarter after quarter, we'd write the same memos and have the same meetings, but nothing changed. We'd spend days and days talking about how important training was becoming, but we'd never actually create a training program. We talked for two years about how to upgrade our aging computing systems, but we could never agree about how to fix them. We wanted to build a legacy, but we spent all of our time putting out fires.

I thought that frustration was just part of the job, though; it was the way things had always been and always would be. Who hasn't left the office at the end of a long Friday and said, "This is crazy. What am I doing?" Yet then we go back to work on Monday and do more of the same. It would take my customers screaming loud and long, and an extraordinary teacher, for me to see that there could be a better way.

In Search of Excellence

I'd come to Marshall in 1983, an eager twenty-nine-year-old area sales manager at Sunnyvale, our largest division. I was convinced that I'd hit the big time; I liked the booming market, the endless string of sunny Northern California days, and the nonstop running around of business day to day and one on one, on the phone or face-to-face, details and deals, strategizing, hand holding, and selling.

And even as our company grew, there was no doubt whose name was on the company door. Although Gordon Marshall had largely delegated daily operations to his senior management team, he still set the company's course, represented us to Wall Street, and remained enormously protective of his original values of competitiveness, integrity, and service. "People should walk on broken glass, fall on their swords, swim oceans—whatever they have to do to make the customers happy," he always used to tell us.

Gordon didn't care if the margins on your memos matched or if your report was stapled perfectly, but other details were nonnegotiable: answer your own phone, so that customers or colleagues can call you directly if they need you; keep your office door open, so that people can see what you're up to. Like the best entrepreneurs, he'd tried to create the kind of company that he himself would want to work in. "No point in screwing around with bureaucracy," he'd say. "Keep it simple. If you see something that needs to be done, just do it." He'd been particularly impressed by Tom Peters's *In Search of Excellence*. "That's the way I want to feel about my company, too," he told me as he handed out copies.

Even as a novice sales manager, I was expected to make a difference. My job was simple: push my eleven salespeople to sell more stuff, with my bonus contingent on my ability to fire them up. But the bonus system that the company had designed for salespeople in Sunnyvale didn't make much sense to me. It set up a monthly budget in fifteen categories, from sales by product line to profitability. If you hit the number in all fifteen, you'd get your bonus, but it was obvious to everyone on my team that there was no way anyone could ever make all fifteen at the same time. So I spent hours in my office redesigning the entire program, creating a sliding scale that allowed for the kinds of contingencies we inevitably encountered. I spent hours more in meeting rooms standing next to a giant chart trying to sell it, first to my bosses, then to my team.

Similarly, during most weeks a supplier would ask to come in to bestow an award—a color TV one week, a grandfather clock the next—at our regular sales meeting, but that was missing its potential, too. As often as not, the winners didn't remember what they'd done to win, whereas the losers all thought that they could have won themselves, if only they'd had better accounts to sell to. Responding to this, I started a monthly newsletter and wrote up everybody in every possible product category I could think of, so that people could see other ways besides selling the most pieces to the biggest accounts by which to contribute to Marshall's success.

Those were both small wrinkles to the system, though, compared to "March into March," a month-long program of rallies, posters, and prizes that I developed after my promotion to branch manager. The mother of all promotions, featuring a different contest and different bells and whistles each day, it spread to all of our offices and would be repeated throughout the company for five years, supported each year by an ever more elaborate kickoff video. One year, I cast Executive Vice President Dick Bentley as "Bond, James Bond," imperiled by the evil forces of the "Grey Schlocker." Another year, I was cast as Batman, saving Marshall from the Penguin, Joker, Riddler, and Catwoman.

To my surprise, though, my enthusiasm for promotions eventually waned. March into March was still the most fun I had each year, and it kicked in big numbers, but as the branch manager I could see that the effect was always short-term. There was no brand development or long-term relationship building, the things that mattered for our branch's growth. "You guys are missing the point," I told my sales staff. "We're not penetrating the marketplace. Everybody is just picking the easiest orders to book. We should be selling all the lines, stressing the features and benefits of the company, our computer, warehousing, and operational resources."

After a while, too, the promotions run by suppliers got absurd. I remember when two major semiconductor suppliers—call them Company A and Company B—each introduced new chips at the same time. Company A gave salespeople a ten-cent bonus on each part sold, a hefty chunk of change for salespeople who were selling thousands of pieces each month. Their sales took off, whereas Company B's chips languished on our shelves. So, Company B upped the ante, promising eleven cents a piece—and their chips flew off our shelves, leaving Company A's behind. Company A then increased their premium yet again: it was like the old gas wars of the '60s, but crazier. Here were two leaders of the world's semiconductor industry, each putting more than a million transistors on a chip, and they were forced to compete in pennies paid per chip sold.

Each time I took a step up the corporate ladder, my perspective shifted. When I was a branch manager, for example, my bonus depended on my branch's P&L performance, so I'd spend hours dreaming up creative ways to allocate expenses to the P&L of someone else within the region. Later, when I was promoted to regional manager and thus responsible for regional numbers, I saw how irrelevant that work had been. That irrelevance didn't matter, though: as a regional manager, I'd go out to corporate headquarters once a quarter for a three-day discussion of the company's problems, and we'd waste two of those three days wrangling over how to revise the expense allocation yet again.

Once I became senior vice president in corporate headquarters, it seemed that I spent all of my time trying to make better rules, hoping to create enough perfectly targeted objectives and incentives to account for everything I wanted everyone to worry about. I sought to find a platform that would make the company successful, something beyond just sizzle and selling that would let me escape the frustrations I felt about our inability to perform. Everyone in the organization knew what we were supposed to do—get the right parts to the right place at the right time—but when we fell short, there was always somebody else to blame. Marketing wasn't allocating right; the salespeople weren't selling right; our credit policy needed revision again. There was no common purpose or coordination between departments: everybody just wanted to protect his or her own sandbox. There were days that I felt more like a cop than a manager.

Meanwhile, promotions had gone still further afield. One day, I came to work and discovered that forty of our top salespeople, one from each branch, were all off on the same supplier's Caribbean cruise prize.

I've been a worrier all my adult life, despite all my success at Marshall. An A student in high school, I'd dreamed of a career in medicine, only to be derailed by my inability to grasp organic chemistry, a premed requirement. Graduated with a degree in psychology from the University of Connecticut in 1976, I had taken everything I had saved from summer lawn work and caddying, after-school jobs through high school, and four years of bartending in college and put it into starting a restaurant/lounge with a former boss turned partner. I'd built some of the sprawling seven-hundred-seat complex with my own hands, trusting my partner to handle the finances, a decision that would land me in bankruptcy after two high-flying years.

I've never gotten over that loss or the nagging fear that the bottom could fall out again at any time. I should have seen the warning signs then, but I was too naive to know how or where to look. This time, though, I had no excuse. At Marshall, the warnings were staring me in the face.

Crunch Time, Just-in-Time, Out of Time

I remember the first time a customer asked me if we could do "just-in-time," delivering different parts of an order at the exact moment that the customer needed each in his production flow. "Of course we can," I assured him. "Let me get back to you."

Of course, we couldn't. I'd read about just-in-time, but it looked too complicated for us to execute. Our best-case scenario showed nine days from the time we printed an order to when it arrived on our customer's loading dock, and even that could be a stretch, given our overloaded computer system and end-of-the-month madness.

"OK," I told the customer. "We're going to do just-in-time for you. Two days to pick your order, two days to pack it, two days to ship it, two days for you to receive it, with a one-day grace period, which gives you time to acknowledge receipt." We couldn't do anything to change the system, so I put the best spin on what we had and hoped that it would be good enough.

It wasn't. And just-in-time was just the beginning: our customers kept raising the competitive bar. If we wanted to stay in the big leagues, they told us, Marshall would have to demonstrate compliance with new external standards of quality, organization, and statistical management. Several wrote letters, announcing that to keep their business, all vendors had to take steps to comply with their Six Sigma Quality Program, the standard Motorola had established in 1981. More still jumped on the Malcolm Baldrige National Quality Awards. "Do you have plans to go for a Baldrige?" they asked. "And would you draft a memo detailing the steps you're going to follow to comply with the requirements?"

I didn't know what to do. We had always presented a good front out in public, keeping the screwups and squabbles in-house. I was afraid that if people—customers and potential customers—saw how strained we were becoming, they'd desert us in droves.

Gordon, too, was worried, but also determined to find a cure for the growing paralysis. But which cure to choose? Should we pick the Crosby path, with its zero-defect focus? Or would it be smarter to pursue ISO9000 certification and learn to reach internationally agreed-upon standards? Gordon, Dick Bentley, and I sat in Gordon's office for hours, debating our options. Nothing too drastic, we agreed. We had a profitable company going here, after all. And nothing that would take too long or cause too much disruption.

Pursuing a Baldrige award seemed to be the flavor that most people liked best, so I sent to Washington for the application and spent a disheartening weekend reading through it. Who were we kidding? There were seven different categories and twenty-eight examination items, and we weren't close on any of them. Still, I sent out a memo to the staff (on red paper so that it couldn't be copied), describing the first seven areas that we were going to have to try to fix.

Then Gordon gave me an article by Dr. W. Edwards Deming, the aging prophet of "total quality management," that he had read in the *Harvard Business Review,* and our strategy zigged. Gordon didn't understand it all yet, he admitted, but he thought that "quality" might be a better fix than trying to win a Baldrige. We'd just find a consultant who could do Deming for us, he said, and our problems would be solved.

I'd heard of Deming, of course: the father of statistical process controls and quality circles, revered in Japan, a notorious curmudgeon. When I read his article, "Fourteen Points for the Transformation of Management," I felt more confused than enlightened. Some points such as "create constancy of purpose" and "institute training" seemed obvious, but others, such as "drive out fear," left me baffled. As best I could tell, we seemed OK on about six and a half of them.

Yet despite my confusion, I didn't like the idea of a consultant, either. While I'm always afraid that a consultant will see me as an annuity, not someone with a specific short-term problem, this time my apprehension went deeper. I didn't know what we were doing wrong, but I was sure that if someone who really knew quality controls came in, he or she would tear us to shreds, and that was intimidating. I felt like an impostor, afraid of this consultant saying, "Look what this guy has done for the last seven years. It has all been useless. Get rid of him."

Our first consultant interview was a nonstarter. After we'd talked about possible terms, he'd tried to explain Deming's fourteen points, but I still didn't see how they'd provide the quick fix that we were looking for. "You just have to *believe,*" the consultant insisted, reaching across the bread basket to put his hand on mine.

I didn't want any part of it. "Look, I can't figure this out right now," I finally told Gordon. "And I don't want to figure it out." But Gordon was determined. He'd come across the name of Nida Backaitis, an associate professor at the University of Southern California, in *The Man Who Discovered Quality,* a Deming biography by Andrea Gabor. As a prominent alumnus and secretary of the USC board since 1970, Gordon had an easy time arranging a meeting with her.

Nida would become a critical player in the Marshall transformation. A Columbia Ph.D. in corporate strategy and an expert on strategic planning and the relationship between customers and vendors, she has been a provocative teacher and inspiring colleague at every step of our journey. But when we met for lunch that day at the USC faculty lounge, she didn't want anything to do with us.

Gordon did most of the talking at first. Handing her a copy of the 575-page Marshall catalogue, he launched into a summary history of the company and a description of our markets and strategies. There were some quality problems, he admitted, some performance issues and tensions. "We'd like you to help us fix them. You know, just 'Demingize' the company."

"What," Nida asked, "does that mean?"

"If you don't know, I don't know what we're going to talk about here," Gordon said, laughing. Then he rattled off what we'd read about process-control methods and techniques for implementing the fourteen points.

Nida listened patiently, then told us, politely, that we didn't have a clue. "Dr. Deming isn't about methods or techniques," she explained. "His whole idea is that to change the way you manage a company, you have to change the way you see the world first. It's not a quick fix. It's changing basic relationships and attitudes, knocking down barriers between different parts of the organization. That means people will feel, at first, that they're losing power and control.

"Deming always says that he thinks it would take ten years for a company to make all the necessary changes," she warned us. "If you're ready to jump into it so fast, you probably don't understand it."

I was impressed by Nida's intellect and poise, and by the fact that she clearly didn't give a hoot who we were. Gordon was impressed as well. He always appreciated straight shooters. We'll do whatever it takes, he promised, offering her carte blanche if she'd take the assignment. "It would be great," I agreed. "If you'd come in, I can go back to selling—and I can sell that Marshall is doing Deming."

Nida just stared at us. "Are you guys for real? You still don't get it."

There was a four-day Deming seminar scheduled for later in the month. She recommended that we attend it, and, if we were still interested in learning more after that, she'd be willing to talk with us again.

Four days of buzzwords? I can barely sit still for an hour. Gordon agreed that we'd go, though, and he was the boss. I just figured that I'd make the best of it: sit in for the beginning, get a flavor, then duck out to work the phones.

Deming for Dummies

"How much longer till cocktail hour?" I whispered to Dick as we filed into the ballroom of the San Jose Marriott for the Deming seminar. "And what can we possibly do for four days here?"

Sitting with a thousand people on folding chairs in a dark room on a sunny Wednesday morning is not my idea of a good start to the day. But it got worse when Dr. Deming started to speak. A tall, bald man wearing wire-rimmed spectacles and an oversized navy suit, he didn't talk, he droned—a low, slow, quivering monotone, shuffling across the platform to his overhead projector from time to time to write out a word or two, laboriously, letter by letter, starting over if he made a mistake. I was fidgeting inside the first five minutes. Half-listening, I started work on a to-do list for my return to work. But then Dr. Deming started to demonstrate the red-bead experiment, and I put my list aside.

It's hard to do justice to the red-bead experiment in a few paragraphs. A classic example of Deming's wit, it's a simple exercise, really, that makes a simple point. But it opened my eyes to a new way of looking at my management frustrations, and that, just as Nida had predicted, changed everything.

In the experiment, Deming, playing foreman, chooses a production team of ten volunteers from the audience. Six are "willing workers," two are "inspectors," and one is "chief inspector." "Congratulations, you're hired," he tells them. "Workers stand on my right, inspectors on my left. We don't want any fraternization or collusion here."

Deming's description of the work at hand is explicit. On the stage is a shoe box filled with beads, roughly 80 percent of them white and 20 percent red. Each worker dips a flat paddle with fifty small holes into the box and pulls it out again with a bead in each hole, then shows it to the inspectors. Each inspector in turn counts the worker's production, writes down the number of red, or defective, beads, then passes the number to the chief inspector, who compares the numbers and announces the result. "The acceptable standard of quality for a day's work is three red beads," he explains.

"Where did the standard come from?" one worker asks.

"Management has determined that, given the financial impera-tives, we need an error rate of no more than three red beads per pull to make our budget."

"Why so many inspectors?"

"Management wants to guarantee accuracy and impartiality. By having each inspector write down rather than announce the count, management ensures that the inspectors reach their observations independent of one another. We need the chief inspector to super-vise that process, to resolve any differences between the two inspec-tors, and to make sure the count is accurate."

Then, Foreman Deming shows the workers exactly how the work is to be done. "Hold the paddle at a forty-five-degree angle," he in-structs. "Do not shake the paddle. Do not agitate the box. Just dip the paddle in and pull it out again, very, very slowly, making sure that all the holes are filled."

One by one the workers try it. "No, no, no," he corrects the first. "That's not forty-five degrees. Don't deviate from the procedures. We've spent a lot of time developing them; they're here to ensure quality."

By the end of the practice session, the workers are already rest-less. With so many red beads in the box, all of them pulled more than three defectives. "You didn't do such a great job during your training," Deming observes. "But now we're going to start paying you, so maybe you'll start paying better attention to your work."

Then he puts them to work, with predictable results. In the first round, no one pulls three or fewer red beads. In fact, most get considerably more, with some counts in the ten-to-fifteen range: "Fourteen!" Deming chides. "Didn't you listen? Management has determined that the acceptable quality standard is three."

Management is distressed. "If you don't get better results than this, we're going to have to replace you or replace the workers," they warn the foreman. "Or maybe we'll just shut down the whole factory and move production somewhere else."

"I've received orders from on high to improve quality," the foreman tells the workers. "We have to lower the error rate, or else." Then he goes around the room putting posters on the wall: "QUALITY IS YOUR JOB!" "Now, remember, you must follow procedures exactly, and there should be no deviation. Our industrial engineers worked hard on them."

The next round's results, of course, are no better, and management is irate. The foreman goes into another meeting and gets yelled at again. "You have to try harder," he tells his people. "So now we're going to give you incentives. Obviously what we've done so far hasn't worked." Then he gives the better bead-pullers a bonus and puts the less adept on probation.

The next round's results improve a little. But the employees who had previously won bonuses pull out unacceptable red-bead totals, while those on probation improve. "Aha," management reasons, "bonuses don't work. Threats do."

By now, the workers are thoroughly absorbed in the exercise. They realize that they can't hit the target, and that it's just a game in any case, but they still feel pressured to try to do their best. Faces flush; palms sweat. One of the workers thinks that perhaps if he changes the angle of the paddle, he might change the number of red beads he pulls. Deming comes down hard when he tries it. "Management has decided that forty-five degrees is the procedure. Do not deviate from this procedure." Another worker tries shaking the box before she puts in the paddle, hoping that that will change the result. "Didn't you hear what I said about procedure?" Deming snaps. "You're fired!"

Seeing this carried out, I had to laugh, although the more I watched the less funny it became. The red-bead experiment was a caricature, absurd and obvious at the same time, but it cut uncomfortably close to the truth of how we managed Marshall. We'd given people "management's procedures" to follow, setting out budgets, designing the promotions, and developing the incentives and MBOs. When that didn't bring the results we needed, we'd produce a more-elaborate video or announce that we were going to compete for the Baldrige. People who didn't get the results we needed did not last long.

Suddenly, now, I was afraid to fidget. I felt as if Dr. Deming were talking right to me, one on one.

The problem with most managers, he explained in his debriefing, is that the techniques that they routinely use to ensure performance actually limit quality and productivity. They stifle innovation, make people fearful and demotivated, and only guarantee conformity to procedures. Quality can be no better than the design of the system allows—people act rationally within the system that's created for them.

A lightbulb went on for me. "My God," I thought, "it's the system, stupid!"

There were ways to solve the red-bead production problem, Deming continued. Adding one inspector to the six-employee work team would have increased production over 15 percent. Or, if the workers had been free to change the process, they might have scrapped the paddles and pulled out the white beads by hand. But management rarely gives workers such choices. Most managers are often so locked in to their compartmentalized view of the organization that they lose any sense of the purpose or the workings of the whole, diminishing everyone's performance as a consequence. Then, when results fall short, they have two choices: distort the numbers or distort the system. Actually, they have a third choice— fix the system—but few ever really recognize, or try, that.

That, too, hit home. When we delayed returns or manipulated a P&L, we were distorting the numbers. When we revised the formulas and changed the incentives, we were distorting the system. But neither got us any closer to solving our real problems.

Over the next four days of exercises, talks, and games, I slowed down and, for the first time in my career, looked at Marshall Industries from a distance. Gordon had started with a good idea: buy low, sell high, and walk through fire for the customer. With a relative handful of suppliers and customers, it had been easy to manage the relationships. As the world had gotten more complicated, however, that simple spirit of the deal had disappeared, obscured by an ever more elaborate edifice of management structures. We were professionals, and we could make the system work, but it took staggering manipulation and brute force to get over, around, and through all the barriers.

I had thought that the problem was *in* the systems, but the problem was the systems themselves. Snappy mottos didn't create customer focus; by themselves they were useless noise. MBOs didn't build teamwork—incentive pay fragmented the organization, focusing people on narrow individual goals. The only result that counted was our customers' and suppliers' bottom lines; if Marshall helped them grow, Marshall would grow with them. Yet our systems kept us focused on narrower internal metrics.

I could see why we were stuck with the same perpetual problems. It made sense for one division to hide inventory from another; they were paid to compete. It made sense for salespeople to ship orders ahead or hide returns; they were paid for monthly numbers. It made sense to sell what sold easily—products that were tried, true, and available—even though our long-term future depended on growing new markets. Salespeople and management focused on closing, although they knew customer satisfaction depended more on follow-up. That's what the Marshall system rewarded. Pep rallies and promotions had become an addiction, but they didn't develop the innovation and added value for constituents that would drive us in the marketplace.

The problem wasn't our people, for they were just responding rationally to the carrots and sticks I'd helped to create. The more we tried to refine the system, the farther away we got from the customer we were supposed to be serving.

Of course, I was frustrated, but I also felt that the buck had to stop with me. For all my good intentions, I'd helped build the very system that was frustrating me.

I walked out of that seminar at the end of four days feeling empty and powerless. I still had the to-do list I'd written on the first day, but the items didn't seem to address the real priorities anymore.

Now I really felt afraid that the bottom would fall out. And when I went back to work after the seminar, I felt worse than ever. The way I had managed before seemed absurd, and that was scary as hell. I knew that we had to sweep away all of the clutter and start again. But I didn't have a clue what a redesigned Marshall should look like or how to start creating it.

Manager's Workbook

For every problem there is a solution that is simple, neat . . . and wrong.
— H. L. MENCKEN

Seven Pillars of Quality

Quality is something you learn, not something you mandate. It's not about statistical process controls, but about building a system that gives you numbers you can trust and react to. It's not about a quick-fix checklist, but wrenching and radical long-term change.

You can't learn quality by trying to manage results. Focusing on the far-end outcome is not an effective way to improve a system's performance. Don't look only at the number of widgets you sold last Tuesday—look at all the different causes that created that result: people, methods, material, equipment, and environment. Don't look at last Tuesday alone, look toward next Tuesday and a year from Tuesday too.

Examine in particular your own performance against the seven pillars of quality:

Context

"Quality is whatever the customer says it is," as quality expert Dr. "Val" Feigenbaum said. The problem is that each customer's definition of quality is unique and constantly changing. Your ability to respond to that moving target depends on evaluating your entire competitive environment: your human, financial, and technology resources, your competitor's strategies and tactics, and the underlying model for competitive differentiation in your industry. It depends on looking outside your industry, too, and evaluating new solutions and technologies to see how they could enhance your own processes.

Collaboration

Quality starts at the top. Only executive leadership has the power to mandate system change. But leadership's role isn't to issue orders and hand down new procedures; it is to pull everyone in to the learning process, connect them to the imperatives of change, invite in their ideas and criticism, and give them the resources, teaching, and support to act effectively. Passion and energy are necessary, but not sufficient by themselves.

Consistency

Quality requires a common purpose commonly understood and common methods consistently executed. Management by flavor of the day can't design processes that create legacy solutions. You need a clear mission and strategy that spreads throughout the organization, grounding individual decisions in a shared understanding of marketplace change. Don't surprise people—it makes them fearful. Communication has to be constant and predictable, particularly when the message is marketplace unpredictability and the necessity of change.

Coordination

Quality comes from aligning your purpose with your people and technology, knocking down the barriers to cooperation and learning. If you want your people to work together, all your systems have to work together, too. People act rationally within the system they're given. If they have incentives to hoard information or if you reward them for short-term goals, that is what they will focus on.

Controls

Forget "ready, fire, aim." You have to plan, implement, and evaluate, then adjust your plan, creating a continuous feedback loop. Your telemetry has to be able to measure and evaluate variation, to separate the market signal from the background noise. Don't try to justify new information. Study it, react, and learn.

Costs

Don't just focus on the expenses you can take out. Focus on the value you can put in—the numerator, not the denominator. And remember, not all costs can be measured. Sometimes the cost of not making a change may be higher than the cost of making it.

Courage

No job is harder than system redesign. It takes vision and dedication, the humility to admit all you don't know, and a personal commitment to learning and change, no matter how painful they may be.

Inside the Management Maze

Ever feel like you can't get there from here? Look at your organization chart, and ask what it takes to get a response from the higher-ups. Your customer wants an answer yesterday, and you're still waiting to hear.

Blame it on management by results—a system designed for control, not speed. Every question, request, or problem has to work up the chain of command, and every level and department has its own objectives and agendas, its own budgets, P&Ls, and incentives—and a vested interest in controlling information, being copied on communication, and signing off on decisions. There may have once

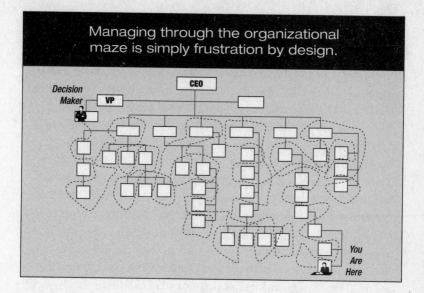

Managing through the organizational maze is simply frustration by design.

been a common mission, but now it is subordinated to narrower goals. This breaks the organization into fiefdoms.

Meanwhile, your customer waits . . . and waits . . . and waits . . .

Who Killed Total Quality Management?

It's hard to say "total quality management" these days without drawing at least a few eye-rolls. The concept, which was all the rage during the 1980s, became the butt of *Dilbert* cartoons in the 1990s. A 1997 Academy of Management survey of five hundred executives in American manufacturing and service companies showed that only one-third believed total quality management (TQM) to have made them more competitive. How did such an apparently powerful idea go from the penthouse to the doghouse so fast?

The trend first hit the nation almost twenty years ago, as American manufacturers struggled to catch up to their Japanese counterparts, who had embraced Dr. W. Edwards Deming's ideas decades earlier, after the same theories were rejected in America. The 1980 NBC documentary *If Japan Can, Why Can't We?* brought home to Americans just how much that initial missed chance had cost. The public became even more focused on the issue of quality with the introduction of the Malcolm Baldrige National Quality Award in 1987. In spite of all the attention, however, TQM proved difficult to implement. Experts have estimated that as many as 80 percent of all TQM initiatives fail. Time after time, the flaws have proven to be in the tactics of the companies adopting TQM, not the ideas behind it. Ineptitude, not irrelevance, killed TQM.

Management missing in action

The number-one reason that quality-management projects fail is a lack of support from top management. The Academy of Management found some unsurprising but illustrative results in a survey of companies using TQM: Managers with successful TQM programs aimed to compete against the best in their respective industries; they saw customers as partners and allies. On the other hand, managers at companies with failed programs believed that the goal of TQM was to meet short-term objectives and "hit the right numbers." These managers saw customers as the enemy—an outside force that bullied them into halfhearted quality efforts. If the managers don't understand or support the importance of system quality, they surely won't be able to inspire their employees to do so.

A recent case recounted in a health-care trade magazine further proves the point. A medium-sized health-care institution, too embarrassed to allow its name to be used in the case study, adopted TQM whole hog. Every department created vision and mission statements, while more than a hundred TQM project teams were created. But by the end of the first year, the CEO had dropped off the steering committee, turning the chair over to a subordinate. Within three years, the program had fizzled—after costing the institution $750,000, not counting the cost of productivity lost from time spent in training instead of on the job.

No culture of quality is created

For TQM to work, it has to be embraced by everyone at the company. Too often, companies have settled for training a few department heads and hoping that the program would trickle down to the line employees. Or, the pay of executives and mangers is not linked to quality, so there's no incentive for them to focus on TQM goals.

Ed Lawler, founder and director of the Center for Effective Organizations at the University of Southern California, has studied nearly nine years of TQM data from *Fortune* 1000 companies, and found that TQM doesn't work unless all employees feel a personal stake in quality. How do you get there? By combining TQM programs with efforts to push information, power, and rewards further down into the organization. Lawler discovered that companies with this kind of quality culture were much more likely to be successful in TQM efforts. For example, Texas Instruments's semiconductor group has created the "Jonah Network," a team of cycle-time experts who are empowered to coordinate information sharing among the company's plants. Since the team was formed and the quality goals established, overall cycle times have been reduced by 60 percent and throughput has increased by 35 percent.

By contrast, companies that fail to make TQM matter to their employees fail at TQM. In another study, a group of researchers from the Manchester School of Management looked at a TQM program at a medium-sized bank in the United Kingdom. Despite the fact that more than 90 percent of employees were organized, their union was not involved in planning or implementation. Training was provided for the managers only, but not for the staff, who were expected to absorb the ideas from their supervisors. Ironically, this bank won an award for its quality training in 1989, but later abandoned its quality efforts, acknowledging defeat. As the training manager remarked, "We won an award for the training, and we came back and put our boxes of books of what we'd learned on the shelf, and many of us didn't DO anything—that was the weakest part of the program. How do you turn these ideas into change?" The motivations to champion the TQM did not exist. And even if they had, employees were not trained or empowered to act on that motivation.

Making quality an island
Quality can't be the province of a privileged few in the company. It has to be everyone's job. But in company after company, you'll find

separate quality divisions and individual quality managers. Dividing the responsibility that way doesn't work. "You end up with these people who travel to the most fascinating countries to benchmark other companies, and there is absolutely no way to figure out how this knowledge applies to their own company," says Eileen Shapiro, author of *Fad Surfing in the Boardroom: Reclaiming the Courage to Manage in the Age of Instant Answers*. "You really just create this elite club of frequent flyers."

Florida Power and Light received the Deming Prize from the Union of Japanese Scientists and Engineers in 1989 for its TQM excellence. Later that same year, a new CEO came in and slashed the quality department from eighty-five to three, after he learned that the company's employees feared that the quality-improvement process had become a tyrannical bureaucracy. He found that the company was more committed to winning awards than serving the customer.

An end unto itself

A blurb in *Forbes* magazine cannily summed up one of the ways that TQM went astray: "High Hopes: Systematically improving the quality of corporate operations toward a goal of perfection can improve competitiveness and improve customer satisfaction and loyalty. Busted Dreams: To hell with profits! We're going to make these damn things perfect."

Quality in and of itself can't be the goal. It has to be the means to competitive differentiation and financial result. Too often, companies lose sight of how TQM fits into their overall strategy and why it was important in the first place. Take, for example, the Wallace Company, a Houston-based manufacturer of pipes and valves. Winner of the Baldrige Award in 1990, by 1991 it had filed for Chapter 11 bankruptcy protection, having spent so heavily on its quality initiatives that it drowned in red ink.

Quality programs, well designed and well executed, can lead to dramatic performance improvements—but only if you focus on the target of competitive improvement, not on the programs themselves.

4
Management on Trial:

Launching Radical Change

Management by Method

The experts will tell you that there are three prerequisites for radical change. First, it has to come from the top, pushed through by a CEO with a mandate of support from the board. Second, it can be launched only in crisis, when everyone inside the organization can see that nothing less than survival is at stake. And, third, it has to start with a concrete strategy clearly defined and explicitly articulated.

Certainly all three were present in the best-known recent corporate transformations, among them Richard Teerlink's reinvention of Harley-Davidson in the 1980s, Edward Martinez's turnaround of Sears Roebuck in the early 1990s, and Louis Gerstner's mid- and late-1990s heroics at IBM. My situation at Marshall, however, was different from these. I wasn't in charge; I reported to Dick Bentley, the executive VP, and to Gordon, who was CEO. Then, for all our headaches, we were still a profitable $500 million company, as Gordon pointed out to me at the Deming seminar. And I didn't have a strategy when I started, just a conviction that something drastic had to be done before the bottom fell out.

As soon as I got back to work, people started pulling at me to tell them about the seminar, curious about what they assumed would be management's new flavor of the month. "What did you learn?" they asked. "What are we going to do now?"

I was asking myself those same questions. Although I knew that we had to reinvent our organization, I wasn't sure what would constitute actually changing the system, as opposed to what would be merely manipulating it. "Rational behavior" and "system analysis," "common variation," "special-cause variation," "optimized" and "suboptimized": my head was spinning with terms. All I knew for sure was that we had to develop a companywide understanding that more of the same wouldn't be good enough. Every level of the company, from the chairman through the ranks, had to see what I saw; that we'd never get beyond the frustration of meeting after meeting and memo after memo if we didn't make a significant structural change.

"I don't think I understand everything that I was exposed to at the seminar yet," I admitted to my colleagues. "I think the company is doing some things well, and it's not doing some things well, but I'm not ready to lay out a series of action items right now.

"There will be no surprises," I promised. "Whatever we do, we'll do together. For the moment, I'm questioning whether contests and promotions serve us well, but beyond that, I just don't know yet."

In retrospect, I was lucky that I didn't have anything concrete to propose. I am not by nature a patient person, and if I'd had what I thought were the answers then, I might have tried to force them through without laying the necessary groundwork. But my uncertainty caused me to be methodical, made me question everything we did and how we did it, pushing my dissection back to core assumptions, values, and ambitions. That, in turn, gave me the time to market the new perspective I was gradually developing. As it coalesced for me, I taught people to see the world as I was beginning to see it. Launching an ongoing and apparently open-ended dialogue up and down the chain of command let me discover who shared my frustration and could be taught my sense of urgency, and helped me identify potential allies and build a broad platform of support.

There are no shortcuts to systemic change. Turnaround artists may slash and burn to push the numbers up for a few quarters, but they leave no competitive legacy behind when they cash out. A competitive legacy, by contrast, takes a radical redesign—not just reengineering specific processes, but reengineering the process of change itself. "Fire, ready, aim!" doesn't work. You have to plan, experiment, then study the result and plan again, working up a continual cycle of design, test, and improved redesign that engages the entire organization.

In school, we accept that we need to go through courses level by level, working from 101 to 201 to 301 and so on to master a complex discipline. But as soon as we get to work, we believe that with bravado and a title we can skip similar necessary steps in the learning process. We can't. And furthermore, an organization, like an individual, needs time.

Before people will care about the how-to of change, they have to believe in the why. A lifelong smoker may ignore all the surgeon general's reports, but if he has a heart attack, he will likely take a new interest in how nicotine patches and clinics can help him stop smoking. Motivation in business works the same way. Before people can develop a method and discipline of change, they have to understand its imperative. Initially, there will be resistance to any drastic shift, no matter how well you explain it. But the more effectively you can bring people into your thought process, the less resistance you'll get and the more likely it will be that remaining resistance will be legitimate and provide a potential sounding board to help you refine your course.

Consensus isn't required; you're not running a democracy. However, you *do* need to get people coordinated to move in the same direction. You can't push them up the hill, whether you manage ten people or ten thousand. There are too many individual biases that will dilute your vision. Instead, you have to market your ideas one to one, patiently reaching out to potential change agents who can help you pull the rest of the company up the learning curve.

Marshall's transformation was launched by questions without conclusions, through an ongoing dialogue that put our management system on trial. What is the world telling us? What could we do to create value? Why aren't we doing it?

Industry margins had eroded ten points in ten years, and from that statistic alone it was obvious that the market wasn't screaming its love for us. What did our customers want? Why couldn't we give it to them? Was it just one customer who was getting hard to do business with, or was it a trend, a force of nature that we couldn't afford to ignore?

Marshall's team had grown up in the business together, developing a set of tools and skills that had served us well so far. But were those likely to carry us into the future? If we on the management team could take a blank sheet of paper, we'd design a different company than the one we were trying to manage. What should we be? What's in the way? Each round of answers focused us on the next series of questions. Why aren't we timely? Where can't we deliver mutual satisfaction? What could we do to fix it?

Marshall had become a web of conflicts; a company of forty different branches acting like forty different fiefdoms. Every time a supplier or customer asked us for something more, we'd try to jump, hoping that luck and skill would hold it all together and keep us from falling flat. Our only chance for the future was to present a common front, a unified identity that made doing business with Marshall different from doing business with anybody else. To do that, we'd have to coordinate our message through everything that could have an effect on the results we delivered, aligning our people, methods, materials, equipment, and environment behind a common goal.

It would take almost a year before we felt ready to act. We spent three months developing a strategy built around the idea of alignment and another nine months defining it operationally and cultivating a companywide acceptance of the need for its implementation. For most of that time I was running on all cylinders, like a novice teacher struggling to master a new curriculum, pushing to stay ninety days ahead of my students. But it was time well spent:

that long roller-coaster year would become the genesis of a different method of management, the method that has guided Marshall ever since. By teaching people to ask the same questions that I was asking myself, we would learn how to find the answers and discover the basis for our organizational redesign, and move from a shared understanding of the why of change to a focused search for the how-to.

Why Not "The Best"?

There was no need to show Dick Bentley the need for radical change. His eyes, like mine, had been opened by the Deming seminar, the red-bead experiment in particular. "It made me realize the way we were managing wasn't right," he told me later, "but I didn't know what that meant yet or how we'd get it across to our people." Dick shared my anxiety, too. He took his wife, Beverly, out to dinner after the seminar to talk about the career risks he saw ahead. "I've been pretty successful doing things my way for thirty-five years, and now I've got to change," he told her, worried. "But can I change? And change into what?"

Gordon was a harder sell. Although he'd chuckled over the red-bead experiment, he wasn't sure how its message applied to Marshall. Ever the entrepreneur, he was impatient for results but wary of anything disruptive of the company he loved. "We don't want to spin off too far," he warned me. "Let's not forget what we've built here."

I had the same kind of conversation with him for several weeks. Mostly I talked about the market forces, margin pressures, and performance shortfalls that I was seeing in my day-to-day duties, puzzling out their possible causes and potential consequences, and trying to get him to agree that something more than incremental improvements might be called for.

"We've got lots of things we could improve right now," he'd insist, then list a dozen specific processes, from buying inventory to selling product.

"We could do that," I'd agree, "and we'd be better for it. But where would that get us? Would it differentiate us from anybody else in the marketplace? Would customers choose Marshall because we'd improved our efficiency by a few pennies or cut our error rate by five percent?"

What we could do right away, I suggested, was give him additional responsibilities and an additional title: chief quality officer. That would send a clear message to both the organization and the marketplace that we considered quality to be one of our prime values, the central responsibility of presidential leadership, too important to be delegated into the middle. It gave Gordon the explicit task of eliminating the barriers between the level of customer service to which we aspired and what we actually delivered, as well as tying him in advance to the system and process redesign to come. And it gave the rest of the organization a basis from which to challenge the direction at the top if that direction ran counter to our quality aspiration. As a side benefit, it provided the makings of a new marketing strategy, too, one that emphasized that from the president on down, we were structured for the benefit of the customer—and gave Gordon a new message to carry to Wall Street.

Meanwhile, the world didn't stop to give us time to figure out what "quality" meant. There were still fires to put out, suppliers to see, and customers to court, a relentless barrage of phone calls and face-to-face meetings to attend to. I promoted my call for change in every meeting and conversation I had, raising the same subjects and questions constantly. One day, I brought in an ad from Roadway Express, one of the leading "less than a truckload" freight carriers. "You know, if we cut out their name and put in Marshall, this ad could be ours," I pointed out. "What do we do that will keep them from cannibalizing our business someday?"

That gave people pause.

"Who else could eat our lunch? American Airlines? FedEx?"

"Do you really think that FedEx could compete with us?" Gordon wondered.

"I don't know," I admitted. "Let me go down and see."

It was a confusing time. I'd talk on the phone to Nida or sit in Dick's office late into the night, trying to distill our business down to its core building blocks. It became discouraging: the more we looked at what we did, the less effective much of it seemed. And when we asked why we did it that way, the answer was always the same: That's how the industry has always done it.

At the same time, I was trying to teach myself organizational design, system analysis, and statistical process control, reading Deming, Hammer, and Drucker, studying during any time I could steal. I was particularly impressed by a simple book about industrial design, Donald A. Norman's *The Psychology of Everyday Things*. It should be clear from the design itself which knob turns on which stove burner or whether a door should be pushed or pulled, Norman argued; the more instruction you have to provide, the worse the design. Likewise, I reasoned, Marshall's business processes should be designed to afford intuitive compliance with their goals. The more memos, oversight, or MBOs you need to make them work, the less well they perform. The key would be communication between processes—but processes can't communicate across a complex organization unless the people who build and use them know first how to communicate, having worked through the design together, sharing a vocabulary, and coming to a common understanding of their larger purpose.

Nida suggested that the best starting point should be to create a Marshall strategy that answered one question: "What do you want to do and for whom do you want to do it?" Over one weekend, I wrote up a few simple paragraphs of unpolished prose. We were a "quality value-added industrial distributor," not a consumer company like Radio Shack. We were looking for customers who wanted "continuous improvement of their technologies, systems, products, and services," not merely the lowest price. Our ambition was "mutual benefit for employees, customers, and suppliers"—and that, in turn, would create shareholder value.

Shortly thereafter, I put the strategy up on the wall for Gordon, Dick, and our 150 senior managers at a special companywide "quality" meeting. "Do you think it's a fair statement of what we're trying to do here?"

There was nothing novel in what I'd written; we'd been talking about "value-added" and "quality" for years. So there wasn't much debate, although we did change a word or two. "But there's one thing it leaves out," someone insisted. "It should say, 'Marshall will be the best.' "

"What does that mean, 'the best'?"

"Well, the best distributor."

"What is the best distributor? Best at what?"

"Well, best at service."

"Best for whom? Best against what standard?"

The longer we broke it down, the clearer it became that terms such as "the best," "number one," and "world class" didn't have any meaning. They sound good, but they can't be defined operationally or turned into a measurable target. Given our fluid environment, today's best might be tomorrow's worst. And if we tried to define "best" as what each person takes to be the best, we'd end up being pulled a thousand ways at once.

"OK, then—we're all agreed that the strategy makes sense? So why can't we execute it? What are the barriers we run into?"

"There's too much paperwork in credit," one person said.

"The phone system in our branch is too old," another complained.

"Our buy reports don't properly reflect quantity on hand, so our main return process isn't very efficient."

"We don't perform well for all our suppliers, just the ones with promos."

I wrote the answers on a flip chart in the front of the room, page after page, 112 different performance barriers before we were done. Then I hung the pages on the wall. This was familiar ground, too; we'd talked about some of them individually for years, but we'd never looked at the whole list together before. What was clear, as I expected, was that most of the problems could be sorted into two categories: the MBO compensation system that drove our behavior, and the operating system that we'd created to serve that system.

"So what do we want to do now?" I asked. "Do we want to work on all one hundred twelve at the same time? Could we work on all one hundred twelve? Are the little ones material for our strategy? If we cut out some paper or fixed our main return process, would anyone care? Would it give us any more horsepower in the market-place?"

I felt pretty good after the meeting. As I'd anticipated, people had agreed that we should attack our two biggest barriers to alignment, which were the way we managed people and the way we managed data. More important, I could hear some excitement bubbling up from the ranks, and Gordon was firmly on board.

"There's no action to take yet," I told them. "We can't go to college until we complete high school. We'll have to study and plan before we do anything."

Unfortunately, though, I didn't deliver that particular message clearly enough. Someone at headquarters ordered a case of Deming's books and sent them out to the branches, as if people were going to read the fourteen points at their desks and decide, "Oh, *now* I'm ready to change." Besides raising the anxiety level, it sent the wrong signals. We weren't "doing Deming." With our company and careers at stake, we had to find a Marshall definition of quality and create a Marshall method of management—not simply mouth Deming.

There was one payoff from my mistake, though: it forced me to follow through on my "no surprises" pledge. Phone calls to branches had always been random. From now on, I promised, there'd be a conference call with all of the branches every two weeks. All the news, good or bad, and any plans before they happened would be addressed. Our meetings had always been called erratically, announced whenever we felt the need arise. Now, though, we'd schedule a meeting of the ten regional managers every ninety days and a meeting of the 150 senior managers each year. There would be no more anxious speculation about what headquarters was up to.

That call has been made religiously every two weeks for the last six years, and meetings have become predictable. So, the calendar doesn't just fill haphazardly with the day-to-day tasks anymore; it's become a proactive low-tech planning tool.

"Two All-Beef Patties, Special Sauce . . ."

For the next few months I worked the road, crisscrossing the country in our aging corporate jet, spreading the message of alignment to every corner of the company. I'd sit down with five or six people and talk for hours, repeating the same conversations, starting with a blank slate, trying to make everyone I spoke to see that what mattered was making sure that all of our individual processes, methods, and people lined up to deliver what our customers really wanted.

While I still didn't know what Marshall should become, the more I studied and questioned, the clearer three design imperatives became. First, once we'd established a shared understanding of the need for change, we'd have to teach people to see our misalignment as systemic. It was not the fault of any individual or department, but a failure of organizational design. Second, we'd all have to learn to look at data differently, and discern which events were meaningful and which were momentary. Third, we'd have to learn how to translate that back into our ongoing redesign process.

How do you teach an abstract concept such as system alignment to an organization of 1,600 people? I did it with the hamburger story.

Whom do you blame if you sit in a restaurant waiting for twenty minutes before your burger appears? The waitress? Maybe the restaurant needs another cook to handle the noon rush. Or maybe the morning's delivery of ground beef is late. Maybe the grill goes out; maybe your order falls off the rack over the grill station.

Not tipping the waitress may feel good, but how fair is it to blame her for the flaw in the system? And does your refusal to tip guarantee that if you come back tomorrow, you won't have to wait twenty minutes for your burger again?

That's what we were doing at Marshall, I explained: we were blaming individuals for our system's shortcomings. If the numbers were down, we'd add a contest—in effect, tipping the salespeople. But maybe the problem lay with how we collected accounts receivable or moved boxes through the warehouse. Or maybe we needed a new way of selling. But whatever it was, we'd never find out if we stopped asking questions and just stiffed the waitress.

I must have told the hamburger story a thousand times over those months, spinning it out in elaborate detail, posing question after question, trying to lead people to say in their own words that the only way to guarantee a happy customer is to make sure that everything from the Fryolator to the pickle delivery works in sync. If the hamburger story didn't click with them, I'd ask about race cars or doctors' procedures or what it takes to win a marathon. Whichever story, though, the punch line was the same: A business is a complex system; all the elements have to be aligned for it to perform at its peak.

Repetition and simplicity are the soul of change marketing. People all process information differently, so you have to develop multiple ways to deliver the same lessons. Few will have the time or inclination to wade through twenty dense pages from *The Harvard Business Review*. Most will nod off over high-end statistical run charts and complex math. Give them an analogy to puzzle over instead, or tell them a parable and let them find the moral for themselves. Then tell them again and again. There's a reason why almost everyone in America can tell you what's in a Big Mac: they've heard it a million times. You have to be just as repetitive.

I needed our people to see, as I did, the fallacy of using short-term results to drive business decisions. By allowing individual data points, such as a quarterly sales report or a branch's P&L statement, set our course, we were squandering our energy, concentrating on momentary numbers while ignoring the larger competitive forces that affected our market. So, here, I talked about football scores.

If the final score of the football game is 17–10, do you know for sure which will be the better team over the season?

It isn't necessarily the team that scored seventeen points—there could be a thousand reasons why the other team lost. Maybe there was a fumble, or a star defensive back pulled a hamstring.

Should the coach bench the quarterback because of one Sunday's results? Perhaps—but not until he has more information than just the score. A great coach will analyze each game's results as best he can, looking for the underlying causes, then use that to prepare for the next game, trying to develop a method that will make the team perform consistently at its peak, game after game.

The same is true in business. You may think a quarterly sales figure marks a big win, then discover that your competitor, who usually never fumbles, actually did drop the ball during that period. Likewise, you could have a low P&L that actually indicates good news, marking an investment in new systems and processes you need to be a better competitor over the long term. What matters isn't the single data point, but understanding its causes and importance in the larger context, then turning that understanding into a strategy that moves you forward.

The goal of systems analysis is to increase statistical probability while decreasing variation, using data to tell you what you need to learn and improve. Many people, however, are befuddled by numbers—they may know how to read a financial statement or calculate an average, but they haven't learned how to plot data points across time, define the margins of compliance within upper and lower control limits, or differentiate between what statisticians call "common cause" and "special cause" variations.

I tried to teach the groups I met with the basics by talking about their daily commute.

Say it takes you about half an hour to drive to work each day. If you graphed your time on the road, you might see that the trip on some days required twenty-eight minutes, whereas on other days it took thirty-two minutes. In statistical terms, those are your upper and lower control limits, which permit you to safely predict what time you have to leave your house each morning. On some days the traffic is a little heavier, and on some days it's a little lighter: that's common-cause variation.

Now, say that one day your commute takes you an hour. Does that mean that you need a different route? Maybe so—it may be the first day of a massive highway project that will clog traffic for months, raising the upper control limits of your common-cause variation for the foreseeable future. Or maybe not—there may be a special-cause variation, such as a five-alarm fire that snarls traffic for hours. In any case, it would be foolish to try to decide what to do tomorrow from one day's data point. Yet that's what we usually did at Marshall.

There's no payoff in reacting to special-cause variations. By definition, they don't change your upper and lower control limits. But there's also no point in trying to beat common-cause variations. We've all seen the road warriors who commute competitively, weaving in and out of lanes, horns blaring. But what do they accomplish? They use up more gas and wear out their tires, and usually end up sitting one lane over at the next red light anyway, their blood pressures soaring. If you need to get to work faster, the solution isn't to try to zip through the traffic on your regular route. The solution is to find a faster route.

That's what we had to do at Marshall, I explained. We'd been trying to beat the system, and the result had been frustration. Maybe it was time to find a better way to work.

"We Have Met the Enemy . . ."

There was one more lesson I had to teach, and it was the most important insight I had taken away from the Deming seminar eleven months before. I'd understood "It's the system, stupid" with my mind, but what had hit me in my gut in that hotel ballroom was the corollary that *I* was the system, the cause of my own frustration and Marshall's performance woes. I'd supported it, manipulated it, and helped create it—and it would thus be up to me to try to change it. Before we'd be ready to act, others had to accept their own culpability and responsibility, too, marrying what we'd learned intellectually about our barriers to performance with an emotional commitment to change our ways.

The teaching tool, once again, would be the red-bead game.

It was different playing the red-bead game with Marshall's 150 senior managers. We weren't strangers; we'd worked the trenches together for years and were colleagues and comrades who had developed an extraordinary esprit de corps. So there was a lot of competitive banter and wisecracks flying from the floor as Nida, playing "management," chose the "willing workers" at the game's start. But the mood changed as the game played out, round after inexorable round of missed production quotas and management threats. Bobby Calderella, a hotshot young sales manager from our Long Island

branch, was nearly apoplectic. He'd try to joke about his performance, but each time he failed with the paddle and beads, he got
more frustrated. He tried shaking the box—and management yelled
at him; he tried changing the angle of the paddle—and management threatened him with dismissal. "If you fail one more time,
we're going to close down the factory and put everyone out of
work," he was warned. So he did the only other thing he could think
of—he slipped five dollars to his buddy the inspector to announce
that he'd hit the production quota.

Bobby was abashed when he was caught, red-handed and red-
faced. He'd known it was just a game, he said, and rigged at that,
"But I couldn't stand that there was no way to do what I was supposed to do."

I couldn't have made the point better myself.

I kept the debriefing light, then sent everyone back to their ho-
tels for dinner and the chance to let what they had seen percolate.
But the next morning, rather than ask for questions, I did something
different. I didn't tell our managers what the red-bead game should
mean for them. Instead, I talked about how it made me feel.

"I've got to come clean," I said. "I look at the red beads and talk
about manipulating the system and I feel embarrassed. I see I have
done some really stupid things. When I was a branch manager, I
used to hide parts for my customers, even though another branch
might have needed them more. I started March into March, even
though the salespeople couldn't handle so many promos, the suppliers didn't like them, and it led to a flood of returns. I used to yell
at people and threaten to fire them for not fixing this problem or
that.

"I can see now that there wasn't anything they could have done.
The system created the problem I was blaming them for. I was
dumb, and the more I yelled or threatened them, the dumber I
looked. I did all that, and it was wrong, and I'm sorry. I feel bad because now with this new perspective I can see I've made some mistakes that really hurt our company, and I never wanted to do that."

Then Dick got up. The red-bead game had opened his eyes, too,
he said, and given him the same commitment to change.

It's hard to stand up in front of your 150 top employees and confess a career's mistakes. It made my stomach churn.

Mostly, I read confusion in the faces around me. Some couldn't believe their ears. Others were nervous, uncertain about just where this might by going. But everyone was listening. Hard. "Let's be honest," I said. "Am I the only one who did something dumb around here?"

"Jeez, Rob, I hid more parts than you ever did," Bobby Calderella volunteered.

That got a big laugh. "I know you did," I shot back, "but I could never figure out where you hid them."

"I'd just enter them into the computer with an asterisk and a double star before the part number. Not in a billion years could you have found them."

That got an even bigger laugh and set off a round of similar confessions. One senior sales manager admitted to hiding $30,000 worth of inventory over a weekend under a mat in his Chevy Blazer. Two branch managers had worked out a deal to ship scarce parts back and forth to each other rather than mark them received. The stories keep getting funnier and funnier, the schemes more and more elaborate, as if people were playing Can You Top This? No one had thought that they'd done anything terrible at the time. They had done it to walk through walls for a special customer, just as they'd been told, or to get their bosses off their backs, or to hit their monthly numbers. Besides, everyone had done it.

I was laughing as hard as anyone. "You guys are giving poor Henry an ulcer," I joked, pointing to Henry Chin, our solemn CFO, sitting with his head in his hands. "Let's remember, though, that we're not a ragtag business here. We're a half-a-billion-dollar company. And all these things are what keeps us from getting better."

I could see the lightbulbs going on in faces around the room. The stories kept coming, but they were more embarrassed than boastful, and the laughter had died.

"People started to realize that they'd been hurting the company, and that was why the company was screwed up," Bobby Calderella remembers. " 'Oh, my God,' I told myself, 'all the little things I've done have really been terrible. I don't want to hurt this company—I love these guys—but I have.'

"That's when the laughter turned to guilt, and it changed from trying to top the next guy to Rob's Bare-Your-Soul meeting. There were plenty of tears at the end, I'm not embarrassed to say. It felt wonderful to come clean. I felt as if my sins had been absolved. I hadn't wanted to do those kinds of things anyway. Now I had a chance to try to do better. Now we were all going to be on the right track and go back and fix everything."

This time, when the meeting ended, I was blunt. "We're all flying high right now, excited about what we've seen and learned," I said. "But the problems we've identified are numerous and complex; they won't be easily fixed. So don't go back and preach to your people, 'We had a three-day meeting at headquarters, and the world is changing.' Be patient. Think how long you've had to learn some of these ideas." Then I passed out a summary memo, a red page with a cartoon captioned, "Stop. Do Not Pass Go. There Is No Action Required. If you want to read, read. If you want to learn, learn. But Don't Do Anything."

Privately, I was elated. I felt that Dick and I had raised people's consciousnesses 100 percent. At last, we were on the road to change, even if we didn't know what we would find along the way. Nida, however, brought me up short. "You're still not ready for action," she insisted. "There's still more to think about and plan."

Looking back, I can see that she was right, although I didn't want to hear it at the time. We had a shared understanding of our market peril, an agreement on the barriers to our strategy of alignment, and a common commitment to change. But I was still trying to skip steps. There was no point starting down the path unless we knew more clearly just where we wanted to go—and had a compass to guide our journey forward. We needed, in short, a mission.

Manager's Workbook

Security is mostly a superstition. It does not exist in nature, nor do the children of men as a whole experience it. Avoiding danger is no safer in the long run than outright exposure. Life is either a daring adventure or nothing.

— HELEN KELLER

Change Marketing

You can't force change on people. If you don't justify the risk, the best you can hope for is grudging acquiescence.

Successful change requires a marketing plan. No matter how good your idea, no matter how carefully researched and brilliantly reasoned it is, you still have to sell it to people, usually lots of people, up, down, and across the organization, particularly if you're trying to change the nature of the organization itself.

People have to see what you see before they'll do what you ask. The key is to get a dialogue started and draw them into your perspective, pursuing a line of apparently open-ended but focused questions and examining the implications of the answers. You have to be methodical and logical, starting with core assumptions and pulling people along through four different steps:

1. Why should we change?

Start by looking outside the organization in every conversation you have. Don't tell people about abstractions like globalization or time-to-market pressure. Point to a specific example from the news or in your marketplace. What's really happening here? What is the voice of the market saying? Should we listen?

Think of yourself as a lawyer presenting a case to a jury: you never ask a question without knowing the answer that the evidence dictates. What's happening to the competition? (*It's getting bigger, better, faster, smarter.*) What demands do our customers have today? (*They want lower prices, higher quality, and faster service.*) What will they want tomorrow? (*More.*) Once you've shown the evidence, you can ask for a verdict. Can we keep doing business the same way? (*No.*) What happens if we try? (*Competitive disaster.*)

2. What should we change?

As soon as people agree that something has to be done, you can start to focus on what that something should be. This is the time to talk strategy—what are we trying to do, who are we trying to do it for, and who has to be involved to make it a success? Think about your customers first—what do they care about? How fast it is delivered? How well it works? How little it costs? Why will they do business with us tomorrow? What will their needs be? What about suppliers? What matters to them?

Write down your strategy and put it on the wall for people to comment on. Is this what we want to do? Is this what we really do? If not, why not? You can't rush the process; take some time on this step. People need to feel listened to if you want them to get involved. So, don't censor, don't blame, don't argue. Don't justify or deny. Listen: the feedback may help you refine your course. In most companies, the problems you'll list are hardly news to people. But writing them down changes these problems from end-of-day grousing to a common understanding of your collective performance barriers.

3. Which ones first?

Now you can start to prioritize. Take another look at the list together. Can we group some items together? Do any common themes stand out? Do we want to work on all of them? Are the little ones material to the competitiveness of our company? Usually, two or three concerns will jump out as most critical. They will become your agenda for change.

4. Who's responsible for what?

Change marketing ends in commitment, closing the deal looking to the future. How should we divide up the work? What's the timetable for each part? How will we coordinate? Where should we start? What will you do? And, most of all, are you in or out?

Then, the real work can begin.

Hamburgers and Fishbones

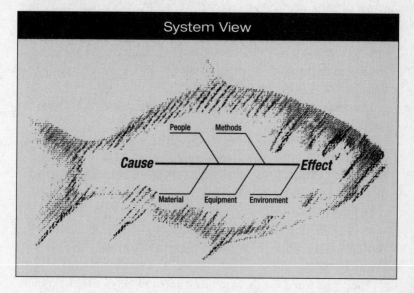

Quality experts call this the Deming Fishbone. It's a system view of cause and effect. I explain it to people as a way to understand why it took the waitress thirty minutes to serve you the hamburger you ordered. It helps you look beyond any specific performance failure to see all of the ways in which a system could have produced it.

Each category breaks down into multiple elements. In our hypothetical restaurant, for example, the people are the kitchen staff, the dining-room staff, and management. Their effectiveness, in turn, depends on their training, compensation, and incentives. Material isn't just hamburger and buns, ketchup and pickles. It's procurement tools and storage systems, too.

So, with all this in mind, not tipping the waitress can't guarantee better results, because she can be only as good as the system that management designs for her. If your hamburger is cold by the time you get it, they're the ones at fault.

How to "Argue Up"

It's hard enough for senior leadership to launch system change, and they usually only have to convince their colleagues and a board of directors. If you're not the CEO, the CFO, the C-anything-O, convincing an organization to try something new can feel like trying to turn the *Titanic* with a canoe paddle.

I know the feeling. Although I'm Marshall's CEO now, I'd been a middle manager for most of my life.

If corporate life were a movie, the task would be simple. You'd just crash the board meeting, present your revolutionary idea, aided by a few flip charts or maybe a song and dance, and in an instant, the board members would see the beauty and brilliance of your vision.

Rejoicing, congratulations, and stock options would follow.

In real life, though, you need more than a surprising turn of the plot and a fancy chart, more, even, than a brilliant idea. You need a foot in the door.

There's no way I can guarantee any method to get a hearing, unfortunately. You may work in an organization trapped by the "not invented here" syndrome. You may work for a dinosaur who doesn't care what you think. Every competent CEO in America knows, however, that success depends at least in part on ideas from the front line. The front liners just have to give the CEOs a reason to want to listen to yours.

Don't wait for a formal meeting

The first time you present a proposal for change shouldn't be the first time that *anyone* has ever heard of it. Don't put anyone on the spot by forcing him or her to respond publicly or make a quick decision. Try to arrange a less-formal encounter first. A breakfast, a conversation on a plane, anything that can give you a less-structured setting in which to make your initial case helps. You want to lay the groundwork, explain the perspective behind your suggestion and gain feedback. That way, you're more likely to have an ally when and if the formal meeting comes.

Think demographic of one

Someone will have breakfast or lunch with you. Who? Someone will read your one-page memo. Who? Someone has the most open mind and open door in your executive suite. Who?

Look at the personality, perspective, and needs of your target. How does your idea address a problem that he or she is facing? How does your idea create an opportunity for him or her individually?

Bait the hook

Self-interest and curiosity are powerful forces, so put them to work. Imagine, for example, that you work at IBM, where CEO Lou Gerstner has publicly announced that he reads the e-mail sent him by his employees. Take him at his word. Send him an e-mail. Introduce yourself and set the stage. "Our industry is going through some drastic changes, as you've said often," you might write. "I see some real opportunity for us to advance our mission and bring content to the marketplace."

Tie your concern to what you've seen firsthand. Talk about your research, people you've met with, or the sources you've read. Talk about the tremendous opportunity for growth and earnings, about the challenges ahead. But keep it short, less than one page. Don't tell enough for anyone to conclude whether your idea is good or bad—tell just enough to show that you've given the issue serious thought. Then, volunteer to meet, in person or with an associate, anytime, anywhere, to discuss it.

No whining

Most executives don't want to hear another critic. So, emphasize your flexibility and eagerness to contribute to the organization's larger strategic goals. Stress the opportunities that you see, as well as problems that lie behind them. Let whomever you speak to know that you're thoughtful and focused, that you're like Teddy Roosevelt's "man in the arena," someone trying to make a difference.

Create your own launching pad

You don't need executive approval to make yourself more competitive. If you see a way to improve your own performance, take it.

And don't just argue up. Try to spread your point of view to peers and subordinates, too. They may not have the power to move the organization either, but they may be able to change their individual part of it. Building a network sharpens your ability to make a case, and provides you with opportunities to test that case in real-world practice. That gives you more ammunition when you finally win a hearing from the people at the top.

5

The $15,000 Pallet Rack:

Building a Common Mission

Beyond the Sounds of Silence

I know that there are Wall Street analysts who roll their eyes when I begin yet another meeting with a slide of the Marshall mission statement. It's not just because they've seen it before, although it has led off every presentation any Marshall employee has made for the past six years. But having seen scores of corporate mission statements each week, the analysts know that most are meaningless, sounds of silence posted on walls or printed in an annual report, signifying nothing.

"Look," I want to tell them, "ours is different. We've changed everything else about the company in the six years since it was written, but we haven't had to change a word of the mission, through good quarters and bad. They're the words we live by, part of a larger foundation of message and method—and I can show you how we bring it all to life."

Mission statements were the hot management flavor of the early eighties, the next big idea of the day, celebrated on magazine covers and in consultants' pitches. In part, they were a response to the public applause for Johnson & Johnson's explanation that their corporate mission drove the decision to pull 31 million Tylenol capsules off the shelves during a poison scare. Unlike other short-lived panaceas, however, mission statements have kept their place of prominence. For the past twenty years they have been the most popular management tool in America; according to a poll of 500 companies by Boston's Bain and Company, they far outdistance such also-rans as total quality management, reengineering, and shareholder-value analysis. Surveying the senior leadership of the country's most admired companies, *Fortune* magazine reported that they "take their mission statement seriously and expect everyone else to do likewise." General Electric's Jack Welch was characteristically blunt about it: "Making your numbers but not demonstrating our values is grounds for dismissal," he said.

Welch's clarity and insistence are the exception, though. Some companies don't stand for anything, mission statement notwithstanding, or, if they do, they don't know what it is. In others, the mission doesn't relate to the way the company actually thinks or runs; it's window dressing, pulled out when the occasion calls for high-minded talk. While surveys show that 90 percent of American companies have a mission statement, less than 50 percent of the executives polled felt that their company's mission meant anything real. Less than 20 percent felt that the purported mission was being actively pursued.

A mission should be concise and direct, instantly clear to everyone inside the company and out. It should look to the future and define what a company believes in, not just what it does or sells; it must help employees and other stakeholders understand their part in the larger purpose. Most fall short. For every great mission statement, such as Ritz-Carlton's "Ladies and gentlemen serving ladies and gentlemen," there are scores more that are numbingly pedestrian, such as Eaton Corporation's "Producing the highest quality products at costs which make them economically practical in the most competitively priced markets." Some are so complicated that not even the CEO can remember them. Others create targets that are too abstract to be meaningful, such as becoming "world class" or "the best." How can people relate what they do in their day-to-day work to such grandiose clichés?

Every enterprise has a guiding spirit at its core, a reason for being that extends beyond quarter-by-quarter profit. I call it the "Spirit of the Deal." But as an organization grows and people's work becomes more specialized, that spirit can grow cloudy. Everyone wants to feel that his or her job contributes to something bigger than himself or herself, but it's easy to lose sight of that. Instead, human-resource, information-technology, or credit departments take on lives of their own, becoming separate universes with their own gravitational forces and concerns. No wonder people are dissatisfied—it's like the young idealist who goes to medical school dreaming of saving lives, only to discover fifteen years later that his days are spent filling out insurance forms. That's not much of a reason to get up every morning.

Marshall's Spirit of the Deal had been clear to everyone when Gordon was starting out. Many of his customers were fellow vets, young and newly minted entrepreneurs like himself. He'd "walk on broken glass, fall on a sword, swim the ocean," do whatever it took to give them whatever they needed. Business was personal. Their success was his success.

Forty-five years later, we still had some of that spirit, some of the time. Too often, though, we couldn't deliver what our customers were asking for. We talked about customer focus and working as a team, but our system kept us concentrated on winning contests, hitting numbers, or keeping the boss off our backs. Think of the energy we wasted manipulating P&Ls or trying to hide inventory: what good did that do customers?

I wanted Marshall's mission statement to remind everyone in our fractured and often-fractious organization that we shared one common purpose. Whatever our speciality or function, our job is to create value for customers. I wanted the mission statement to link us all together by expressing our values and setting the direction of our future. I hoped that eventually it would give us some differentiation in the market, too, a unified message we could brand. But, first,

Marshall had to stand for something, and we had to consistently deliver it from every department of every branch.

Remember the strategic ambition we'd agreed on in the wake of the Deming seminar: take down all the barriers that keep Marshall from responding to the new demands of the marketplace. Our mission statement would have to articulate that purpose as eloquently as possible. But the words by themselves wouldn't be enough; we were trying to change behavior. If we wanted customer focus and employee involvement, we'd have to design a system in which everything was aligned to support those values operationally, through processes and structures that afforded intuitive compliance with our goal. Our mission statement had to be a method as well as a message, a tool that everyone could use, a compass to guide management decisions, and a touchstone for individual actions.

Mission statements can be a bear to write. It would take me three months to draft ours, although most of the final version came to me in an instant one morning as I stood under the shower:

Marshall Industries
serves our business partners
by adding value with a commitment to
continuous improvement, innovation,
and mutual satisfaction.

Just words, you say? Too close to the dead prose that a solitary walker in a big-city park finds carved at the base of some forgotten politician's moss-covered statue?

Far from it. Look at the actions it mandates: serve, add value, commit; improve, innovate, satisfy. Our customers have become our business partners. We don't just sell them *things;* we work with them to improve their businesses, whether we work in bookkeeping, the warehouse, or the sales bull pen. Everyone shares the same purpose, regardless of his or her individual specialty: Find a way to add value to the partnership.

Look, too, at what it doesn't say. There's no mention of distribution. Given the forces of change reshaping our marketplace, there was no way to predict what distribution might mean in the future. It's not a mirror reflection of our strategy, either. Strategies have to change with circumstances, but who we are and what we stand for should always stay the same.

More important than the words, however, is how we teach people to take those words off the wall. "Put yourself inside the mission," we tell our employees. "Don't say, 'Marshall serves . . .'; say '*I* serve . . .' " Then the mission tells you what questions to ask: "Who are my business partners? How can I add value for them?"

Our colleagues are our business partners, too; we serve them the same way we serve our customers. When warehouse foreman Bert Hernandez talks with Rita Megling, one of our vice presidents, for example, he makes the mission personal and interactive, serving a demographic of one: "How can I serve you?" he asks. "Where can I add value?" She, in turn, asks Bert the same questions back. If everyone inside an organization asks those same questions over and over, of customers and colleagues alike, the answers can define a company's future.

Too squishy for you? Think of the mission in basic statistical terms, then, as a way to increase predictability by driving down the range of the common-cause variations. Any change is going to be rocky, but people most often make mistakes at the beginning of the learning curve, like when a new customer relationship begins, a new employee starts work, or the company offers a new service. The mission is a way to move people out of that rocky period faster. Teaching people to use the words interactively gets everyone saying the same things, asking the same questions the same way, and leveraging what we've already learned while gathering fresh and robust market and process-efficiency data.

"You've Got to Keep the Lights On . . ."

There's no escaping the Marshall mission. It's on the back of our business cards and at the front of every sales pitch and employee meeting, in our financial presentations, Web pages, training handbooks, and annual reports. It hangs in every hallway and office in all of our forty branches and on the walls of our alliance partners in thirty-six countries. Accompanying the mission statement are our guiding principles and values, which were written at the same time.

When I started the project, I didn't know that the mission would be the first step toward creating a larger foundation of message and method. Once the mission was written, though, Nida pushed us to develop guiding principles and values to support it, two more tools to link people to the Spirit of the Deal and to blend our strategy with our mission. Once they were written, in turn, we needed a new organizational chart and a new concept of quality to support them, for they would be useless without a way to define our blended mission and strategy operationally, as part of the larger system we were trying to design.

As always, we were running flat out. Even as the principles and values were being discussed, planning teams were already at work researching compensation alternatives and working on the computer systems. Meanwhile, Dick and I were still talking about hamburgers, football scores, and the perils of the daily commute—and trying to keep our $500 million company moving at the same time. I'd work on the mission for an hour or two while flying home to Pasadena, or steal a weekend afternoon behind closed doors in my study to do it.

Initially, I tried to write the mission by shortening the strategy itself, asking myself what ideas I could edit out without too much compromise. But after three months I realized that I couldn't make it work. The shortest I could get was still over fifty words, too long for me to memorize. If I couldn't remember it by heart, why would anyone else bother to try?

Then, one day in the shower, it occurred to me that I was going about it the wrong way. What I had to do was make the mission bigger than the strategy, not a summary but an umbrella. It had to be bigger and bolder, to look beyond the strategy, both back to the six forces of marketplace change that drove its creation and forward into the future. After that, the first seventeen words came easily: "Marshall Industries serves our business partners by adding value with a commitment to continuous improvement and innovation."

There was one problem nagging at me, though. Continuous improvement and innovation sounded great, but they didn't have any boundaries. Just how far were we prepared to go to add value? Would we put our survival at stake if that served a business partner? Who would believe us if we said that we would?

I talked with Dr. Deming about it, and his advice was simple. "Well, son," he reminded me, "you've got to keep the lights on."

That's why I added the last two words, making our commitment to "continuous improvement, innovation, and *mutual satisfaction*." It grounded the mission in the facts of life.

Once the mission was done, I wrote guiding principles, four axioms that explicitly combined the mission with our alignment strategy:

• Continuous Improvement and Innovation are central to our pursuit of excellence.

• Customer Focus aligns our organization, resources, and strategies to exceed total customer satisfaction.

• Employee Involvement is essential to create an environment in which each employee is willing and able to contribute his or her efforts, knowledge, and ideas to achieve the corporation's mission and strategy.

• Supplier Partnerships are a foundation of our business strategy as we continuously seek new ways to add value, develop, maintain, and enhance mutually beneficial relationships.

Then I wrote out our values, essentially a list of the hot words that mattered most at Marshall:

Quality. Customer focus. Market leadership. Pursuit of excellence. Integrity. Timeliness. Resource management. Safety. Innovation. Bureaucratic avoidance. Entrepreneurialism. Employee teamwork.

Seem like a waste of time? Too "Mom and apple pie"? Who's not in favor of quality and customer focus? Why write them down and put them on the wall?

Because doing that works. Putting these values on paper says, most obviously, that somebody thought these ideas were important enough to hang in every Marshall office. But our values are more than a symbolic message: like the mission statement, they are a tool for reducing the amount of variation in our system. They work because we teach people to use them every day, in matters both mundane and profound.

Consider recruiting, for example. We depend on line employees, not just human-resources staff, to interview potential hires. The values give interviewers a checklist for evaluation, a uniform method that coordinates the process across the organization and ensures that everyone looks at the priorities we think are important, such as resource management and entrepreneurialism. Some people don't need that help; they'd know to collect that information automatically. For everyone else, though, there's a system to guide their course.

More important, the list of values guides how we behave internally. People know that we won't say, "To hell with the customer, just ship it." Anyone who did—including Gordon, Dick, or me—would get called on it. The list reminds all of us how to critique ourselves. It invites legitimate criticism of senior management, too, framing the terms of the debate while giving line employees a platform from which to challenge our decisions.

People challenge us all the time to live our words. Over the last five years, I must have gotten hundreds of letters from employees that refer to the values directly. "You say we value integrity, but this person wasn't honest with me," or "You say Marshall wants to avoid bureaucracy, so why does it take me six weeks to get an answer to my question?"

I don't need the words on the wall, but they remind me, and others, of what we've agreed on and why it's important. You could talk to any of Marshall's employees—warehouse staff, executives, salespeople, and support staff alike—and all of them could describe who we are and what we believe in. They might not be able to explain the latest semiconductor technology on our shelves, but they'll know what the Spirit of the Deal means at Marshall and what they have to do to make it real.

"What are you trying to do?" one customer asked me after a tour of our El Monte headquarters. "Start a cult of Rob Rodin clones? Everyone that works for you says the same things and asks the same questions you do."

I had to laugh: clones are the last thing we need. Our system depends on people taking personal responsibility for the results we deliver. We give our people a message to take to market and a mandate and method for action, but execution depends on their own entrepreneurialism and focus, creativity, sweat, and guile. "I'm proud of that," I told him. "The *Fortune* 500 has to pay swarms of consultants big bucks to get everyone to sing from the same hymn book. Look how much money we've saved."

The World Turned Upside Down

Back in the 1970s, when I started in business, the organization chart was still sacred writ, a seemingly unshakable pyramid ascending from the mailroom to the man at the top. Those days, fortunately, are long gone for much of corporate America. Now the model is a matrix: although the CEO is still at the top, there are fewer levels up the hierarchy.

We created something different at Marshall. We flipped the pyramid over, inventing a new corporate form that puts customers in their proper place in the system and places the CEO in a more effective position to deliver strategic leadership:

Customers, everyone's ultimate boss, on top

Suppliers next

Sales and marketing, our link to both

. Assorted vice presidents

CEO Gordon Marshall, with the new title and responsibilities of chief quality officer

"A marketing gimmick," one competitor groused—and he was half right. The inverted org chart was another attempt to differentiate the Marshall brand in the marketplace. It gave us a new story to tell customers; it gave Gordon a new story to tell Wall Street; it even got us a splash of ink in the trades. But it really wasn't a gimmick—it was another tool, another step toward an operational definition of our strategy to align everyone in the company to the customer.

The conventional hierarchy, particularly when supported with a system of MBOs and traditional compensation, teaches people to keep the boss happy. Listen to the language of corporate America: "We've got to hit these numbers—make the month, make the quarter," people say, "or else my manager will go ballistic." That's not where we wanted our people to focus or what we wanted our system design to reinforce. Of course, results and the numbers that measure them are critical, but chasing numbers alone can create frustration and distortion, as we'd learned firsthand. And I'm not saying that keeping your boss happy isn't important, either. However, it's not what we agreed mattered most.

Our inverted org chart symbolizes the changed relationships that our mission, principles, and values mandate. It doesn't reflect reporting structures, where policy is set, or who makes capital decisions. Instead, it depicts where the organization has to look for sustenance, whose needs we should anticipate, whose feedback we have to solicit and heed.

It changes everyone's role. Primary responsibility, it says, belongs to the front line. They have the closest interaction with the customers, so they are more likely to know what customers need and to have better ideas for how to deliver it. Meanwhile, as the shareholders' stewards, senior management doesn't give up authority. Strategy is still set in the boardroom, and we control the purse. But our job is to listen and ask questions, to give people the tools, resources, sponsorship, and support they need, then let them go to work.

Best of all, the conventional role of the middle manager disappears. There is no need for a bureaucrat to police behavior, monitor the MBOs, or get the expense reports in on time. Those functions would have disappeared within the next five years anyway; they're predictable enough to move into the software. Instead, the opportunity for middle management is to embrace leadership responsibilities like teaching our message and method to less-experienced colleagues and working as a coach and mentor focused on employees' professional development. That's certainly more valuable to the organization, and is a more attractive career path than playing CYA with the boss.

It was Jacob Kuryan, a young engineer whom we courted away from McDonnell Douglas, who gave us Marshall's first operational definition of the nebulous term "quality"—then showed us how to put it to work for real-world process design. "Quality," he said, "is where the voice of the process aligns with the voice of the customer."

That sounded right to me. Easy to explain, it tied right back to our strategy and mission. It was another tool to help focus people: the greater the gap between what the customer wants and what our process delivers, the greater the opportunity to serve and add value.

Jacob had been hesitant to leave the glamour of the aerospace industry for a warehouse filled with boxes; he was apprehensive, too, about leaping from a structured environment into Marshall's ongoing experiment in change. "How serious could you be," he asked, "if your existing quality program is a twelve-page manual sitting untouched on the shelves?"

"It never matters where you start," I told him. "What matters is where you end up."

Jacob began his search for quality in the warehouse, working with the people who would use the processes, assembling a design team that included information-technology director Raj Jha, then warehouse manager Mike Lelo, and six hourly employees off the warehouse floor. He asked them the questions he was trying to answer himself. "What is the voice of the customer telling us? Where don't our processes deliver?"

Perfect quality meant more than defect-free, they agreed. No defects was just a minimum, the first and easiest target. The bigger challenges and opportunities lay in what Jacob dubbed "the upside of perfect," the creation of new features and benefits, customized services that would help clients with their current problems and anticipate their future needs.

The result exceeded anything I could have imagined. The warehouse team designed a system that combined state-of-the-art robotics and computerized statistical process control while driving out inefficiencies and reducing costs. They cut our error rate in half—and then cut it in half again. Our customers asked for six-sigma quality levels, 3.4 errors per million, and the warehouse team exceeded it. Customers wanted an ISO9002-certified warehouse; that was accomplished in four months.

"Redesigning the warehouse was a joint learning operation," Jacob explains. "There was a vision of alignment from the top—but the fun came from making it work lower down.

"How do you nurture continuous improvement and innovation? It's easy to say: Go hire Ph.D.s and you can get some bang for it. But quality comes from leveraging everyone up the learning curve. It's not a lightning bolt. It's built on an understanding of who you are and what your purpose is.

"Our mission statement forces me to sit down with all my partners in the company and ask how I can add value to what they do. We ask it relentlessly, everywhere. In the warehouse, for example, we say, 'Receiving serves picking. What can we do to serve you better? How can I add value? Where do you want me to improve?' If you have those conversations enough times, people will tell you what they need."

Visitors are often astonished when I show them the Marshall warehouse today. They expect dingy walls and dusty boxes, but what they see looks more like an engineering facility. It's that immaculate and efficient.

While we're there, I always take time to point out the blue pallet racks. "There's a story here," I tell them. "It speaks directly to the culture and capability we've built."

One day, about three months into their design work, the warehouse team came to me with a request. They wanted Marshall to buy them custom-colored pallet racks for the warehouse, Marshall blue to match our logo, rather than off-the-shelf gray. They had debated among themselves, they told me, but they'd agreed in the end that the $15,000 extra would be money well spent. The warehouse had to send a message of pride, inside the company and out. Alignment wasn't just about infrastructure, they argued. It depends on look and feel, too.

What is the return on investment for $15,000 worth of blue pallet racks? I didn't know then and I don't know now.

But the warehouse team had the experts responsible for designing a system that moves $300 million worth of inventory in and out the doors with unprecedented speed and efficiency. Their design process had showed us all, for the first time, how management by method could work operationally, bringing Marshall's org chart, values, mission, and strategy together to deliver on the Spirit of the Deal. If they wanted blue pallet racks, they'd get blue pallet racks.

Manager's Workbook

People talking without speaking,
People hearing without listening . . .
— PAUL SIMON, "THE SOUNDS OF SILENCE"

Imagine a scenario in which anything any customer heard delivered the same intended message . . . every employee in every branch or division pursued the same goals with the same focus . . . and every process, method, technology, and procedure aimed at the same end.

That's alignment—simple to show on a chart, but difficult to execute. Alignment comes when everything in your organization can be stacked up like a tower of power connecting your vision with the results you deliver to your customer. But alignment doesn't happen by accident—it has to be designed.

Alignment is a process as well as a state of being, a step-by-step journey to consistent results. It starts with a vision of an ideal customer connection, the "Spirit of the Deal." That, in turn, drives your mission, a definition of your purpose in the world.

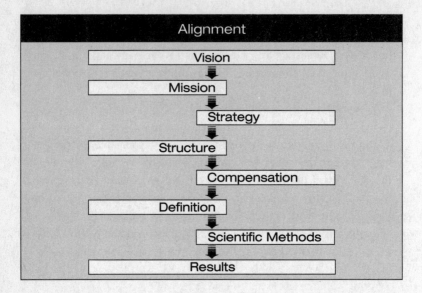

Strategy is mission in action. It creates the framework for your organizational structure, your compensation system, and the operational definitions you'll use in the marketplace. Consistent methods—aligned with strategy, mission, and vision—produce consistent results, and enable you to create the telemetry to monitor your performance against your goals.

Mission Control

A mission, ideally, should be a way to bring people together, a strategic and tactical touchstone for everything attempted by the organization. It should preserve the guiding values of the company through the tumult of change and rally people around a common idea, whether they are in human resources, information technology, or accounting.

Make it simple

If it's too long to memorize, it's simply too long. People can't internalize what they can't remember.

Make it personal

Everyone, from the CEO to the front line, should be able to see his or her individual job in the mission you share. If it doesn't help them relate to their customers or colleagues, it doesn't work.

Make it usable

A mission has to be more than words: it should be a tool, a blueprint for action. If people cannot get a list of "go-do's" from your statement, it isn't practical enough or smart enough.

Make it timeless

Your strategy may change every year or two, but your mission has to remain consistent. If you're paying attention to the forces of marketplace change, what you do and sell today may not even show up in your annual report five years from now. Your mission should reflect your values, not the mutable, gritty details of here and now.

Make it real

Don't drift away in words that are too flighty and vague to have real meaning. Use verbs, not adjectives and adverbs. Don't promise an open-ended "whatever the customers asks for, they'll get." Your mission has to be both believable and doable.

Use it

If *you* don't, why should anyone else?

6
Money Matters Most:
Designing the Right Incentives

What Counts and How to Count It

A day doesn't go by that I don't have to explain Marshall's controversial compensation policy to someone. Usually I give the short version—"I'm the heretic who took the entire six-hundred-person sales staff of a half-billion-dollar publicly traded company off commissions, overnight, and lived to tell the tale"—but the full story is a little more complicated than that. The process was more time consuming, the change more radical, and the anxiety level higher.

We didn't just change how we paid our salespeople, although that's how it looked to the outside world. We changed how we paid everyone, salespeople and secretaries, new hires and senior staff, product managers, credit personnel, and warehouse employees alike. Out went the old metrics, the old reward systems that had governed all of us. Out went all the contests, promotions, and March into March, too. No more management by objectives (MBOs). No more individual incentives at all, in fact. Instead, everyone would be paid the same way: straight salary with company-wide profit sharing.

We didn't change overnight or in a single step. It took us nine months to design and implement the new pay plan. We started with our thousand management and support personnel, then moved to the sales staff, raising the heat exponentially at each stage. Putting the plan in place differed greatly from our previous initiative, for while agreeing on our list of strategic barriers and creating a mission statement had been critical work, it was still somewhat abstract. In contrast, compensation was personal, visceral, and immediate to everyone. We were talking about people's money—and betting the company in the process.

The payoff from our change was bigger, too, although no one could have predicted the specifics at the time. Marshall's success has come from innovation, harnessing technology and the Internet to create customized solutions that anticipate our customers' constantly accelerating demands. But we couldn't have delivered on virtual distribution if we hadn't changed how we measured and paid people first by aligning compensation with our mission's customer focus and commitment to partnership.

Could we still sell on the Internet? Sure, but our model of electronic commerce as a seamless and frictionless connection couldn't have worked so well if we'd had to waste time worrying about how to split commissions on the new business we developed.

Could we still have introduced Lotus Notes and an intranet to link the company together, putting all our numbers into the plumbing and making them available to everyone? Sure, but it would have taken longer. People would have fought the new technologies were they still paid to monitor other people's results.

Could we still have built the entrepreneurial team that created those innovations, a knowledge-driven culture constantly searching for new ways to deliver free, perfect, and now? Probably not: you get what you pay for.

That's an obvious truth, of course, but it's a truth many managers seem to ignore. Too often production people are asked to focus on quality, then get paid for units produced. Department heads are asked to share resources and cooperate, then are paid for their department's profit and loss (P&L). Salespeople are asked to meet higher customer-satisfaction levels, then get paid for booked orders. No wonder we're frustrated. We're trapped in a red-bead game of our own making.

To retool the system, you've got to go back to the basics. The point of an incentive structure is to motivate behavior, and people will respond rationally to the system that they're given. What you pay for is more important than anything you say. The challenge, then, is to create a system that aligns your people with your organizational goals and rewards employees for increasing your company's ability to cope with change.

Compensation is your best motivational tool, not just one of your biggest expense items, and the most effective method you have to send a message about what you think is important. However, it doesn't give you much leverage on your human capital if it is not part of a larger agenda of employee development. The easy thing to do, of course, is to give all employees a few annual numerical objectives and then reward them if they hit their targets. It's harder to evaluate each employee's growth needs; make sure that everyone understands the changing aim of the organization and how that changes his or her role, responsibilities, opportunities, and value; and then to establish a comprehensive plan of feedback and coaching to help each person realize their potential. But that more-difficult process is far more valuable if you are trying to prepare your organization for the unpredictable future. Nurturing a broader range of skills opens up a broader range of opportunity for employees while deepening your talent pool, and it builds loyalty at the same time. While you can't promise employees a job for life, or even for tomorrow, you both win when you pursue a strategy to develop the skills necessary to add value in the present and future marketplace.

Marshall doesn't set anyone's income; the marketplace does. The better all of us learn to serve our customers' changing needs, the more we will be worth to them.

Six years ago, when I first started to study compensation practices, conventional MBOs on the Peter Drucker model were considered state of the art. As Drucker prescribed, companies designed their pay processes to meet tactical imperatives like managing costs, assuring employee equity and recruiting competitiveness, and minimizing taxes. Since then, however, competition has increased and compensation is now widely recognized as a strategic issue, a means to create the higher service levels and increased teamwork customers demand. Yet because service and teamwork can be notoriously hard to define numerically, as we've seen, and harder still to connect to the bottom line, a majority of companies are committed to incentives linked to pure financial measures such as profit and loss. A smaller number of companies, driven in part by what Charles Peck, a compensation specialist for the Conference Board, calls "the time-consuming administration required for a multiplicity of individual plans," have implemented some form of group incentives, most often team-based pay or productivity-based gain sharing.

Those changes are fine, as far as they go, but they don't begin to address the currents of change cascading through the world today. This is the era of bandwidth explosion and global competition, of demographic shifts and shrinking time to market, mass customization, and supply-chain management. If you believe that sooner or later those forces will radically transform your world, like a second big bang that creates a whole new competitive universe with new suns and moons, gravitational pulls, and rules of physics and chemistry, you need a more radical response than just tinkering with the numbers.

Remember the goal—you're trying to design an organization that can anticipate the inevitable shifts in customer values, chasing a moving target through an increasingly competitive cosmos. No simple set of measures can accurately reflect the complexity of sales, marketing, and service strategies that these shifts will demand. There are too many relationships and handoffs involved; there are too many customers with too many unique needs, each a demographic of one, each with a different definition of service and satisfaction. Your pay system should be flexible enough to meet that challenge. It should reward people for responding to your customers' voices, no matter where they lead. It should also be customized and collaborative, rewarding individual initiative and team-work alike, and it should encourage people to share learning. It must be sustainable, tying people to a common purpose even as strategies change, and focus on the marketplace rather than internal company issues.

It was clear to all of us at Marshall that our old system wasn't working. We'd seen the distortions and frustrations that it produced. We tried our best to create incentives for individual performance by incorporating more and more elaborate objectives, but we still had to send out a steady stream of "I need you to do this" memos asking people to perform tasks unrelated to or not covered by their compensation plans. We held seemingly endless meetings and pep rallies to talk about what we *really* wanted—for everybody to work together, satisfy customers, improve processes, increase productivity—but our old metrics had become so complex that people had lost sight of Gordon Marshall's original Spirit of the Deal.

More of the same, we agreed, wouldn't be good enough. We needed to motivate people to work smarter, not harder. Our product managers, for example, ought to be thinking of new ways to create demand, not just taking more phone calls for price and delivery details. Our warehouse staff had to be looking at changes in the environment, such as new packaging requirements or automation potential, not just packing and shipping boxes.

We knew the behaviors we wanted. We'd written them into the mission statement: serve our business partners by adding value; commit, improve, innovate, satisfy. We needed a method to produce that result, a system that would support intuitive compliance with our enterprise goals, a way to reward the words we'd put on our walls.

So, to develop that method, we followed the same design model we had used in formulating our alignment strategy. Like then, we began with fundamental questions: What are we trying to accomplish? What are the barriers we hit? How could we eliminate them? The implementation process, too, was much the same as it had been when we initially introduced the idea of system redesign; we marketed change one on one and in small groups, trying to draw people into the thinking process, translating abstractions such as organizational performance and professional growth into everyday analogies about sports or doctor's visits, then repeating them over and over.

Performance today means adding new value, developing service improvements, creating market updates, or winning technical certification in a discipline or product line, so that is what we concentrated on building into our method and compensation system. Employees advance by what they learn, what they teach, and what they accomplish. They're promoted on the basis of growth in a matrix of fundamental abilities we think all our people need, no matter what their function: business skills, sales or communication skills, product knowledge, system knowledge, knowledge of the company, personal development. We review them, and they review the company, twice a year, based on growth in these six skills and their ability to use them in executing and advancing the company's evolving alignment strategy. In time, as we changed our technology applications to create a new customer interface, that collective knowledge would be organized into a database, a corporate dictionary that we add to every day, which allows anyone with a good idea to leverage his or her intellect through the entire organization instantly. (I'll detail this in chapter 10, "The Upside of Perfect.")

Admittedly, it took less time to measure performance by numbers alone: monthly P&L results, inventory levels, what someone booked or shipped were easy to find and superficially evaluate. But our new process gives us a more comprehensive look at our people and the ways in which they interact with our business partners.

Don't misunderstand me. We still track profits and losses (P&Ls) and monitor inventory reports; we talk about day-to-day performance all the time. But if that were all we talked about, we might have missed the more-important early-warning signals of change in the marketplace: the customer value shifts that lie behind the numbers and have become our greatest source of competitive advantage.

Today, six years after we got rid of performance incentives, Marshall's pay structure remains unique in the industry. But I know that customers don't choose Marshall because of our compensation system. They don't care how we get paid or even if we get paid.

They're too busy trying to compete to care about Marshall's internal issues and systems. All they care about is results, that Marshall's commitment to value-added partnerships, customized solutions, and new ideas shows up on their bottom lines.

That's what we pay our people to deliver.

What do you pay your people for? Have you designed a compensation system that motivates them to drive you into the future?

We believe that we have. I'm not suggesting that you should imitate Marshall's specifics, though. What works for us might not work for you, because every company faces individual challenges and has to design accordingly. But the design process itself has to begin where ours did, with the core questions: What counts and how do you count it?

Rethinking the Numbers

Still think that paying people solely by their numbers can work? Think again.

Think forecasting and planning

Ask yourself this question: If you took the compensation incentives out of your people's quarterly forecasts, how much more accurate would they be? People who are paid to hit a forecast usually project a number they think they can exceed, but your planning depends on their read of the market. How often have you looked at forecasts and wondered who was sandbagging? Wouldn't you rather be able to plan your staffing or cash-management requirements with reality-based telemetry?

Think market analysis

Would you entrust your health to a doctor whose pay was based on how well he or she could perform against profitability standards? What incentives would there be to run that extra test that may uncover the early-warning signs of illness? To spend the time asking every possible question that could help improve your health? If we pay our employees for their performance against profit targets alone, aren't we limiting the range of questions they ask about their customers in the same way—and limiting our ability to understand the health of the marketplace as a result?

Think responsiveness

What happens when your customer announces, "I've found a better way to do things"? Say those customers are outsourcing their manufacturing or moving purchasing from Manhattan to Montana. How supportive will your people be if those necessary competitive changes mean a hit to their sales targets or P&Ls, and those are what their pay is based on? Would they be more effective business partners if their incentives were based on the customer's bottom line instead? If you were a customer, who would you want to do business with?

Think handoffs

Today, businesses compete supply chain versus supply chain, with elements spread around the globe racing one another to market. Success depends on the smoothness of the collaboration. Say a customer needs your Boston operation to work with your San Jose operation to deliver a new product being manufactured in Austin and shipped to Beijing. How seamless can the connection be if people define their roles territorially and worry about who gets the reward?

Think time management

Pull out your appointment book. How many hours of meetings have you sat through while people argued over which expense went on whose P&L? No one likes expense allocation; it takes too much time and too often feels shoved down people's throats. And the compromises it often requires may be worse than the time and frustration. If there is a leak in the roof, you've got to fix it, not argue about how to split up the cost.

Think innovation

No one knows the return on investment of the new; what's important is its potential. The explosion of bandwidth is transforming content and delivery alike, changing the nature and face of your customer connection. What happens if you need a new computer or phone system, an EDI feed, an intranet, or an extranet? Those technology expenses have to be front-loaded; it may take years to see the profit payoff. What do your people say? They may see the need and jump on board, championing change if it increases the company's long-term strength. That's certainly what you would wish for. But how would their enthusiasm for absorbing such expenses be colored if their compensation review is based on this year's P&L performance? There's a new business dynamic being born; you want them to help you deliver on its promises. Is that what P&L incentives promote?

Dollars and Sense

Changing how we paid our 600-person sales staff wasn't even on the agenda when Gordon, Dick, and I first starting talking seriously about redesigning Marshall's compensation system. Then, the whole sales staff was, like almost everyone in sales everywhere, on straight commission with a small draw, stoked by promos and contests to keep their competitive fires burning. Changing that long-established system would have been challenging holy writ, a riskier move than any of us were willing to contemplate at the time.

Changing how we paid our thousand-odd management personnel, on the other hand, didn't seem like such a giant step. They were all already on base salary with an incentive bonus of usually 20 percent or 30 percent. Many of them, too, had agreed that our old system didn't work, so there was a consensus that our metrics had to be changed. No one knew yet what they should be changed into, though.

For more than a year, ever since the managers' meeting where we'd identified our MBOs and our operating system as the prime barriers to strategic alignment, two separate task forces had been at work. Dick and I, along with Nida, sat on both of them. Together with other managers, we dissected why our old ways didn't work and researched possible alternatives. However, despite the panels' considerable work, most of the incentive redesign was done less formally by Dick and me, working late into the night in his office or mine, trying to translate our ongoing discussions about customer satisfaction, quality, and value into concrete and definable methods. We didn't know what an effective pay process would look like; we only knew the results that we needed it to produce. We're a service business, and, like a restaurant, we're only as good as the last meal we serve. So, we as an organization had to be nimble and quick, able to respond effectively to the changing voice of the customer without a memo from on high or endless and pointless turf wars.

At first, Dick and I looked for some derivative version of our old targets that we could apply throughout the company, a more-sophisticated set of numbers that would measure everyone against the same objective standard. But we couldn't decide what it should look like. Make the incentive smaller? Bigger? Divide gross profit dollars against some hypothetical nine or ten measures? We considered scores of systems and read numerous books on the subject, but in each case there was some component that blocked change. There was just no way to get our arms around customer delight. We had 60,000 customers, each with a different definition of "satisfaction" and "follow-up." Even if we could find some narrow measures that worked today, we'd probably have to change them as soon as the system was introduced, given how rapidly the competitive bar kept being raised.

So why not just go to plain-vanilla profit sharing? Logically, it made the most sense. The only reliable gauge we have of customers' satisfaction is whether they keep doing business with us, so the more satisfied they are, the more we grow. Profit sharing seemed the simplest way to feed that back to the organization and send the clearest message about our interdependence, the need for flexibility and cooperation, and the importance of results.

It made sense to Dick and me personally, too. We were both on incentive programs based on total company profitability, and we both came to work every morning looking for new ways to make the company great, worrying about everything from personnel to cash flow to turning off the lights in empty offices. Profit sharing, we thought, would motivate everyone to take the same broad perspective. A profit-sharing system was so simple, too, that we wouldn't have to change it every six months, either; it could be "built to last," a legacy system like our mission statement.

So who should get a share? Senior staff? Sales and marketing? The warehouse?

Only one answer really worked: Everybody. If all employees are important to the process of serving our customers, then all deserve a piece of the action. And if they aren't important, why do we have them?

No one, we agreed, would make less money. Changing our incentive system would be an alignment strategy, not a financial manipulation, a way to take down barriers, not to cut costs. So we'd guarantee that the conversion would be, at worst, revenue neutral, at least for the first year. After that, who could predict? The size of our profit sharing would depend on how well we all performed together within the new system.

We knew that employees would have questions. "What's in it for me? If I'm doing a great job, shouldn't I make more money than somebody else who isn't so great?"

That made sense, too. So we decided that individual excellence would be reflected in salaries that could range significantly, even in the same job category. The more value people added, the more they could make.

As our technology task force got closer to introducing our new operating system, we could see that our definition of value would have to change as well. For example, I undertook an informal study that found, among other things, that our product-marketing people spent about 85 percent of their time each day executing mechanical tasks such as expediting price or delivery details and pulling data sheets. Yet, as our information-technology capabilities advanced, the value of answering more phone calls or passing papers faster would disappear—everything transactional would happen automatically. Then what value would these employees have?

We believed then, as we believe now, that Marshall's future is based on doing things we haven't done yet, not on doing things we already do. So the product-marketing people's value would depend on their ability to grow and help us design the company of the future, their learning to listen better to the many voices of the customer, their teaching us to use new technology applications and new ideas to meet their needs, and their training and nurturing of others to do the same.

In addition to employee-performance measures, we'd been talking about quality for years, not just as a statistical process control in the warehouse, but as the responsibility of everyone in the organization. What is a quality product manager? A quality accountant? A quality telephone operator? Each of them has to excel in a different discipline, but all of them grow to leadership by developing a common set of abilities: business skills, sales or communication skills, product knowledge, system knowledge, knowledge of the company, and personal development. Those skills, then, would constitute our performance matrix and provide the basis for our system of evaluation and development. We didn't know exactly how it would work yet, though, we'd leave the details of the process to be hammered out by the people who would use it.

I don't mean to make our design decisions sound as easy as a few logical choices that can be captured in a page or two. The work was harder and more painstaking than that. We were in uncharted waters, making critical decisions about our individual and collective futures, with no models and no benchmarks available to guide us. Thus, each decision was broken down, analyzed, and weighed against a score of alternatives. What behaviors did it reward? Would it align people with both our strategy and, more important, our mission and values?

"This isn't going to fly," some on the compensation task force worried. "Incentives are the reason people work so hard."

"Look at the risks," Gordon Marshall counseled. "You could lose your top performers and breed mediocrity."

"Think of the expense," Henry Chin, our chief financial officer, warned. "Switching incentives to salaries turns a variable cost into a fixed cost."

I shared their concerns. "Let's reality-test the numbers," I suggested. So we did a statistical analysis tracking five years of incentives paid against the results we'd been hoping to get. Interestingly enough, whether we hit the target or not, we usually paid most of the incentive. There was a whole group of people, our top performers, who virtually maximized their dollars over a five-year period, even though they might not have hit any of the sales-versus-forecasts and gross-profit-dollars targets we'd set. There was always some special reason for the override, an abnormal customer request or an unexpected glitch in delivery, but the real reason was always more simple. Companies always find a way to make sure top performers get their incentives. If they don't, that talent will get snapped up by the competition.

Change is always tumultuous, of course, but there didn't seem to me to be any danger that the bottom could fall out. Why would people leave? We weren't going to be changing how much they actually took home; we were only changing the method of payment. And look at the upside: we'd have a better management process, and we'd get a better way to coordinate all our people as a result.

Or so the thinking went. We were really never as confident as it sounds on the page.

Our best people wouldn't be bothered by the change, we hoped, thinking that they'd never worried too much about their specific incentive targets. Instead, they'd assumed that the incentives would take care of themselves if they took care of their customers' needs. That's how we wanted everyone to perform. The people who called corporate every week or two to argue about some expense allocation had far too much time on their hands and far better things they ought to be doing.

Overthrowing the Peter Principle

By December 1991, we were ready to make our shift. We held our regular performance reviews over that month and awarded annual raises, sitting down one on one across a table with all of our thousand-plus management personnel. After that, we reviewed our figures one last time, double-checking the accuracy of our salary adjustments against our forecasts of the profit and incentive pool. Then, on January 1, 1992, we formally announced the change to the company, using a video from headquarters and meetings in every department of every branch to explain the basics.

We knew even then that we were changing people's careers. The new matrix would wipe out the traditional departmental silos and conventional paths to advancement. Everyone's future, like Dick's Gordon's, or mine, would depend on the ability to learn. Eventually, we'd have to sit down and develop a career-investment strategy for each employee, along with a curriculum to speed each one's way up the growth curve. But that was more than we thought that people could digest at first, even if we'd known the details of how the matrix was going to work.

Instead, we kept our explanations simple, focusing on the issues foremost in everyone's mind. "We aren't talking about the amount you'll get paid," we kept repeating. "We're talking about the method you'll get paid by. If you used to get twenty percent of your base salary on the old method, you'll get twenty percent of your base salary on the new method.

"Our strategy as a company is to try to take down barriers to performance and growth anywhere we see them. That's what we're trying to do here, adding value with a new process designed to increase mutual satisfaction, just what the mission mandates."

By now, people were familiar with my management method. So, in keeping with it, I tried to draw them into my thinking process, moving from the why of change to the how-to, asking them the same open-ended questions that I'd asked myself. I tried to sell the new system on its structural logic and the opportunity it created, but rather than talk abstractions like incentive distortions or the need to reward cooperative behaviors, I presented it in terms of medicine or sports.

"Remember Rick Mirer, the Seattle quarterback whose bonus depended on his number of attempted passes? How confident could his teammates be that he'd call for the run if that were what the game demanded?

"It's the same here. We'll win more games if people have the incentive to call the right plays at the right time, not just run up their personal stats.

"On whom does your life depend if you're wheeled into an operating room? Is it just the surgeon with the scalpel, or are the anesthesiologist and nurses critical, too? How many other people have to do their jobs well to give you the best health care you can get?

"It's the same here. We aren't practicing surgery; we're professionals, creating critical customer solutions. But the customer's health depends on all of us, and we all depend on one another. Anyone who shares in the responsibility deserves a share of the reward.

"Why did baseball fans start talking about slugging percentages along with batting averages? Because the slugging percentage is a more accurate measure of how valuable a player is to a team. Batting average measures only how often he gets a hit, but slugging average measures total bases divided by at-bats.

"It's the same here. Our new matrix is a better measure of how you help our team score by creating value for customers."

I got a little help, too—some god of distribution must have been smiling down on us. That winter, newspapers and television broadcasts statewide were filled with stories about the California Attorney General's investigation into allegations of deceptive consumer practices at thirty-four of the state's thirty-eight Sears Auto Centers. It didn't seem to matter which auto center you visited; they'd try to sell you a muffler whether you needed one or not.

Sears management was mortified when the news broke. Back at headquarters they'd been preaching how customer friendly the company wanted to be. Edward Brennan, then the Sears chairman, who had initially denied the charges, used a national advertising campaign to apologize. In it, he explained that the Sears Auto Centers had just introduced a new incentive plan that tied branch managers' pay to the number of mufflers sold, and a few managers had gotten overzealous.

It was a perfect story to prove my central points: Incentive systems drive behavior. What you pay for is more important than what you say.

Through the six years since then, I've been talking about compensation practices inside Marshall and out. And there has always been a story similar to the one at Sears in the headlines to help me drive home my points. Remember the scandal that shook financial giant Kidder Peabody a few years back? Thirty-six-year-old bond trader Joseph Jett was awarded a $9 million bonus as Kidder's top performer in 1993, as a result of reporting trading profits over $150 million—and then was fired the next year, accused of inflating his figures by $350 million in "phantom trades and profits" over two years in order to fatten his own checks. Remember the investigation into military recruiters? To keep standards high, they were expected to test every potential enlistee for literacy and basic arithmetical skills, but they were paid for the number of warm bodies they signed up. So they closed their eyes to test scores and fudged the paperwork or forged test results, flooding the system with substandard recruits, expensive washouts that cost the government millions. And remember the recent investigation into "excessively aggressive" IRS agents? They were supposed to operate for the good of the taxpayers, with strict procedural guidelines to follow in their audits, but they were rewarded for the number of people they nailed and how much they nailed them for. So the rules went out the window.

Still, as I'd expected, "What's in it for me?" remained the big question among employees. "Why should my bonus be tied to someone else's?" "How do I make more money?"

"Your incentive is tied to company performance," I explained every time, "because you are a part of a chain of dependency, no matter how good you are at your job. Even Michael Jordan went six years without winning an NBA championship, until the Bulls put a complete team on the floor.

"That doesn't mean we aren't going to pay you what you're worth. If you're a superhero performer, we'll reward you accordingly. We're just not going to pay you for every basket you sink.

"If you're great, you'll establish a market value for yourself. Let's say it's $50,000. That's what you'd get paid if you shopped your skills on the street, so we have to pay you at least that much. But you've been with the company a few years. You understand what we're trying to do. You know how the systems work and where the coffee machines are. So you have an additional internal market value that we have to pay for, too. The more you contribute, the more we'll have to pay you. Then, your profit sharing is an additional bonus you'll get as we learn to win championships together.

"Look at the new opportunities. Under the old system, there was only one route to the top, from sales manager to branch manager to president. With just thirty-eight branch managers and one president, how good were your odds of moving up? With the matrix, there are new ways you can grow in the company.

"We're overthrowing the Peter Principle [the rule that says people rise to their level of incompetence]. We all know a general sales manager isn't necessarily a good branch manager, but that was the only step open with the old system. With the matrix there's no longer just one way up the ladder. If you're good at training sales staff but not at managing people, we can create a job function there. If you're good at market analysis but not at administration, then that should become your speciality. The more value you can add, the more you'll be rewarded. Now are you willing to be part of that team?"

The reaction was mixed. A lot of people thought that what we said made sense. Others thought that the new system was no big deal, that it didn't really change things much. But there were no extreme negatives, at least initially—everyone seemed willing to try it and see.

What was a big deal was finally getting rid of sales promotions, a measure that we announced at the same time that we put in the new pay plan.

Promotions, remember, were ingrained in the system, scores of them running simultaneously as our suppliers spent millions trying to push their products into the marketplace with the help of contests and prizes. As far as we could see, though, the system didn't work for anybody. Our biggest suppliers spent the money because they had to keep the playing field level, but they were offended that they had to compete with cruises and television sets, not the features and benefits of their technologies. Many of our employees resented them, too; scrambling through our March into March madness was fun, but it didn't feel very professional, and, besides, the same people won over and over again, not because they worked harder, but because they had the biggest accounts. The warehouse staff would work until 2:00 A.M. night after night, and no one ever gave them an appliance for their contributions. Most important, though, promotions didn't make sense for our customers: they needed custom-designed solutions to their competitive problems, not a generic pitch from a salesperson pushing a product to win a prize.

Some of our suppliers balked when we explained the change to them. "We've always used promotions," they insisted. "Why should we stop now just because you've kissed Dr. Deming's ring?"

In reply, I asked each of them to go to the 150,000 customers in our marketplace and find just one who would call me to say that he or she thought promotions were a good idea. That call never came.

Suppliers still ask Marshall to run promotions today, six years later. And I still say the same thing: Find me one customer who will call in defense of them. It hasn't happened yet.

It's hard to gauge the bottom-line result of Marshall's incentive conversion. We've paid profit sharing every year, and in some years it cost us more than our old incentive system, while in others it didn't. By itself it might have been an impossible financial burden, but it was just the first of many process redesigns, a necessary foundation for broader changes that would cut costs companywide and enable us to double our productivity while also doubling our sales. So, in the total scheme of things, the payoff was huge.

We did lose a couple of people along the way, however. Some left by their own choice, some by ours. It wasn't over the money though; it was over the ideas behind the method. No one ever quite said, "I don't want to be a team player," but that's how some acted.

We needed everyone to see that Marshall's new system was one more important way in which we differed from anybody else in the marketplace, another step closer to alignment with the real needs of our business partners, customers, suppliers, and employees alike. But some people could not or would not buy in. No matter how much support and training we gave them, they refused to spread the message of interdependence, and we had to let them go.

Here's a point worth remembering for any leader who is trying to implement change of any kind: Some people will never get it and others will never accept it. That's a fact of life. However, you are not handicapped by values of trust and integrity to carry your dead. It's better to leave them behind.

The truth is, it's probably good news when they go. Would you rather have an employee who quits and leaves or one who quits and stays?

The Final Barrier

For all the internal tumult, Marshall's incentive makeover stayed largely invisible to anyone outside the company. There was gossip in industry circles, as always, but we didn't send out a press release or anything, and there wasn't much attention paid in the weeks that followed, except for occasional jibes from visiting suppliers. ("Look at this hot VCR we're giving away—Ooops! I forgot. You don't take prizes.")

Remember the so-called Hawthorne effect? In that celebrated case study, management turned up the lights in their warehouse and employee productivity increased. Then they turned the lights down and employee productivity went up again. Conclusion? As long as management tried something, anything, employees would work more productively. "What you've done with incentives at Marshall may just be another example of the same phenomenon," a Harvard professor wrote me.

That made me feel terrible. I thought we were designing radical change; he thought we were flipping light switches.

Likewise, I had felt honored when Dr. Deming asked me to speak at one of his seminars, and I nervously prepared a fifteen-minute talk on all we had done over two hard years developing the strategy and mission and creating our new incentive plan—but even that presumably sympathetic audience sat unimpressed. "Why didn't you include the salespeople?" someone in the audience asked. "If you're talking about logic and alignment, don't they have to be included, too?"

I knew she was right, of course. I just didn't know how to incorporate salespeople yet, and couldn't face the risk.

People inside the company had been pushing the same arguments since our earliest discussions. "We've got to include the sales staff," they'd say, but I'd insisted that we already had enough on our plates: "Abolishing commissions is a lot more complicated than just changing an incentive. No one's ever done it successfully. I'm not sure it can be done."

Meanwhile, our six hundred salespeople, not surprisingly, had been getting more and more restless. All of their managers were talking about their own compensation, all the time. Then we'd gotten rid of the contests, and after that, some of our competitors started saying that we were going to eliminate sales commissions, too. Everyone was edgy. What was coming next?

"I honestly don't know what, if anything, we're going to do," I admitted to them, trying to sound reassuring. "I've told you every step of the way what I was thinking. That's not going to change. But this is one question I really don't know the answer to.

"I don't want to screw up the company by doing something stupid. So we aren't even going to consider changing anything until next January—and we might not even change anything then."

Regardless of everything I said, though, the pressure to move sooner kept growing, first from a handful of people, then from many. We'd introduced a flood of collaborative support material, videos and workbooks and teaching guides, and enthusiasm was starting to build. I was meeting with small groups of managers every night, giving the rap about system alignment, Michael Jordan, and the possibilities in the matrix, and the question was always the same: Why not do the salespeople? By the spring, when we held our regular ninety-day management meeting, it seemed as if everyone was pushing the idea, and pushing and pushing, including Gordon, who had initially counseled caution.

Nothing had gone wrong so far, after all. No suppliers had left; there had been no mass defections of employees. The market was strong, and business was growing. Morale had never been better.

"This is sort of working," people said. "But it would work better if we'd see it through."

"I don't know," I wavered. "I'm just not sure. This is big, really big. Besides, I said we're not going to do anything for a year."

That's when it hit me: maybe this time I was the barrier to change.

So we thought it through. First, the practicalities: How many people would we lose if we abolished commissions? Could we afford to go revenue neutral? Would we lose any customers? Then, the basics: What kind of salespeople do we want? How can we motivate that behavior? Could we design a system to help them sell better? Do we even need salespeople in the classic mold?

By the time our June management meeting rolled around, we had the outline of a plan. "We'll do it in January," I said, "just as I promised." But most of the management personnel wanted to do it sooner, and so did the sales staff. Thirty percent of them had already bought into the whole idea of system alignment; another 30 percent would be glad just to have the uncertainty resolved. So we moved the date forward, to Monday, August 24, 1992, less than three months in the future.

It would be the hardest day of my career. Although taking our salespeople off commissions was the logical next step in our attempt to align compensation policy with the voice of the customer, that change would launch a battle I still fight every day.

Manager's Workbook

It is not the employer who pays wages—he only handles the money. It is the product that pays wages.

— HENRY FORD

Mapping the Competitive Path

Paying people to hit a number is easy, but it doesn't do much to improve your competitiveness. That depends on adding value and differentiating yourself in a world of accelerating change.

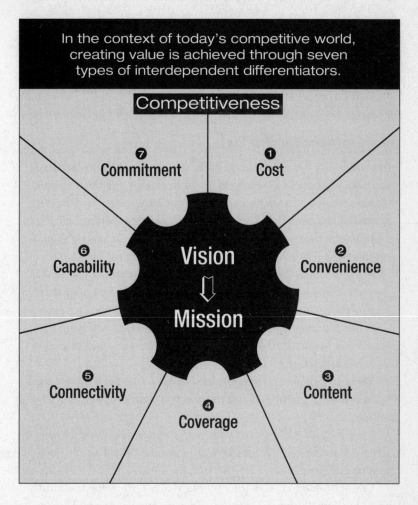

In the context of today's competitive world, creating value is achieved through seven types of interdependent differentiators.

Competitiveness

❼ Commitment

❶ Cost

❻ Capability

Vision
⇩
Mission

❷ Convenience

❺ Connectivity

❹ Coverage

❸ Content

As our chart shows, there are seven paths to differentiation: cost, convenience, content, coverage, connectivity, capability, and commitment. They all start with a vision and a mission, and for definition depend on the marketplace context. Each will change as the competitive context changes, driven by individual customer's unique and insatiable demand for free, perfect, and now, and by the forces of change discussed in chapter 2: bandwidth, global competition, demographics, compressed product life cycles, build-to-order, and supply-chain management.

That's a complex challenge. What conceivable numerical measures could you use to evaluate all the different ways in which you need your people to contribute?

Getting What You Pay For

No single pay plan, in and of itself, is best. As with any strategic weapon, what's best depends on the individual competitive context. But everyone has to ask the same basic questions to begin with: Who are we selling to? What do they want? Is what they want changing?

To work effectively, your compensation system should be aligned on four different levels:

First, it should tie behavior to your *enterprise model,* and leverage your mission and ideal message consistently and without short-term distortions.

Second, it should tie behavior to your *customer model,* and advance your strategic understanding of who you serve and how their perception of value is changing.

Third, it should support your *delivery model*, or the job and functions you need performed and the way you want people to work together.

Fourth, it should support your *performance model*, or the standards of excellence and methods of execution you'll use to judge and reward people.

I'm not asking anyone to copy Marshall's system for the fourth step, but I would submit that if you pay people by individual objectives or departmental and job description, those will be the targets everyone worries about most, not your mission, strategy, delivery, or performance goals.

7

No One Asks for a Salesman:

Customers Want Solutions

The Rush to Close

Unlike those lucky holy men who always seem to find revelation in a flash of light, I was slow to see the central truth about selling until it more or less conked me on the head, embarrassing me with its simplicity.

No one asks for a salesman: they ask for someone to help them.

It seems obvious to me now. When any of us goes out to buy something, whether it's a new computer or a new car, we want someone to help us sort through the often-dizzying options. We want this person to take the time to listen, to protect us from mistakes, and to have our best interests at heart. That's particularly true in my business, where our customer's best technology choice can change in a nanosecond.

Unfortunately, most salespeople see their jobs in different terms. They're closers, trained and paid to get your name on the dotted line, then move on to the next potential sale.

There's nothing wrong with closing, of course—it can

be exhilarating for both the saleperson and the customer. But if it's not part of a larger process it's not likely to lead to long-term satisfaction for either of them.

Think about what you want from a visit with a doctor: If a specialist gave you a pain pill for a sore shoulder without asking what your ailment was, you'd sue for malpractice. You want to be diagnosed, listened to, and analyzed before you are prescribed to; then you want your recovery to be monitored, with treatment adjusted as your health improves. That's how doctor-patient trust is built—holistically, over the long term.

Customers want the same relationship with a salesperson, but they don't often get it, because it's not what the system rewards. Rather, commission programs drive a feel-good quick fix instead. The short-term incentive is to skip diagnosis and analysis, and ignore follow-up care.

Why do you bring your spouse or your kids to the showroom when you buy a car? Because you want an out if the pressure gets too intense. Your salesperson may be charming, with a great gift of gab; he or she may know as much about cars as Mario Andretti. But because his or her only financial motivation is to close the deal, you're at cross-purposes as soon as you sit down. There may be a better car coming out in a month, but you're not going to hear about it. And you're never going to see this salesperson after you take delivery, either, no matter what kind of service problems you encounter. In addition, you're thinking long-term ownership, while he or she is thinking short-term transaction and the ever-powerful and status-raising commission. No wonder more than three-fourths of all Americans think that the process is a scam, or that salesmen rank third on the list of America's least admired professionals, right after politicians and the press.

We talked a lot about effective selling that summer of 1992, sitting in my office or Dick's, asking the same kinds of questions we had asked about management by objectives (MBOs): What counts in the selling process? How can we count it? What makes a salesperson great, and what makes a great salesperson? How can we help our people deliver more sales for our suppliers? What are the barriers to performance, and how can we get rid of them? How should we pay our sales force, and what should we pay for?

The more we thought about customer alignment and the Marshall mission, the less sense commissions made. Closing a deal doesn't build value for customers: a salesperson can close a hundred people on a hundred different computer parts and not help any of them find the one perfect solution to their particular problem. In fact, for our customers, the close was usually the least important part of the experience. They were more likely to need help staying current with new product and technology choices, and want followup after the sale to make sure that the new technology delivered to its maximum potential. Why had we created a pay system that focused effort solely on one step of the process? Was it because we believed that without the commission incentives, the sales staff wouldn't work hard enough? That they wouldn't be aggressive or pursue new business? That they didn't understand the full scope of the buying decision? Or was it because we'd just never considered the possibility that there might be a better way?

The goal of any compensation system, remember, is to motivate behavior. The design challenge is to create a system that supports your larger organizational goals by aligning people, technology, and processes with strategy and mission. Aren't numerical quotas a rather blunt instrument whereby to manage something as complex as the customer connection? Could we find a way to get rid of the distortions that they create? Could we design a system better focused on serving each customer while making sure that our features and benefits were well presented and follow-up ensured? If we could learn to anticipate our customers' needs and develop the ability to deliver, order flow would take care of itself. Maybe we could, but to do so, we'd have to teach everyone to listen better to what our customers were trying to tell us.

First off, the close personal relationships our sales relied on in the past weren't sufficient anymore. Our customers wanted a professional partner, not just a buddy to have a beer with—a businessperson, not a salesperson. That distinction is more than semantic: a salesperson looks for the order on the customer's desk, which is good, but a businessperson looks for the solution to the customer's problems, which is better. A salesperson sells; a businessperson practices multidimensional sales and marketing skills, and draws on an understanding of the customer's product or service and finance, credit, and operational needs. A salesperson makes deals; a businessperson builds trust by working with a customer as a colleague, helping him or her wrestle with long-term competitive issues such as time to market, product road maps, and the cost/benefit of emerging technologies. That's infinitely more useful to a customer than a salesperson with his or her eye on the day's number alone.

We had 60,000 customers, which meant that we were serving 60,000 demographics of one, all with increasingly demanding and idiosyncratic requirements. We had to hear more clearly what standards individual customers were using to measure our performance, then follow up to make sure that the results we delivered exceeded each customer's expectations. Commissions weren't allowing us to do that job. Some of our salespeople pushed the same easy sell to everyone—"SWAT," or "sell what's available today." Because there was no incentive to tie them to the larger process, the temptation, inevitably, was to overcommit, to promise more than our system could deliver. The result, too often, was seller's remorse—and a scramble to find a way, whatever it took.

Most of all, we had to learn how to hit a moving target. Our customers' value definitions were shifting; we had to adapt or lose our customers to a competitor who would accommodate them. Organizational survival depended on developing new and better solutions that would differentiate Marshall in the marketplace, but most of the changes we made in the past were imitations of processes and innovations that our competitors had tried first. If we wanted to be known as the industry innovators, as our mission promised, we needed better market intelligence from our sales force, a richer database of more-detailed and more-timely customer information that we could use to develop our strategies and manage our resources. The more we knew about our customers today, the more we could do for them tomorrow, if we could see the trends and flex our considerable marketing and operational strengths to harness them.

In the early 1990s, Marshall wasn't the only company thinking about the linkage between sales compensation and the customer connection. Our competitors, too, were talking about the difference between "money made" and "money earned," acknowledging the growing complexity of long, multiple-contact customer relationships and trying to adapt their commissions accordingly, moving away from measuring straight gross-volume dollars toward calculating more-intricate credit costs or freight expenses. Outside the industry as well, companies were talking about "consultative selling," "relationship selling," and "customer intimacy," and adding new figures such as new business development, range of products sold to an account, or that most immeasurable metric, customer satisfaction, to their commission bases.

As far as I could tell, though, all those attempts to tinker with the system ran into the same barrier: the fact that quality customer service and sales quotas always clash. When market competitiveness heats up, commissions encourage people to reach for the low-hanging fruit, regardless of the long-range consequences for the customer or the company. So we abolished the old system—we got rid of commissions altogether and put our entire sales force on the same system of salary base plus companywide profit-sharing bonus that we used to pay everyone else.

Our logic was the same as when we took our managers off MBOs. We wanted a more-sophisticated measure of performance than a simple single figure, a better way to evaluate, develop, and reward talent for adding value. Once again, we promised revenue neutrality, at least for a year. We weren't changing the amount we paid anyone, just the method by which we did so. And for the sales force, our analysis, planning, and implementation processes were, if anything, even more methodical and painstaking than when we made our earlier management-compensation changeover.

With the sales force, the risk felt higher. This time, we knew that the bottom really *could* fall out, and that was scary as hell.

Methods and Brands

Here's a question to ask your salespeople: If your competitor charged one dollar for your particular service or product, how much more could your company get?

For most of us, unfortunately, the answer is not much. Unless we make Pentium processors or own the rights to Mickey Mouse's ears, we compete in a world where many others sell products or services very much like our own. On-time delivery, low costs, or defect-free quality control are merely the price of entry. Your best competitive efforts become marketplace givens overnight, and no good idea goes uncopied. So what can you do to get $1.01? Does anything make you stand out in your customer's eyes?

That is a strategic question, not just a tactical one. Hypercompetition keeps pushing margins down, and opportunistic customers will desert you in a heartbeat if someone offers them something better. Differentiation is the key to survival. You can't protect yourself anymore just by winning a bigger share of the market; you have to win a bigger share of the customer by offering more attention, more time, more trust. You earn the right to serve customers by learning to anticipate what will serve them better.

There are a handful of products targeted at one-time buyers. I know—I sold vacuum cleaners door to door one summer in college myself. For most of us, though, building and sustaining our brand equity is critical. And with the cost of new customer acquisition running three to ten times the cost of existing customer maintenance, we need to create what businesspeople today call customers for life.

Customers experience a company through their connection with its sales force. So, how do you want them to feel after your salesperson leaves? What do you want them to think about? A customer who has a good experience may tell ten people, if you're lucky, but a customer who has a bad one will surely tell a hundred. How can you make sure that your message and value proposition hit the marketplace cleanly and consistently with every salesperson at every sales call to every customer?

I love salespeople, and I love good selling practices. But it was clear that the paradigm that was in place had to shift. We wanted customers to think of Marshall as a partner, not just another salesperson with a line card and a price list. Thus, the design challenge was to create a system that would focus our sales force on win/win solutions that help both sides of any deal. Abolishing commissions removed the greatest barrier to customer alignment, the excessive concentration on the close, but it was just a first step toward creating a larger system to motivate, train, evaluate, and reward our people. We gave them a new selling method to follow, too, and a new way to add value and make more money.

Everything you've ever done well in your life has been grounded in a process. Whether you were learning to juggle or to speak a foreign language, you had to master the basics before you could aspire to proficiency. That's as true for organizations as it is for individuals. We couldn't make people smarter, more empathetic, or better listeners overnight. But we could push everyone up the learning curve faster if we gave each person a better tool. So we created the "Marshall Process," a method of learning how to expand business opportunities and build stronger relationships. The Process guides people toward an understanding of each customer's critical issues, teaching the key questions to ask, step by step and one to one, and thereby ensuring that the solutions they develop will truly address their customer's specific short-term and long-term business needs.

If I can sell a mediocre product with a great story to a naive customer, that doesn't make me a great salesperson; it just means that I can work the transaction. The best salespeople, by contrast, can work the process; they find the right products to satisfy a customer's needs, and do it over and over and over again, looking beyond the short-term incentives of their system to the long-term rewards. I've known scores of them over my career, men and women with a wide range of personalities and styles in all kinds of businesses, but they all shared the same essential skills: they knew their markets cold and knew where to hunt for opportunity; they were good at listening to customers' needs and at explaining solutions; and they knew their competition and its pricing, as well as its operational strengths and weaknesses. And when they made a deal, they exceeded expectations—and turned that result into still more business.

We wanted everyone at Marshall to follow those same steps: market research, marketing, prospecting, qualifying, presenting, closing, and following up. Rather than emphasizing just one step, though, we gave all seven equal weight. Then we replaced the word "closing" with "commitment," because signing a deal should be the beginning of a relationship, not the end. It's an opening to follow up, and perhaps proceed to the next opportunity, part of a virtuous cycle of problems solved, opportunities created, and growing mutual satisfaction and reward.

The Marshall Process distills our collective best thinking about how to listen to the changing voice of the customer. It takes each step and breaks it down into smaller parts, teaching people what they need to learn and giving them the questions to ask to build trust and credibility, one customer at a time. Our salespeople begin with market research and marketing, through which they earn the right to stand in front of each customer by mastering the necessary specific product, industry, and market knowledge needed before trying to sell anything. This learning then continues even past the sale through follow-up, and includes evaluation of Marshall's performance and suggestions about how to make the whole sales process more cost-effective, productive, and convenient.

Like a turbocharged customer-qualification form, the Marshall Process teaches salespeople the things they need to know most. Who are the target customers, and what do they want? What is the customer's unique definition of quality? Do they have supply-chain problems? What do they want that's different from what we've given them in the past? Like a compass, the process points inquiry toward a better understanding of customer needs and the details that lead to more-focused, customized solutions. Like a self-teaching curriculum, the Marshall Process poses questions that encourages deeper questions, progressing, as it were, from Problem Solving 101 to graduate study. Some of the specific questions it mandates appear in the Manager's Workbook at the end of this chapter as the Seven Steps to the Never-Ending Sale.

There is nothing new about "qual forms," of course. Managers have always nagged salespeople to fill them out, but usually they sit in folders in a drawer or in the trunk of a car. But we collected this paperwork and turned it into a database.

Today, driven by Lotus Notes, that market intelligence is the backbone of Marshall Industries: it's the answers to all the questions any employee has ever asked any of our customers. "Marshall Account Planning Profiles," we call them. Linked to the Marshall Process, they inform our marketing choices, govern our organizational direction, and guide our tactical decisions, resource allocation, and strategic execution. The Marshall Process allows senior management to see into the marketplace through the eyes of a sales force focused on changing value, continuous improvement, and innovation, one that asks the questions we need answered. Our account profiles, in turn, give us a means with which to use what they hear, respond to trends, and spread anyone's good ideas throughout the organization instantly.

Rather than evaluating salespeople only for their volume numbers, we reward and advance them based on how well they execute the Marshall Process. The more they learn about our marketplace and teach others, the better solutions they can create and the more value they can add, for customer and Marshall alike, and the more money they can make. That's a more-sophisticated measure of performance than plain commission, as it is focused on each individual's creative problem solving. And, in the end, it produces better numbers. It also gives sales managers a better way to lead and coach, for it grounds them in the immediate critical issues facing salespeople serving particular customers.

Could we have developed our account-profiling system and the Marshall Process with a commission-pay program? Sure—but there would have been no incentive for people to fill these forms out had we not changed the selling model first. Even at Marshall, where every salesperson has a laptop and where asking better questions is the path to advancement, people still occasionally grumble about the need to record data.

Here's a question to ask your marketing department: Would you do your job differently if you had just one salesperson, one customer, and one thing to sell?

That's an easy one, I know. You'd train that one person relentlessly, teaching him or her everything anybody in your organization knows.

Why would you discard that ideal process if you have multiple customers, salespeople, and products or services to get to market? No one can remember everything, of course. But that's a problem that bandwidth can help solve. Technology makes that ideal design model possible, and enables you to connect with your sales force individually. Salespeople, like customers, can be treated as demographics of one and given customized interfaces with all the information, direction, and prompts they need to learn greatness.

The Signal-to-Noise Ratio

Even now, sitting in the quiet of my home office, my whole body gets tense when I write about commissions. It's been over six years since we shifted our pay system, and I've had to defend the decision every single day to skeptical and often passionately opposed suppliers and employees, competitors, reporters, and academics. By now, I know that almost everyone will disagree with everything I say, at least initially. I've been misrepresented by competitors, sniped at in the marketplace, and hammered in the press. At times, I feel I'm trying to negotiate peace in the Middle East: there is no end to the dispute, more heat than light, and no understanding among the parties.

I'm the heretic. There are hundreds of great sales teams in America, powerful and respected names such as Cisco, Procter & Gamble, General Electric, and Merck. But so far as I know, there's only one that doesn't work for commissions: Marshall.

No one disputes our results; it's the idea that bothers people. A salary-based sales staff, they think, is somehow subversive, a shortcut to mediocrity. Commissions and sales have always gone together, and by this point in history, they are almost one word. "It just doesn't mesh with my philosophy of selling," the skeptic says.

I say look again. Our system grounds each member of our sales force in the selling process with each customer. It has marketing, database management, leadership responsibility, entrepreneurial behavior, teamwork, profitability, and growth written all over it, along with rah-rah, raw meat, and beat the enemy—it does everything you want an incentive system to do. But, at the same time, it is a different method of payment to corral a different behavior and focus—and its consequences, as we've discovered, are radical and all embracing.

I'm not trying to be evangelical. I don't think that we've necessarily found the only way to create a customer interface, or that your commission program may not already be working to motivate the customer-focused behavior you want. However, ask yourself if the commission-driven emphasis on the close doesn't distort your system and misalign your people. Think about how opportunistic your customers are, and how fast their definition of value can shift. Can you afford to ignore what might be a better way to listen to their voices? Are you so confident in your market position and share of customers that you're willing to miss hearing everything you can about new concerns and opportunities?

Fortunately for Marshall, our customers understood the value of our system from the beginning. They can see how it works day by day, and like being served by a businessperson focused on their needs, not a salesperson who needs to sell them something to pay the rent or win a new TV. Our system is an easier way for them to do business, a more seamless connection with less friction and more trust. It also is the key to our results—and results, in the end, are how we've differentiated ourselves in the market.

We don't always execute perfectly, and commissioned salespeople can certainly create deep and trusting relationships with their customers—the very best salespeople do it every day. There are some individuals who already understand the importance of adhering to every step of the sales process, including qualification and follow-up, just as there are individuals in our system who still rush the close. But the question is which system is most likely to produce the behavior that you want consistently displayed throughout the organization. It's not about whether this person or that would work better on commission or on a salary with profit sharing; it's about designing a method to govern and guide the behavior of ten or one hundred or one thousand or fifty thousand people. I believe that the more a method is aligned with the organization's mission and strategy, the more that organization is committed to listening, to remembering, and to exceeding expectations, the better a customer interface it will produce. One order or one day or one quarter isn't the important thing. The important part is creating a legacy process, understanding the Spirit of the Deal and bringing it into the marketplace over and over again, building customer trust as the foundation of an organization designed to last.

"Wait a second," people say. "Without commissions, you won't get people to work hard."

Let's get real. Go look at some of your commission salespeople. Beep them at 7:00 A.M. or call them one morning and say, "I want to travel with you today." You'll see that even your best don't work every second of every day. There's not enough money in the world to drive people that hard. Some will kill for every nickel they can get, but for many, that's not enough.

What would happen if you doubled your commissions? Would people work twice as hard? Why do you have to run a contest or a promotion on top of a commission? If incentives were all it took to get people to sell, wouldn't the commission alone be enough?

Like salary programs, it isn't commission programs that work or don't work: it's people that work or don't work. No system by itself solves any problems. What counts is how it is designed, managed, and led—how its people work with it.

Why is our company better without commissions? Because when we listen for the voice of the customer, we have a higher signal-to-noise ratio. Although we do thousands of transactions every day, we don't just hear "buy low and sell high." We hear about problems because we're asking questions more multidimensional than what we can sell you today. Because we're committed to every step of the process and because all our incentives reenforce that commitment, we understand the marketplace better and develop better solutions for customers. We're more innovative. Our sales force pushes the envelope as soon as it hears where Marshall is misaligned with a customer need. No one has to force a square peg in a round hole to hit a quota. Instead, people are paid to figure out ways to help Marshall add value for customers over the long term—and to push the organization to make it happen.

Look, for example, at how we built our sales muscle on the Internet.

People ask me all the time, after I explain how our sites work, whether the Internet was the reason we took people off commissions. The short answer is no, not exactly. I'd never heard the word "Internet" in 1992, and Web browsers hadn't been born. But even then, it was clearly just a matter of time before we could connect with our customers electronically, given enough bandwidth and the capability to execute transactions digitally. "It could be huge, creating a whole new dimension for the business," I told Gordon Marshall at the time. "But no commissioned salesperson is going to tell customers it is a good idea, no matter how much more competitive he or she becomes."

Today, some commissioned salespeople compete like this with their company's Internet sites all day long. They're just responding rationally to the system they work in: electronic commerce may be good for their company and their customers, but it takes money out of the salespeople's pockets. Our sales force doesn't have that worry, because they're paid to help our business partners find better, more-competitive solutions. They saw the Internet's potential early and championed it in the marketplace, giving us the feedback and design direction that defined how virtual distribution should work.

It was the same when we recognized that the world was awake around the clock.

"OK," we said, "let's answer our phones twenty-four hours a day."

That's not a revolutionary idea in service by a long shot, although Marshall is still the only company in our industry to use it. Under commissions, what incentive, beyond their dedication to their customers, would salespeople have had to promote that new easy access? None. But our sales force embraced it. "Why don't we add credit clearing twenty-four hours? My customer would love that," some said. "If we take orders on Saturdays and Sundays, why shouldn't we ship on Saturdays or Sundays, too?" another suggested.

That's adding value, helping us see the opportunities and seize them, pushing our strategy and mission forward. That's how individuals get ahead at Marshall and how we prepare for the future.

Leading Questions

Here's a question for CEOs, vice presidents, marketing managers, and sales managers: How come when you go on a customer call with a member of your team, you're usually able to sell a broader program for a higher price than your salesperson could have? Why do you always find another hook? Better opportunity? More continuation?

Are you just that much smarter than the people who work for you? Probably not. Or are you more successful because your perspective on your job is broader? Probably—you understand better what your company is about, what you can do to solve a problem, how to factor the industry trends and pressures. After all, that's what you're paid for.

Would you develop that perspective if your income depended on what you sold that day? If the primary message delivered by your incentive plan was to sell more?

Ever had salespeople overcommit? Maybe it is the end of the month or the end of the quarter, and they have to hit their numbers, so they promise something that your shipping department or manufacturing plant can't deliver without working until 2:00 A.M. every night for a week. How much does that strain your systems? What does it do to your quality control? Your follow-up programs? Your customer's satisfaction? Does any of this widespread distortion of the system cost money or decrease competitiveness? Does a commission motivate a salesperson to consider those costs?

Whose planning needs do you focus on? In most cases, salespeople measure their sales objective with an account in dollars. But dollars aren't usually the customers' prime concern. Customers need to know how many units to buy to keep production running. And dollars aren't what the suppliers need to know, either. They need to know how many units to build.

Moreover, thinking in dollars, not units, creates more than a simple translation problem: it distorts the entire system, leading to mistakes and waste, last-minute reschedules, and U-turns in tunnels —and all the strain gets dumped on the backs of customers and suppliers in the form of high costs and increased work, not to mention not having their long-term needs thought about. The salesperson may have sold $1.2 million and earned a trophy or bonus, but the critical issues of supply-chain management are never addressed—for supplier, distributor, or customer.

We eliminated the translation problem at Marshall. Our salespeople, like our customers and suppliers, forecast in units. That's tough enough in an industry driven by time to market, shrinking product life cycles, and build-to-order, but factories need as much predictability as possible to maximize returns. Customers need to keep their manufacturing lines moving, fast. Aligning a supply chain around the same numbers allows for more speed with less time wasted in the useless work of phone calls, expedites, and rework.

Look at your PC or VCR. Think about all the parts inside. Now, imagine that it is your job to buy all of those parts at the best price in the most efficient way possible. How do you make sense of all those different dollar forecasts, particularly when each is distorted by promotions, contests, and end-of-the-month madness?

And what of your own planning? How often has a dollar-sales forecast influenced action that was wrong, while a unit forecast would have told you something useful about competition, demand, or product road-map technology?

Here's a question for sales managers: Are your best salespeople the two or three who take home the biggest commission checks? Maybe. But maybe their big numbers depend less on their skill than on the size of their accounts, the credit limits, and how much corporate support they get to close the deal. Do they recognize their dependency on others and their place on the team? If they are your best, could you move them where you needed them more—to a smaller more difficult customer with greater potential, for example—or would they scream that you were taking money out of their pockets?

Remember *Glengarry Glen Ross*? "I just need more leads," Jack Lemmon kept pleading to Alec Baldwin. In a commission system, people live or die on their individual accounts, and they think of them as their own, not the company's. What does that do to your organizational flexibility? What happens when you need five people to work together to service a demanding customer, or if you need expertise in a narrow segment common to twenty different accounts? How do you divide commissions then, and how much energy does it divert?

Abolishing commissions allows Marshall to use our sales force wherever and however we think it can have the most impact. If someone is great at presenting but not at qualifying, he or she can specialize and still find ways to advance by adding value to the system. Salespeople can take a break if they get stale on a particular account, take time for training without worrying about not being out moving product, go on vacation without phoning back three times a day to see if their next commission check is going to cover the American Express bill. And most important, they can nurture the startups that promise to become supernovas, without worrying about short-term numbers—they can call on a single account for months, even without a single sale, if our account profiles, the Marshall Process, and leadership agree that it is an investment worth making.

"Salespeople Are Different"

I played my cards close to the vest during that summer of 1992. As we geared up to the August 24 announcement of our new pay plan, I was still out in the marketplace constantly, still talking about Marshall's customer-focused mission to anyone who would listen, but I didn't say a word about what we were going to do with commissions. I wasn't ready to go public yet; my anxiety level was too high.

There were times when I could picture the bottom falling out. Our customers would like the new plan; I was always sure of that. And our suppliers, I thought, could be persuaded at least to give it a chance. But in my worst nightmare, I saw our sales force deserting en masse, leaving Marshall a gutted shell and my career in ruins. Gordon had named me Marshall's president earlier that summer, and I would be blamed, fairly, for the debacle.

In the light of day, though, I thought that we could just maybe pull it off. We had momentum on our side, the experience of changing one pay system, and a growing internal enthusiasm for the radically redesigned Marshall that we were creating. The key would be to get the sales staff to understand the thinking behind the change.

Our managers had been glad to be rid of MBOs; they liked being judged and rewarded on a more-sophisticated matrix of skills. Why would the salespeople be any different? No more being judged on a single skill; no more skullduggery over account assignments. No more worrying that a key account will move production to someone else's territory. We were offering our sales force a future tied to their talents, more flexibility, and more opportunity—and the chance, if everything worked, to revolutionize our industry and reinvent the customer relationship.

The clincher, we knew, would be the money. Once again, we committed to revenue neutrality, at least for a year. Except for our top fifteen salespeople, who presented a special problem, no one would make less money, and many would make more. Dick and I sat at my office table and reviewed all six hundred salespeople individually before we set their salaries. If someone had been getting a $1,500 per month draw with an added $3,000 in commissions, we moved his or her salary to $4,500 per month, guaranteed—or more, if we thought that their performance trend or value in the market was moving up.

It would take a second book to credit all of the people who threw themselves into preparing for the change. Marshall has always been a seat-of-the-pants company, but this process was methodical and detailed, a concentrated and coordinated three-month effort. One task force designed what would become the Marshall Process; a second designed how account profiling should work; a third puzzled out how to integrate the Marshall Process and account profiles into our converted computer-operating system, which was scheduled to be launched that coming December. Meanwhile, Dick, Nida, and I were wrestling with how to teach our sales managers, general managers, and regional managers to use their new tools, and Les Jones, our vice president of human resources, was developing a monitoring program to make sure that everyone felt mothered after the change and to adjust salaries if necessary. For ninety days, each salesperson would meet individually with his or her manager every two weeks, with a report sent to headquarters; after that, one-on-one meeting reports would be due each quarter.

Despite this preparation, I knew what the sales force would ask first, though, no matter how much salary we paid: "How can I make more? What's my upside?"

I knew what I would tell them, too. I had rehearsed the arguments and advantages of our new pay plan so often that I could recite them in my sleep.

"We don't want to keep you from hitting the mother lode, but you can't just *make* more money, you have to *earn* it. If your business grows and you add more value for your customer—and Marshall, of course—your salary will go up, just as it would for any business professional with more responsibility.

"Volume is critical, but there are other things that are important, too. Think about how dramatically the world is changing. If all you do each year is book more business because you're chasing upside, if you aren't learning all the time, preparing for those changes, you'll be obsolete."

This would work for the majority of our salespeople, whose incomes wouldn't change, but our top fifteen performers presented a problem of a different sort. They were terrific salespeople, critical to our future, but some of them were cashing commission checks worth $250,000 a year, and we couldn't rationalize guaranteeing that level of income—the deals involved were bigger than any one salesperson, really, for they involved dozens of people at Marshall and millions of dollars of inventory credit and corporate support. So we had to adjust those incomes down, closer to what we considered market value.

Dick or I talked with all fifteen individually, and, in most cases, we worked together fairly easily to come up with a salary level that we could agree on. A few people, however, were very upset. "We don't want to argue about nickels and dimes here," Dick and I told them. "We've got a big program ahead of us here, and we want you to be part of it. So go look at your market value in the world. Put your résumé out on the street. Talk to a headhunter. Then we'll negotiate."

Today, six years later, all fifteen of them are still at Marshall, still among our top performers, and all are earning more money every year.

The last few weeks before announcement day were spent in the trenches. Enterprise redesign is a fine and exhilarating thing, but, like any management effort it ultimately comes down to grunt work. We made checklists of all of the key constituencies we served and all the idiosyncratic needs of the individual players, deciding who would tell whom, when, and how they would explain it, then made checklists of our checklists. We put together a video to show to all of our salespeople on the big day itself, and prepared a package of support material for each of them individually. Dick and I double-checked all six hundred salaries again, then triple-checked and reality-tested them with each salesperson's direct manager. Then, as best we could in a two-day meeting, we trained those managers on how to use the video and pay-package worksheets to make the day run smoothly.

At last we were ready. All that was left was to tell the outside world.

No one would have come to a Marshall press conference; to most people, we were still just one more distributor. But ours is a gossipy industry, a small network of people who talk all the time. So, if I didn't explain loud and clear the reasons behind our change, people would deem it a cost-cutting move, and rumors would fly. For that reason, we decided to make a public announcement in our industry's weekly trade paper, *Electronic Buyers' News*. We bought space for an open letter to explain our goals to our valued business partners.

We must have written that letter seven zillion times, passing drafts back and forth between Nida, Dick, and me. Writing it was easier than deciding who should sign it, though. Just Gordon, the founder and chairman? All three of us, a united senior-management front?

"It should be me," I said. "Gordon's built a great reputation over thirty-five years. Why risk tarnishing it? If we all sign, we could all go down in flames together. Why not have just one guy go down? If the company crashes, Dick can step in and try to pick up the pieces: 'Hey, Rodin had a bad idea, but it's gone and he's gone.' "

I flipped and flopped in bed all through the night before announcement day, unable to still the adrenaline-fueled what-ifs in my head. I was terrified, but excited, too. Though it had not dawned on me until now, I'd been pointing toward this change since the red-bead game eighteen long months before. I knew I'd have to defend the decision, but no matter how hard I looked, I couldn't see where it was wrong. Every change we'd made so far was working; maybe we could make this work, too.

"What's the matter?" my wife, Debbie, asked me sleepily at 3:00 A.M., eyes half open. "What are you doing?"

"I'm taking all the salespeople off commissions."

That woke her up fast. "Rob, are you crazy?"

Crazy or not, the die had been cast.

Dick and I both came to work early the next morning, before 6:00 A.M. in Los Angeles, 9:00 A.M. back east, when our Boston and New York branches were opening. It was eerie just to sit there in the silence, waiting for who knows what to happen. In Boston and New York, people were playing out the most drastic gamble in Marshall's history, but in headquarters everything was still. No phones. No footsteps. Nothing. "Now they're watching the video," I thought. And we waited. "Now they're opening their pay packages." And we waited some more.

Finally, when I couldn't stand it anymore, I called Boston. "How's it going?" I asked.

"OK. A few questions, but nothing we didn't anticipate."

Then I called New York.

"It's OK here, too, I guess. No one seems particularly disturbed or anything."

I was astonished, but the more I thought about the calm, the more sense it made. Nobody was going to dump a good job with a hot company in five minutes—they'd quit tomorrow, after they'd had a chance to hash it out at home, or next week, after they'd found a place to jump to.

The next day, as I'd expected, the supplier calls started coming—first a torrent, then a flood—all asking the same questions. "I don't get it; this is crazy. What will keep your people motivated?" So I'd explain the whole Marshall Process to them, from "No one ever asks for a salesman" through the importance of teaching people to listen better to how account profiling would make their connection with Marshall more productive.

Salespeople called me, too, but fewer and less agitated than I'd feared. "Explain it to me again," they'd ask. "How do I make more money? What if this happens? What if that happens?" It seemed like a pretty fair deal to most of them, actually. If they'd been making $55,000 before, most were making $55,000 now, guaranteed. Some were taking home more. They'd give us the benefit of the doubt, at least for a while.

I remember that week as a high-speed blur, spent pacing back and forth in my office, talking into my telephone headset, explaining, explaining, explaining, working through every analogy and open-ended question in my repertoire. The gossip in the marketplace was intense; our competitors took nonstop potshots. Day after day, Dick and I worked the phones, rallying the troops, quashing rumors, and soothing fears. By the weekend, I felt totally drained, but relieved, too. No suppliers had withdrawn their business. No salespeople had quit. The bottom hadn't fallen out after all, at least not yet.

Then, when I came back to work on Monday morning, disaster. The latest issue of *Electronic Buyers' News* lay on my office table, open to the editorial page. "THIS ISN'T TQM!" the boldface headline thundered.

I was beside myself. I'd been reading that paper my entire career, and they'd never once let a writer criticize any company's policy. Here, slugged "Executive Comment," was a diatribe against Marshall, specifically and by name. "Now's not the time to demotivate salespeople," the editorialist warned. "I'm sure Marshall Industries has made adjustments in its sales compensation to offset short-term concerns. But salespeople are different from other people; to take incentives away from them is to pull their legs out."

Short-term concerns? Give me a break. We were trying to align ourselves with the forces of the future; we'd been talking, thinking, and planning for months. Salespeople are different? Get real. Are they so different that if you came into a room of fifty people, you could pick out the ones in sales? Money isn't all they care about; they're motivated by many things, just like everyone else is, not just carrots and sticks. The editorial was wrong on all counts. But every supplier and every buyer for every customer we did business with would read it, and dismiss Marshall as doomed to mediocrity. Our competitors would have a field day.

Outraged, I called the paper's publisher, demanding a retraction, but the best he'd promise me was equal space to mount Marshall's defense on the editorial page of the next issue. I tried to write it myself, but every draft sounded more defensive than the one before. So Nida and I worked on Marshall's rebuttal together. Then she wrote and signed the final version, an elegant summation of Marshall's ongoing search for ways to forge beyond the old barriers to customer service, quality, and performance. Our branches wrote letters, too, unsolicited but appreciated.

Looking back, the *Electronic Buyers' News* attack still makes my blood boil, but, unwelcome as it was at the time, it turned out to be a blessing. We had wanted differentiation, and now, thanks to the dueling editorials and the debate they set off, we had it. Morale went up, too: pulling through the crisis had pulled us together.

Letters came in to me for months after that, at least two hundred or three hundred of them, an outpouring that none of us had expected. "I foresee higher prices, slower service, and quality salespeople leaving," one critic warned. "The whole idea sounds like communism—no competition and no incentives!" The vast majority of the letters were complimentary, though—congratulations on our boldness and courage, and pledges of support for what we were trying to do.

For all my fears, Marshall didn't lose a single salesperson when we made the change, either. Many of our people liked getting off of the commission roller coaster, and more still liked the broader range of career paths our new system opened up for them. Today, Marshall is the only company in the industry without commissions. Our turnover has gone down, and our productivity has gone up. Our sales force uses the compensation system as a selling point; human resources uses it as a recruiting tool.

"It lets me be more professional. I can focus on the customer's benefit, not on pushing something at them so I can pay the rent," account manager Steve Macina explains. "We can work on long-term objectives without being distracted solely by what needs to be sold this month," product sales manager Leigh MacQueen adds.

"I never would have allowed myself to be put in the position of having only one account, like I do now," Randy Ferguson says. "But it could be important, and I can make it work. I'm not sitting around thinking: 'Oh, my God, how am I going to justify my existence?'"

Not every salesperson bought in at first, though. I remember our top guy in Boston asking me to go on a customer call with him six weeks after we made the change. So I flew into Logan airport, and we drove to the call together. For forty-five minutes in the car, he told me everything he thought was wrong with our new plan. Then, when we were in the customer's office and he was finishing his presentation, he said, "Oh, by the way I'm not on commission here, so you can trust that I'm not trying to manipulate things." Then, when we got back in the car, he started ragging on the new plan again.

"Wait a second," I said. "If you think it won't work, why did you just use it to sell that customer?"

"I know customers love it," he admitted. "But I still don't see the point."

Manager's Workbook

Everyone lives by selling something.

—ROBERT LOUIS STEVENSON

Unless you are selling Ginsu knives or swampland in Florida you want more from a customer than a signature and a check. You want a relationship, and the chance for still more sales.

You earn that by solving problems, not selling products. You have to listen, ask questions, and learn.

Think of selling as a cycle, not a straight-line rush to close. It's a continuum of equally critical steps, from market research to marketing, prospecting, qualifying, commitment, and follow-up, and it leads to new opportunities for new market research. You're not trying to close the customer. A "closing" is an ending, and the best sales never end. You're trying to create mutual commitment to a process, working together as partners to understand the need, design the best solution, and profit together.

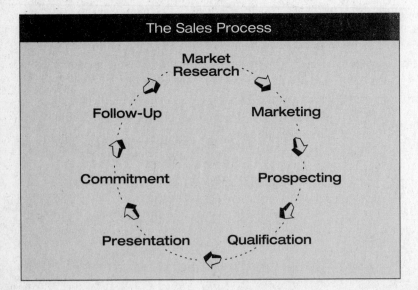

Seven Steps to Never-Ending Sales

Too many salespeople talk too much, babbling away in honest enthusaism about this new product or that improved service they have to sell. But that misses the point: customers want you to solve their problems, not sell them things. Don't tell them what you have. Find out what they need.

Effective selling is a conversation, no matter what you sell. At least half of your time should be spent listening. Most of the other half should be spent asking questions, exploring, and trying to understand the customer's problems and opportunities so that you can design a better solution together.

It's a process built around a seven-step cycle:

1. Look outside

Market research means becoming expert in your customer's businesses. That's the first step toward understanding his or her needs. What are the primary market forces affecting the customer's industry? How is competition changing and how does that change affect them? What knowledge does the customer need from you in order to compete better?

You can find answers in conventional sources like annual reports and Securities and Exchange Commission filings, industry and general business publications, and advertisements for your customer's products. But don't ignore on-line information sources, such as industry Web sites, your customer's site, and the sites of its competitors; Deja News searches of Usenet news groups; and personalized information services like Pointcast.

2. Look inside

Marketing means more than knowing all the products or services that you have to sell. Beyond those basics, you have to understand how those products or services help customers solve their business problems, improve their profitability, and free up time and resources. The goal is to see what you sell as an integrated group of solutions.

Think differentiation. What is unique or special about what you're selling? Is it the content? Delivery? Interface? Is there something that could add customer value in the way your product is designed, ordered, delivered, installed, invoiced, or packaged?

3. Choose your opportunities

Prospecting is the way you listen to the market tell you what to do next. It saves you time, resources, and opportunity cost in two ways: it keeps you alert to every opportunity, but, just as important, prevents you from wasting energy pursuing leads that will not prove mutually beneficial.

Prospecting is the time to make decisions. Is there an opportunity for you? When should you address the prospect's need—now or later? How important is this opportunity, and how much time should you invest? Who at the prospect, among your vendors, and internally should you keep informed?

4. Help customers buy

Qualifying is the heart of effective selling. It requires asking questions to establish what the customer needs in order to solve his or her problems. At this point, you need to listen to your customer describe problems and opportunities from his or her perspective, even if you've already been asked about a specific product.

Start with basic fact finding abour your customers' business. How have they segmented their markets? What are their top priorities? What are their performance goals for next year? Then get strategic. What problems does the customer want solved? What are the consequences of not solving those problems? What does the customer believe is needed to solve the problems? What is the value of solving the problems?

By assisting the customer to quantify the value of solving the problems, you set the stage for an understanding of the value of any solution you eventually propose.

5. Solve problems

Presenting is your opportunity to link the features and benefits of your products or services to the customer's issues and concerns. It's also a chance to provide any tangible or intangible proofs, from test results to references, illustrating that you can deliver the benefits promised.

Don't try to promote your products or services. The focus of your presentation should be on the customer's issues and needs, not on the wonderful features of your widget. Say your customer wants to reduce rework. Your widget is longer than your competitor's and comes in seventeen brilliant colors. So, your presentation could show how your widget addresses the problem of rework caused by too-short widgets.

After showing that your widget is one inch longer than the current widget (a feature), you would explain how the extra length would reduce rework and then quantify the cost saving derived from reduced rework (the benefit). Then you'd wrap up with proof of previous success, like references from other manufacturers who have benefited from using the longer widget. You wouldn't address the color choices, which are irrelevant to this particular customer's problems.

6. Forge a mutual commitment

Commitment differs from closing. It's a two-way street, not just a signature on a bottom line.

Sometimes the customer isn't ready to agree on delivery dates or sign a contract, and that may well be your problem. Ask more questions. Does the solution still fit? Needs may have changed since you made your initial pitch. If so, you need to revisit step three, prospecting, to see if you still have something to offer. If the delay is because of something external, like budget allocations or purchasing procedures, look for ways to work around these barriers. Ask more questions. What might be the consequences of not moving ahead now? How might delay affect the project? If you don't move ahead, how might your customers be affected? Does delay give a competitor an opportunity?

7. Stay for the finale—it's the overture

Follow-up is potentially the most important step of the process; it's your chance to build on the goodwill, trust, and credibility you have worked hard to establish. At this point, you have to look back at the original problem, making sure that the solution worked as promised and expected, and that any glitches are being openly and immediately addressed and resolved. You have to look ahead, too: to the marketing and market research that begins the process all over again. How could changes in the market affect your customer's needs? How could changes in your internal capability affect your ability to meet them? Where is the next opportunity to add value?

Talk Is Cheap

Persuading salespeople to endorse relationship selling is easy. The hard part is getting them to walk the talk every day.

American companies spend $7.1 billion annually on training salespeople, according to *The Journal of Business & Industrial Marketing*. That translates into an average of thirty-three hours per year for every salesperson in America. Too often, though, it is time and money misspent. Companies still concentrate their sales training on teaching their own products and services. They'll pump up the enthusiasm and help people learn a more persuasive pitch, but they don't address what customers need from the salespeople who serve them.

Successful training programs focus on problem-solving skills. At Fidelity Investments Institutional Services Company, for example, salespeople practice how to sell through role playing that has them asking questions to identify customer needs, then writing proposals to address those needs. IBM concentrates on understanding the needs of the industries to which the salesperson is selling. And Xerox teaches interactive listening, according to Mignon Williams, its director of sales education and training, "because people are ultimately building trust."

Our training goal at Marshall comes from our mission. We want to teach people to become their customers' business partner and aim to add value with a commitment to mutual satisfaction. That means that our salespeople must learn to see the world from their customers' perspectives.

We use all the conventional teaching methods: lectures, small-group discussions, and case-study workbook exercises. But two simple tools have proved the most effective.

The first is a twenty-minute video called *The Voice of the Customer.* Its format is disarmingly straightforward: a series of Marshall customers, talking directly at the camera, explaining how it feels to be "sold." Some are resigned, others are angry or frustrated. But their messages are remarkably consistent: "I want you to listen," they say. "I want you to help me to think about my business. I want you to be centered around my business problems, not your sales goal."

Their voices are more eloquent than anything any trainer could say. We don't just show our salespeople what it feels like to be a customer, though. We give them a chance to feel it for themselves.

So, rather than providing only practice selling, our role playing is a two-way simulation. Students play both salesperson and customer. And it's the time they spend in the customer's seat that people remember most. For it's then that they're the one being talked at, trying to explain a problem to a salesperson who doesn't seem really interested. They're the ones feeling manipulated and rushed to close. It's a practical lesson in empathy, and constitutes the first step to understanding the customer's perspective.

No training program is magical, of course. When the going gets tough, it's tempting for salespeople to drift back to their old methods. But once they see that the old ways don't work, they're likely to regroup and try listening to the customer more thoughtfully.

8
The Uses
of Tools:

Technology Without Tears

Enterprise Technology

I'm continually amazed by the number of American managers, particularly at senior levels, who remain techno-skeptics. They're not Luddites, resisting change merely because it is new; they'll use the best tools they think they can afford, if only out of fear of being left behind. But they often don't see much tangible benefit for all the confusion, expense, and headache of their multimillion-dollar investments.

I'm here to testify that technology can transform a company. Since 1992, when in a single tense night we replaced all seven hundred of the computer programs that processed our 750,000 daily transactions, we've spent over $25 million in information-technology (IT) research and development and infrastructure implementation. We've changed every piece of hardware and software that we use. In an era of thinning margins and relentless quarterly earnings pressures from Wall Street, that's a huge investment for a company of our size. The payoff, however, has come in performance: our sales per employee climbed more than 131 percent over the next five years. Our intangible returns have been more valuable still.

Technology is the engine that drives our organization forward, and it is constantly evolving to support as well as help shape our corporate strategy. It is one of the strengths that differentiates Marshall in the market and provides the basis for our brand and growing national visibility. Customers may not care how we pay our people—their eyes may glaze over the hundredth time they hear the Marshall mission. But they do care about our technology—or, to be accurate, they care about what our technology enables us to do for them.

I empathize with many managers for the anxiety that they feel when the talk turns to technology investments. I also worry about spending too much too soon, buying the latest generation of the Betamax, or spending too little too late, losing customers to a competitor who leverages a new idea faster. In addition, too often discussions of technology are too technical to be comprehensible; they degenerate into a rolling cascade of names and initials like CPU and DB2, OLTP and OLAP, domino servers and push and pull, data warehousing and data mining, smart agents and bots. No wonder people throw up their hands. Technology seems like black magic, arcana best left to a chief information officer or vice president of information services, information technology, or electronic data processing.

That way lies obsolescence. Technology offers too critical a range of tools for investment decisions to be left to the experts: it is the fundamental path to connectivity. To succeed, though, it has to be part of a larger enterprise architecture, a system that integrates technology with people, methods, material, and environment. Such a design imperative makes technology the responsibility of every manager in the organization, starting at the top. Daunting as it sounds, there's no need for anxiety—if you'll throw out conventional thinking. At Marshall, we've developed a less-painful way to climb the technology-adoption curve. We've banished the black magic and broken down the walls that separate IT staffers from their colleagues, replacing the traditional mandates, structures, and metrics with a new method more in tune with the forces of change.

I don't pretend to understand what it takes to make a complex computer system perform. The last time I did any hands-on coding was in high school, when I convinced my teacher to permit my classmates and me to write a dating program in BASIC on the classroom IBM. But I don't need to understand how the X's and O's work to use a new technology effectively any more than I need to understand how my TV's remote control changes channels wirelessly. I need only to know what it can do, and how it could change Marshall's ability to execute our strategy.

Don't think technology—think application. How do you want to manage your work flow? Where could you cut out cost or put predictable repetitive tasks into the plumbing? How do you want to connect with your customers? What interfaces would be best? How could you make it easier to work with your customers as partners or speed their time to market? Don't ask what kind of drill you want to buy; ask what kind of hole you need to drill. That's a strategic question, not a technical one.

Assume, for the sake of argument, that if you're willing to invest the time and money, you can create virtually any application your heart desires. Absent such time and cost concerns, you can make a business choice about which investments make the most sense, weighing the cost against the features and benefits that they would let you bring to market. You could, for instance, send a three-dimensional hologram baby with your company's logo dancing across desktops around the world, although it's hard to see what the payoff would be. But don't ask the dollars-and-cents questions too soon. If you don't explore all of a new application's capabilities first, you'll end up shortchanging yourself. Could the application improve your competitive profile? Make you more efficient, accessible, responsive, or creative? Sometimes the cost of *not* spending money is higher than the cost of spending it, even if you can't predict any hard return on investment (ROI). Could you add new customers if it gave you a new capability? Could you lose current customers if a competitor developed the same capability first?

If you ask frontline people what technologies they need, they'll usually say that they want more horsepower. However, that's the wrong answer—and the wrong question, too. Using technology to speed up a flawed process is like trying to help a drunk get home by giving him the keys to a Porsche: he'll still crash; he'll just be going faster when he hits the wall. Ask instead what your organization needs to do to add value. Then you can look for the tools needed to deliver it.

Our customers told us what they wanted: speed, communication, and coordination, a seamless and frictionless connection with the Marshall junction box—free, perfect, now. Technology enables us to pursue those goals. It breaks down the barriers to partnership and defines alignment operationally. It also gives us better telemetry, because, by improving the quality and accessibility of our business intelligence, it increases the predictability of that business. Furthermore, our technology allows us better communication and thus helps assure that intelligence gets to the right people at the right time and that a good idea is leveraged throughout the organization. And finally, it improves the quality of our connection to customers by allowing them to access any of Marshall's services any time, any way, and from any place they want—by electronic data interchange or fax, phone or Internet, twenty-four hours a day, seven days a week, with the interface individually tailored for each customer.

Few companies our size—and no other distributors—have developed such a wide range of capabilities: twenty-four different Internet sites, shareware, an intranet and an extranet, data warehousing, data mining, and expert knowledge-management systems. We didn't create our technology infrastructure with some detailed design in mind, though. Instead, we assembled it in small steps, on the fly and on the cheap, driven by our mission and strategy and the rapidly changing nature of technology itself. We started by removing cost and error and adding speed, then leveraged the capacities of our existing systems to create new systems, along the way harnessing evolving technologies such as the Internet and multimedia to add new value and open new ways to satisfy our customers' insatiable demands.

Although we sometimes call Marshall's technology our plumbing, it is the lifeblood of what we are today. It allows us to function organically and respond to a myriad of stimuli from suppliers, customers, and employees instantly in real time, with self-awareness wired in. But it is, and always will be, a work in progress. Only our enterprise focus and the development method that supports it stay the same.

Applications, systems, and standards are changing too fast to follow a traditional slow-development cycle. Today, any long-term blueprint is obsolete before it's created. What matters, then, is adaptability, flexibility, scalability, and speed. So, rather than aiming for huge leaps, we take small steps, looking for applications that combine tangible value the day they are introduced with long-range potential. Typically, we'll implement a new initiative in less than three months, then start to enhance it the day after implementation, leveraging our way up the learning curve.

We don't expect to be perfect on the first try. Too often, the best is the enemy of the good. We find that it is better to implement a new tool fast than it is to try to perfect it first—and perfect, like free and now, is a moving target. What will get us new business or more orders? What can we turn on next week? We don't waste time looking for the best technical solutions; we look instead for what works best for the specific business problem we're trying to solve. Some solutions are developed in-house, while others are bought off the shelf. What matters is how easily and effectively whatever we hammer together can be integrated into our existing system—a "plug and play" approach, in technospeak.

We're organized differently as well. Rather than having a single information-technology department, Marshall works in naturally evolving work groups designed to reflect the short-term nature of each project and the need for quick decision making. Responsibility is spread among five different team leaders, focused by IT initiatives, like mainframe infrastructure, or by application responsibility. There is no explicit delegation of tasks on teams, and each team's mandate is the same as everyone's at Marshall: Find better ways for the company to listen and respond to the voice of the customer. The mission doesn't say, "Go find the best technologies"; it says, "Serve your business partners by finding ways to add value." Teams are groups of specialists using technology to push our strategy forward, but to fulfill that role effectively, they have to be businesspeople first and possess clear understanding of the needs of the organization as a whole. Without that enterprise focus, even the best team can't consistently create systems that fit together and work. With it, anything is possible.

Our systems don't always fit together and work the first time, of course. But we're usually pretty close, and we learn enough to score a hit with the next try. Then, after initial implementation, the real learning about how an application might develop begins.

Money, of course, plays a part in all of this, but we don't manage that in a traditional manner when it comes to technology, either. We won't bleed the company, chasing state-of-the-art technology— there are places where Marshall still uses old 286-generation computers. We aren't big spenders, either. Although we've invested considerably more since then, we created our Internet prototype for under $25,000. We don't have an annual budget, because technology opportunity doesn't move by calendar year. Projects are funded, modestly but fast, whenever a new opportunity arises. Each is judged on its individual merits, based on long-term corporate strategic goals rather than short-term return-on-investment targets, as we try to predict the potential value of an application twenty revisions forward.

I like the comfort of hard numbers as much as most managers do, but when you're investing in innovation, numbers can be impossible to figure. When we automated the warehouse, we could look at concrete productivity data; when we upgraded our mainframe memory, we could pencil out capacity-planning calculations. But when we decided to launch our first Internet site or introduce Lotus Notes, there was no data to help predict the payoff.

The Internet, as it turned out, would become the "killer app" of Marshall's technology toolbox, as we'll see in more detail in chapter 9. In the summer of '94, however, when we opened for business on the Web, electronic commerce as it is evolving today had barely been imagined. Mosaic, the first popular browser, was still a novelty. Few companies had registered domain names, most of them for stockholder relations.

We didn't have to make the investment. None of our suppliers were on the Internet, although they sold the most sophisticated electronic products in the world. Only a handful of our customers had heard of it, and many of them thought it was a waste of money and time.

We thought otherwise. Despite not knowing where it would lead, we could see in the Internet a way to add value from day one; we could post data sheets for our 250,000 products on-line. The key was getting started fast.

Being among the first on the Internet established momentum for us as well as set standards and expectations—and won Marshall a national public-relations bonanza in the process. There was nothing prescient in our investment decision, though. We had a practiced method to follow to minimize our risk, one based on the lessons we had learned on that disastrous day when we had tried to change our operating system eighteen months earlier, on December 7, 1992— Pearl Harbor Day.

The Crash of '92

Even back in 1991, before I went to the Deming seminar, everyone had long since agreed that Marshall's twenty-year-old computer operating system would have to be scrapped. Like an old jalopy held together with duct tape and bailing wire, it sputtered, barely able to process Marshall's 750,000 daily transactions, let alone handle the growing customer demand for mandated quality standards or high-speed responsiveness.

The distribution industry had been different when we bought our old system. Marshall was divided into divisions serving separate local markets then, each identified by a different letter on the keyboard and operated like a separate business with its own supplier franchises, inventory, and profit and loss. By the late 1980s, the days when we could function that way were long gone. Our survival now depended on a coordinated national response to the market, and our computer couldn't even communicate data from one division to another.

How bad was it operationally? Each morning someone from the management information systems (MIS) department would wheel a handcart into the executive offices with a three-foot stack of print-outs containing the numbers that we were supposed to use in monitoring and guiding the business. Then, each night the computer would go silent for eight to ten hours so that it could batch process the day's data. At the end of the month, batching could take twice as long, so on those days, if customers called before noon, wanting a simple stock check or price quote, they were out of luck. "Sorry," we'd tell them. "The computer is down."

The system stunted our growth, too. When we ran out of letters, we started calling new divisions "pound" and "back slash," but inevitably we got stuck: no one wanted to run a division called "colon."

Over the years, people had figured out lots of ways to work around the system's limitations. They'd go to extraordinary lengths to serve individual customers, rerouting an order entry or marking their parts with an asterisk to fool the computer into hiding their inventory. "Tampering," Doctor Deming called such short-term fixes; it was manipulating a failed system rather than analyzing and redesigning it. These tactics had left Marshall with an undocumented maze for work flow and was the source of perpetual inventory-management, customer-service, and quality headaches.

We'd known for years that we had to replace our system, but we had never been able to finish the project. The leadership of what was then called MIS had promised us a cure for all our ills, something called "COBRA" (customer order booking resale applications), but after years of work in progress without completion, it was hard to believe them anymore. They'd met with user groups from every department and division in the company, trying to establish goals and objectives for the new system, but no two groups could agree on what we needed.

Part of the problem, in fairness, lay with management. We'd sit around a table with the COBRA team trying to describe the business so that they could write the appropriate software code, and the best answer to all their questions was always "I don't know":

"How many change orders a day do you think you'll need in two years?"

"I don't know. It depends on lots of things."

"How many branches will you have?"

"I don't know. Maybe none. Maybe a hundred. Could the system let us go either way?"

The system, I realized, could be designed to do almost anything, if we were willing to pay for it. But we had no way to figure out where our money would be best spent.

Take, for example, something as critical as the database-management system, a multimillion-dollar choice we'd have to live with for years. Hour after hour I sat in a room listening to people ten times smarter than I'll ever be debate the virtues of VSAM versus DB2. VSAM, they said, was established and traditional; DB2 less tested and more contemporary in design. VSAM would save money and use the central processing unit (CPU) more efficiently, but DB2 would be easier to program. How were we supposed to pick? They were just letters to most of us.

The Deming seminar changed our perspective. Our redesign of the company as a whole began when we recognized that Marshall's performance depended on a complex system, an architecture that aligned our people, processes, methods, materials, and environment. Technology, we realized, was the engine of that system, and as such, it had to be a part of everyone's life, not a department with its own separate purposes.

The months we spent discussing Marshall's future, going back to when we put the strategy on the wall, gave us the guideposts and clear purpose we needed to go forward with technology improvement. Whereas we'd been looking internally for our design principles, Deming showed us that we instead had to look outside, at our customers' changing needs. We'd been trying to make decisions based on technological attributes, but now saw that we needed to make them for business reasons. There were always going to be "I don't knows"; creating the flexibility to manage those uncertainties had to be our prime design mandate.

So, of course, we chose DB2 for our database management. Our mission said innovate, and DB2 was easier to change faster. It seems obvious, in retrospect, that its inefficient CPU performance would be improved as the program matured through its revisions, but it felt like a huge gamble at the time.

It took scores of people thousands of hours to design, code, and test the new system. After all, we had to write the seven hundred different application programs that run Marshall today. To coordinate everything, we put together a new team, and renamed the system QOBRA, for "quality order booking resale applications." Then the detailed work of figuring out how all the X's and O's should flow began. Every single interaction and transaction occurring whenever anyone touched a keyboard, from stock check to order, invoice, packing slip, accounting, and finance, had to be graphed step by step in bubble charts.

The QOBRA team built our values into the design. They opened up the information flow, reasoning that the more access people had, the better decisions they could make; and they eliminated repetition to cut down on drudgery and reduce error. They looked ahead, too, anticipating the computer clock changes at year 2000, creating multiple language and currency capabilities, and laying the groundwork for virtual distribution—even though we couldn't see how it would work yet. Each application had to be designed to enhance the larger system, then built with enough infrastructure support to handle the technology evolutions to come. We must have been successful: we still have the original charts, a wall's worth of bulging three-ring binders lining the office of Diane Bull, one of Marshall's IT directors who sparkplugged the thirty-month project, and we refer back to them even today.

We were finally ready to change over to the new system in late 1991, and chose December 7 to do it—not out of any sense of historical irony, but because business was always a little slower before the holidays, and so we'd have some breathing space. In addition, December 7 fell on a Friday, which would give us the weekend to work out the bugs.

I remember how anxious I felt that day. There would be no turning back; our old system wasn't documented well enough to reconstruct. We had no real backup plan, either: not only did the X's and O's have to get converted to QOBRA over the weekend, but on Monday people had to be able to come to work and use it to run the business. I went down to look at our IBM mainframe before I went home on Friday, but there was nothing to see but a large machine humming beneath the fluorescents.

Dick and I both came to the office at 5:00 A.M. on Monday, 8:00 A.M. East Coast time, as the first users started logging on. The system was fast and responsive for the first few hours, running like a high-performance luxury car loaded with options, but by 11:00 A.M., when the company was signed on from coast to coast and usage climbed, QOBRA stalled, then stopped dead. We'd overloaded the capacity of the computer's CPU. It took twenty minutes from the time you hit the ENTER key to get an answer.

We'd been our own worst enemy, as we found out later. People had been so excited about all the bells and whistles we'd designed that they swamped the system, trying out exotic searches that ate up memory or playing numbers-crunching "what-if" games on-line. One branch decided the QOBRA was so robust that it could print its Christmas card list out of the system mainframe. It was a miracle the lights didn't dim.

At the time, though, all we knew was that our expensive new computer was down. We were moving boxes to shipping without even printing invoices. Inventory worth $5 million could have disappeared without a trace. People panicked, then started pointing fingers. What was killing the response time? Why hadn't we done more testing? Why did we chose DB2? Who was to blame? It was as emotional a scene as I've ever witnessed in a business office.

"What if we rerouted this way?" someone suggested, and started drawing new bubble graphs in marker. "What if we entered data differently?" another argued, and hurriedly sketched still more graphs.

By 7:00 P.M., when they were done jury-rigging a possible fix to try on Tuesday, they'd covered the wall with a jumble of new charts.

What did I know? They were the experts, and we had to do something. But that night, driving home, I had my own flash of panic. Marshall, I realized, was chasing disaster. I could almost hear Dr. Deming lecturing at the seminar, warning me against "tampering"—trying to manipulate the system before we even knew what was wrong with it.

We'd worked too hard on our design to toss it out so quickly. If we weren't careful, we'd end up back where we started, with an incomprehensible maze of shortcuts and quick fixes. We'd tried to build a luxury performance car, and now we couldn't make it run. But rather than patch it with duct tape, we had to scale it back to basic transportation, turn off the air conditioning and turbocharger and CD player, and see what happened. All we really needed were stock checks, invoices, and packing slips. Once we got those working, we could start to add some of the more-advanced functions back in.

So that's what we tried, beginning the next day. I asked Jacob Kuryan, who had led the team that designed our automated warehouse, to sit with the crisis group through what I knew would be a long grind. I wanted him to make sure that we stayed true to our design.

For Marshall's sales force, already stressed by the abolition of the commission system just three months earlier, the next few weeks were an ordeal. Imagine trying to maintain a multimillion-dollar business with 150 suppliers, 60,000 customers, and 250,000 different technical parts working with just pencil and paper and elbow grease. Customers calling with questions didn't want to hear that the computer was down. So, Marshall's salespeople looked up prices by hand or checked with the warehouse to see what inventory was available when. Some sat bolted to their desks for twelve hours a day for days, steely eyed, fueled by caffeine and adrenaline. Others cornered me in the halls, pleading for relief. "What are we going to do?" one sobbed. "My customers are going to drop me if we don't do *something.*"

"I know it's hard, but we will get through it," I answered. "We cannot fix this in a day. It's too a big problem. But Dick and I *are* going to fix it.

"I understand what's at risk. We could lose customers. We could lose employees. We'll just have to win them back. The only way out of this is through it."

The Soul of Our New Machine

In the end, happily, we didn't lose any customers. As in the old days, when Gordon Marshall urged employees to "walk through walls," our people found a way, somehow, to keep Marshall working, although it took us six gruesome weeks to get our basic applications up to speed and another month and a half to restore QOBRA's full capacity. Revenues held steady for the quarter, but due to cut-over expenses, our earnings were below analysts' estimates—so our stock price took a hit, although that, too, was temporary. Sales and profits started to climb in the next quarter, pulling our stock price with them, and the crisis, finally, was past, remembered today, almost fondly, as one of our finest hours.

Looking back, though, I often wonder if Marshall could have survived if we'd still lived with MBOs and sales commissions when the computer went down. Could we have cut our operating system down to basics if we'd still had to keep track of everybody's individual performance? We wanted to know how people were doing, of course, but we didn't need to know the exact numbers to keep the business running. Our sales force was already upset with management: we were the bozos who'd created the mess. Would the salespeople have hung in with us if their paychecks depended on our ability to generate commission reports?

As it happened, our salespeople were heroes. All of the stress, commotion, and confrontation focused on them. They faced constant demands, frustration with response time and service levels, tears, anger, and impatience—and they pulled us through.

It struck me then that there was a message in their response, a validation of our new incentive-and-compensation strategy. Skeptics had insisted that our new system would breed complacency and mediocrity—but how, then, to explain the sales force's performance? Why didn't our salespeople just call in sick, take vacation time, or simply take it easier? Wouldn't that have been the rational response, if the critics were correct?

It turned out that the people were committed, dedicated, and conscientious. They were motivated by responsibility and pride; incentives and commissions were not the issue. Mediocrity and complacency were not options to them.

I made a promise when the worst had passed, to myself and to Marshall: Never again would we let the company grow dependent on an obsolete operating system or put our employees through the ordeal of trying to replace such a system. Bringing QOBRA on-line would be the beginning of the system's development, not the end. QOBRA would be Marshall's permanent engine, to be improved forever.

Today, six years after the crash, we still work on that engine every day. Changing as technologies evolve, QOBRA supports and propels our strategy, providing us with new ways to align Marshall's processes with the voices of our customers. We've cut the mainframe batch time, added new capabilities and applications on eleven new client servers, and improved our connections with the Internet, our extranet and an intranet, and Lotus Notes. We have a networked infrastructure, all built on QOBRA's foundation and developed in small steps that responded to opportunities as they arose. The target—free, perfect, and now—has stayed the same, and so have the critical questions: What can we do next? How fast can we do it? Our goal isn't to create the best technology possible, although I think we often come close. Rather, our goal is to marry people and technology to our enterprise vision by creating tools that everyone will use. Then the real learning can begin.

QOBRA's core function was to manage process data, which included calculating invoices and counting inventory, but its real power was its ability to move that data quickly and accurately to whoever needed it, absent any handoffs or filters—"leveraging the intellect of the organization," as Tony Roberts, a Marshall board member at the time, called it. Our sales force was flooding us with information, the answers to all the questions we wanted asked, as they worked through the Marshall Process with their customers and pinned down individual buying habits, quality mandates, and competitive imperatives. With 60,000 customers, we might well have drowned in all that detail, but DB2's accelerating database muscle enabled us to put it to work. With DB2, we could keep track of each customer individually and serve them as a demographic of one, while at the same time it helped us track the shifts and patterns in the marketplace as a whole, the voice of the customer writ large, and pointed us toward the process improvements we needed in order to stay competitive.

The warehouse, automated in 1990, was the obvious place to start up the technology learning curve. We already stored and retrieved parts robotically; the next step was to bolt the tracking system to QOBRA with a client server. It took over three months to complete, but when we were done, customers could check backlog or inventory status instantly. Then, we connected to our major freight forwarders, UPS and FedEx, through a single, paperless manifest system. That, too, was done in ninety days—and it enabled customers to track their orders right up to their assembly plant door without leaving Marshall's server platform.

Our robotic warehouse didn't just track where parts were, however. It also tracked how many moved, how fast, when, and where. With this information, we could turn a mechanical measure into a cognitive tool and build a forecasting system for our customers based on our modeled usage trends and seasonal variations. "SMART," we called it, for "supply management and response technology." SMART took the speculation out of customers' purchasing decisions, thereby improving both efficiency and cash flow.

That's when the real enhancements began. We weren't just increasing the quantity of information we shared, we were improving its quality as well, turning data into business intelligence. We could see our customers wrestling with ever more complex financial, manufacturing, and logistic puzzles as the competitive pressures in the market accelerated, and now we could help them find answers. We had the capability to design software applications that would analyze such critical issues as strategic forecasting, time-phased order planning, account profiling, and supply-chain management, all of it hooked into QOBRA's real-time transactional data.

Could we have created SMART and its sister applications if we still sold on commission? Sure—but the applications would not have fit our customers' needs so well. SMART, for instance, projects volume in units, not dollars, for units are the only numbers that matter to our customers' purchasing agents and manufacturing managers. Commission-based companies, in contrast, usually forecast a customer's volume in dollars, then use that figure to forecast their own revenue streams. It's easy enough to convert dollars to units, of course, but dollars are a different mind-set as well as a different metric. Dollar forecasting looks inward, at the organization's need. Unit forecasting, though, by design, looks out at the customer's needs, as our mission mandates.

Decisions on what to do next and how much to spend are made in my office, in an ongoing dialogue with Marshall's IT teams. As CEO, I have the responsibility to set the company's strategic course, but I count on them to define that strategy operationally and to figure out how to make it work. I don't tell them specifically what to do. They understand our capabilities, processes, and purpose; they invent what they know we need. But the target keeps moving, for new technologies constantly create new strategic opportunities and change the operational definitions of existing ones. And success can't be measured until after implementation, as people in the field actually start to use the new tool they have been given.

Take a simple strategic decision like staying open all the time. That's easy enough to define—24 hours a day, 7 days a week, 365 days a year—but it takes a huge amount of infrastructure engineering to execute. Someone has to reroute the switching system for all the phones in our branches to make sure that after-hours calls roll automatically to be answered in our Nevada call center, "@ONCE," within three rings, by a human being. Someone else has to worry about our mainframe batch time. Before QOBRA, our computer was down for ten hours each day so that it could batch, twenty hours or more on the last day of the month. Today, the system runs 24 hours a day, 6.8 days a week each week.

I didn't ask IT director Mi LeHoang's team to figure that out, and I don't know how they did it—I just said, "I want to be open all the time." I didn't ask Kerry Young's Internet team to add live-chat capability to our Web site, either. We agreed that our virtual business should be as open as our real one, with a human connection a customer could talk to twenty-four hours a day, seven days a week, and Kerry made it happen.

Lotus Notes, introduced in March 1995, was incorporated in much the same way. I didn't ask, "What's the best groupware platform?" I'd never even heard the term. Instead, I said, "We've got to take advantage of bandwidth; let's connect everyone to the system."

It was embarrassing that so few people in a company specializing in selling computer parts actually used a computer themselves. We'd been on the Internet since July 1994, but we hadn't even given our own people a way to log on. Eventually, we'd all have to become computer literate, or risk obsolescence. Why wait? The future is now.

Harnessing the bandwidth available to us would let us maximize the value of the Marshall Process and keep our message crisp, with a consistency of communication. We could take all the learning behind the questions the salespeople asked, along with all the knowledge in our database, and put them directly into the hands of each salesperson on every call. And also at their fingertips are all the details about any of our 250,000 different products—all current, all in real time.

Connecting everyone would allow us to change our work flow, too, by eliminating the need for handoffs and checking up. That meant no more passing papers or circulating memos—we could put the predictable, mechanical tasks into the plumbing, thereby giving everyone more time to work at the real job of looking for new ways to add value for the customer. We'd talked about getting rid of the hierarchy, flipping over the organizational chart, and putting the customer on top, and if everyone were connected, we could make that ideal real. Information could pass instantly, with no distortion. Everyone in the organization, employees, suppliers, and customers alike, could see anything they wanted and communicate with anyone they wanted to.

Once I saw them, the strategic imperatives seemed blindingly obvious. So did the urgency. And since I'm not a rocket scientist, I assumed that if I could see the potential, our competitors could see it too. So I told Kerry Young's team to make it happen. I didn't know what the hardware or software should be or what we could do with them, I knew only that it had to happen fast.

Forty-five days later, everyone in our Silicon Valley branch had Lotus Notes installed, and each of our forty-five salespeople there had a Toshiba laptop. Then we started to roll the system out companywide, putting Lotus Notes on desktops and distributing laptops to the rest of our six hundred salespeople.

Giving so many people laptops is easy. The hard part, as anyone who has ever introduced a new technology will attest, is getting them to use them. There are tree-huggers in every company who get upset if you try to move their desks, let alone change the way they do their jobs.

Resistance among Marshall's sales force was particularly high and rather vocal, but our managers were anxious, too. This was four years ago, remember—many of our employees had never even touched a computer before, and dreaded the prospect. And while a few understood what we were trying to do, most wanted no part of it.

"None of our competitors have computers," people complained. "Why do we have to?"

With that question, our two days of training began. We set out to explain the why, just as we had explained all the earlier changes Marshall had gone through. We had no choice, I told them. We'd either adapt to the forces of change sweeping through our world, or we'd die like the dinosaurs.

Then we moved to the how-to: This is a computer, this is a battery, this is a disk. The heavy sledding came late that first morning, after we had shown them how to turn their computers on and introduced them to Windows. By the end of the first day, though, the laptops were starting to make sense to people, although a few younger employees were on the edge of tears from their frustration. The second day went more smoothly as we looked at what Notes would let them do when they actually went to a customer's site with a specific part to sell. Once again, just as we had when we taught them the Marshall Process, we stressed problem solving and role playing.

Then, the real test began. Information-technology designers can create the most intuitive navigation paths and put in infinite bytes of data, and sales managers can train people till the cows come home, but the success of any technology can be measured only by how much it is actually used in the field. People are the soul of any application; the more they learn to exploit it, the more they will push its evolution forward.

Lotus Notes was popular from day one. Everyone liked the novelty of e-mail and Internet access, and the more they used the brainstorming, work flow, and database applications, the more comfortable they felt depending on them. No more searching for data sheets or fumbling for details on a call; no more time wasted totaling daily figures for a monthly report; more time to sell and more ways to sell more effectively. Mary Obot, who'd fought back tears on the first day of training, became an early convert. "Just wanted to send you a note to let you know I have made significant improvements in my utilzation of the wonderful tool you have provided," she wrote me. "I was a tree-hugger. I wanted to cling to my old ways rather than go through the uncomfortable transition of having to learn something new. Thanks again for not allowing me to remain in the age of the dinosaur."

The conversion of the last skeptics came later that year, when Advanced Micro Devices (AMD) signed Marshall on as a new franchised distributor.

Every supplier wants to send a clear and consistent message to the market, but by the time the sales presentation gets put to work, it has already gone through three different handoffs, from supplier to supplier's rep to salespeople at a Monday-night meeting in each individual branch. It can take weeks just to sort out all the paper and make sure that the right data sheets and price lists, engineering studies, technical reports, and marketing peripherals get into the right hands.

Lotus Notes gave us the leverage to change all that. We got the AMD franchise on a Thursday, and by the next day, every person in the Marshall system had the full presentation in front of them, exactly as AMD wanted them to see it, with all the supporting detail just a click away.

Then, without further ado, they could begin using what Lotus Notes gave them to build AMD's business.

Free, perfect, and now? Not quite. Marshall's new tool didn't cost AMD a penny extra, and it moved the AMD message instantly and error-free. But perfect, as always, remains a moving target. That's where opportunities lie, where technology connects with the imagination.

Technologist Round Table

Every morning, no matter where in the world he or she turns on the laptop, there's an e-mail waiting for every senior Marshall manager. It's a report on the company's 750,000 daily transactions, telling each of us individually what's new in the numbers we've chosen to track. I watch exceptions on sales, productivity growth, and profit performance, as well as how many people are using our sales force–automation tools and the figures from our human resources department, but I could watch any numbers I want.

That's Marshall technology today, pushing information I need to a customized interface, turning raw data into information I can use to monitor our strategic performance. But that's just one of the tools our infrastructure presents to me. If I want to know more about what's happening with a specific customer or with the market as a whole, I can tap into our broad range of database applications. If I want an unfiltered look at our customers' immediate concerns, I can click into live chat at www.marshall.com, where engineers at work—customers—discuss their design problems with Marshall's support staff.

There isn't a day that passes that I don't wish I better understood how these technologies work. As bandwidth explodes and time to market shrinks, their importance can only increase. Fortunately, though, I don't need to know: I'm blessed with an astonishing team of people who do, and who use that knowledge to reinvent the company every day. Thus, it made sense as I finished this chapter to give the last word to them.

Information-technology director Diane Bull joined Marshall in 1990, after twenty years creating applications systems in the retailing industry. She led the team that designed and implemented QOBRA, and is currently responsible for applications development.

Roy Chang, another information-technology director, has been at Marshall for eight years. After undergraduate training in Taiwan, he earned advanced degrees in math and in computer science at Kansas State University and the University of Tennessee. He is responsible for IT operations and telecommunications.

Our third information-technology director, Raj Jha, has been with Marshall since 1994. A former team leader for the artificial-intelligence group at McDonnell Douglas, he is currently responsible for Marshall's supply-chain management and warehouse automation.

Mi LeHoang is Marshall's director of intranet applications. Trained in computer sciences in Europe, he joined Marshall in 1991.

Kerry Young is Marshall's vice president of information technology. A former manager of information systems (IS) and quality assurance at McDonnell Douglas, he joined Marshall in 1993. He is responsible for the entire IT department, including a broad range of technology activities, including electronic commerce and the Internet, groupware, and sales force automation.

I asked them the same question I'd asked myself when I'd started this chapter: What's special about Marshall's technology toolbox?

KERRY: The difference here is that IT is focused on a strategic enterprise perspective. We listen to the voices of the users, collecting their input and trying to be responsive to their needs, but our thinking revolves around how to improve the company as a whole, working with management to envision what our business will look like in the future.

DIANE: In other places I've worked, individual departments decide what they need and go to IT to execute it. Here, our job is to see the big picture, to understand how all the parts of the business and technology fit together. That's a perspective individual users just don't have.

MI: I think the most important thing is management's support and vision of the new technology. If you don't have support from leadership you can't get anything done.

ROY: There's no red tape here whatsover. You just have to prepare, to be ready to present your case, but once the project is approved, you're on your way.

KERRY: Because we think application, we don't get caught up in the idea that one technology is better than another. There are some differences, sure, but for any application need, there are probably one hundred good solutions. We look for the one that solves our specific business need, concentrating on value added, flexibility, and time to market.

RAJ: Most IT departments define themselves by a small range of technologies that they'll use, so that's where they look for solutions. We aren't that limited. Keeping our options open shortens our cycle from idea to prototype to implementation.

DIANE: Our job is to study our industry, study our business, then find ways to put people and technology together. The opportunity to be business analysts as well as technologists forces us out in the field, to spend the day with salespeople, living in their world, trying to figure out how to help them be more effective.

We start by looking for ways to take non-value-added work out of their jobs. Our business and markets are changing constantly, so we always have to be looking for new features and functions to try.

KERRY: A lot of companies measure an IT group by how complete their solution was or how few errors there were in the code. Here, those things are important, but they're less important than getting to market and starting the learning process fast. I hate saying that, though: it makes people outside of our culture very nervous. Nevertheless, software development is a work in process. You never fully learn about an application until you're actually using it.

We have an advantage there, too. The way our organization is structured means we don't get our input channeled through a single source or through a narrow chain of command to be rearticulated to us. We get it directly from real-world users, inside the company and out, every day. Being able to ask questions and understand exactly how people are using applications affects our ability to design the right solutions more than anything else.

RAJ: It gives us a better hand on the pulse of any changes we make, too. Whether we make a mistake or do everything right, we'll hear about it right away, unfiltered. That real-time feedback means we can understand a problem before it is too late to fix it.

We're so closely tied to people's objectives in the field that we understand their day-to-day responsibilities most of the time. They may even call us to help solve a general problem that isn't technology related.

KERRY: IT's job is to be their business partner. We try to understand their pains. We brainstorm with them all the time, whether they feel like talking about technology or about operations and marketing. Our mission is the same as theirs, and all our successes are joint successes.

Manager's Workbook

Technical knowledge is not enough. One must transcend techniques so that the art becomes an artless art.

— KARATE SENSEI DAISETSU SUZUKI

Road Rules

There is no one, me included, who can provide a cookbook full of recipes for your investment decisions. You have to find the answers for yourself, based on where you think you're trying to go strategically.

Consultants can help you kick the tires and blue-sky new ideas; most are smart and current with the trends. But they don't have any stake in the game. Even the most knowledgeable can unwittingly mislead you by misunderstanding your company's individual history, culture, or needs.

Instead, you'll find your answers in the marketplace itself. The better you can listen to your customers' needs and experience your own service, the clearer you'll see where you have to spend. It helps to keep six basic rules in mind while you look:

1. Let ROI reign, not rule

Return on investment matters, but sometimes the cost of not making an investment is higher than the cost of making it. Hard numbers are always best, but some technologies are too new for anyone to predict what the concrete payoff will be a year down the road. If the initiative fits your strategic needs or adds to the value you deliver to your customers—and you can keep the investment incremental—it may be worth the risk.

2. Easy does it

Technology isn't just about access to information. It's about *easy* access to the *right* information. You could pump out numbers and stats to people all day long, but all you'd do is drown them in data.

It's more important to identify which information is critical and make sure that everyone who needs it gets it in a way that's convenient and simple. Don't make them pull out what they need—push it to them, customized, user specific, and exception based.

3. Become bilingual

Do your IT people speak only technobabble? Ever wonder why? At most companies, IT people are herded into one isolated department and venture out only to interview users and demo prototypes. The best IT professionals, though, *live* with the business units. They spread out across the company and work side by side with the business folks. Direct access to the customer and the user every day helps them learn the organization and its processes inside and out, and they bring that knowledge to every project they lead.

4. Keep your options open

The key to building great IT systems is maintaining flexibility. Don't buy into one type or brand of technology if it will stop you from adapting to the changing business environment. The best solutions balance time, cost, scalability, and user requirement. They're easy to add to what you have, and will be easy to add to in turn. Think incremental steps, and keep your eye on the ideal end state— free, perfect, and now—but chart an iterative course.

5. Faster is better than better

Too many IT projects fail because developers with feature-itis insist on getting it complete before they roll it out. They quibble over the drink cup holder instead of making sure that all the cylinders fire; or they delay the start so long that the race is half over before they're on the track. But instead of striving for such completeness, it makes more sense to implement a basic, quality version of a project, then incorporate user feedback to add and enhance features as you go. The faster solution may be technically less elegant, but when time to market matters, you have to bite the bullet. And don't build everything yourself—take advantage of useful technologies that already have large existing user bases.

6. Put muscle behind it

If your IT projects don't have buy-in and visible support from senior managers, you might as well throw in the towel before the rollout. Most new technology requires some adaptation from users; it asks them to step outside their comfort zone. If no one backs up the IT project and explains why the change is necessary, you'll end up wasting your resources.

The Steps of Learning

Maintaining competitive differentiation is a full-time job for everyone in the organization. To be successful, you have to climb three learning curves simultaneously.

Initially critical, continuous improvement by itself eventually delivers diminishing returns. But it focuses people on problems, and that is the path to innovation. Innovation moves an organization to a new level of learning and to new levels of capability, connectivity, and creativity. It's "learning to think outside the box," to invoke the current cliché. That ability, in turn, becomes the path to growth, by welcoming in the new collaborators, tools, and ideas that come from outside the organization and help to initiate quantum leaps and digital learning.

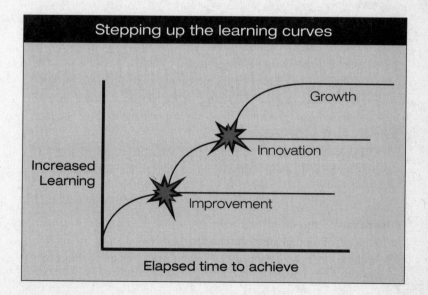

How to Get to How-to

Which technology is right is the last question to ask. If you want to make sure that your choice is right, you have to start with basics.

What are you trying to do? Step back and think about your end goal. Are you sure that technology is the right way to get there? What problem are you trying to solve?

How will this IT initiative affect the process? If it doesn't change the way you do business—allow you to move faster or do more— why would you do it? You can't expect technology to fix the flaws in your system. If you automate a broken process, you get an automated broken process.

Who is the sponsor? A project without a senior business executive as champion is dead before its launch. If you can't find anyone who will support an initiative publicly and passionately, you've probably picked the wrong project.

How will you measure success? You know your goal—is there a hard or soft return you can expect to see from it? If you don't know what it is yet, you aren't ready to invest in anything.

TrendWatch

Talk to technology adapters these days and the term you'll most often hear is "knowledge management." That's a high-end way to refer to how a company uses its information. It incorporates how well relevant data reaches the right people, as well as the system in place to ensure that the know-how employees have in their heads is shared with the rest of the company.

A simple idea, perhaps, but it depends on the convergence of a new attitude toward IT with two rapidly developing technology trends:

The death of "the wizard"

After years of mutual misunderstanding, businesspeople are starting to understand the importance of technology, while IT folks are learning that their technology must have a business purpose. We're moving away from the time when technology was the province of a few wizards practicing their magic off in the corner—and moving away from the time when IT executives were blocked from participating in senior management's strategy discussions.

The numbers tell the story. In a 1998 survey conducted by *CIO* magazine at one of its conferences, 62 percent of information-systems executives polled said that they reported to the highest-ranking executive at their company. Of that same group of IS execs, only 19 percent ranked themselves among the top five executives in their companies five years ago; only 6 percent ranked themselves among the top three. Today, 48 percent rank themselves in the top five, 12 percent in the top three.

The magazine tells the same story editorially, too. Historically a publication for technology executives alone, the editors have launched a new section for "the other O's." Their logic was simple: everyone, not just the specialists, has to understand what technology can do before it can do very much.

The rise of the warehouse

"Data warehousing" is an awful term for a useful process, for it implies that information gets packed away in a musty warehouse, where it never sees the light of day. In truth, though, it's merely a way to make information accessible to everyone—which is why a data warehousing capability is the tool at the top of most IS managers' wish lists.

A data warehouse collects all the X's and O's from various computer systems, inside or outside the company, puts them into the same digital format, and then stores them all together. So, instead of purchasing, accounting, and marketing departments all having their separate database fiefdoms, unreadable to anyone lacking the same platforms and applications, data comes from a central source that everyone can access, navigate, and analyze easily. That way, everyone works with the same most-current picture of business reality.

Data warehouses can have more than operational uses, though.

Harrah's, for example, has built a data warehouse that stores information on its six million customers. If one of its regulars hasn't shown up for a while, the casino can entice him or her with a free hotel stay.

The National Association of Securities Dealers uses their giant warehouse as a regulatory tool for the NASDAQ exchange. Some 555,000 registered traders buy and sell an average of 700 million shares per day, generating 4 gigabytes of data a day. It used to take at least twenty-four hours and as much as two months to sort and analyze those numbers for violations. Now, most regulatory reports are issued within thirty minutes of market close. The number of violations flagged has risen 30 percent since the automation went into effect.

The explosion of intranets

Considered a novelty less than three years ago, internal communications networks are fast becoming the circulatory system of choice among American businesses. Intranets today are either in development or on-line at more than two-thirds of the *Fortune* 1000, according to Forrester Research.

Cheap and efficient, intranets use the same kind of technology as the Internet. Employees can use the same browser software they use to surf the World Wide Web to surf a company's internal servers, where Web pages can serve as gateways to the organization's databases.

Hewlett-Packard is one of the pioneers of the intranet. The company had an internal network nine years ago, long before the commercial browser had been born. Today, HP uses its intranet for global electronic communication, personnel training, and support for distributed teams. But its most impressive application is as a software distributor. It used to take HP two weeks and countless IS staff hours to roll out a new software program to the company's 100,000 internal users. Today, thanks to the intranet, rollout has been automated and cut to two days, saving the company $2,000 per PC each year in technical support and related costs.

9
Captain Internet and the Tower of Babel:

Get Wired

The Electronic Marketspace

I got a whiff of the coming gold rush in the fall of 1997, when the Silicon Valley–based CEO of one of Marshall's large suppliers called me on the phone, looking for advice on how to upgrade his Internet capability.

He'd watched his competitor's beefed-up Web-marketing campaigns take customers away long enough, he told me, and it was time to get serious. He wanted to hire the best techno specialists he could afford and set them up as a separate profit center that reported to him directly. There was money to be made on-line: Why shouldn't he make some of it?

He'd thought a lot about the metrics, he said. His competitor was spending $1.3 million annually to get 12 million hits a month. Since he could only budget $1 million, 75 percent, he'd set his target at 75 percent of his competitor's result, too: 7 million hits. Now he wanted advice on specifics. Which statistical-report writer should he use on which server? What was the best way to retrieve data—cookies or mouse droppings? What kind of profit-and-loss return could he expect, and what return on investment (ROI)?

The conversation made me squirm. Hits are a dumb target to begin with, and who plans a strategy for anything that aims to be 75 percent as good as the competition?

He'd done his homework, but he was asking all the wrong questions. There was no attempt to integrate the new Internet capability into a larger enterprise strategy; no attempt to design an interface tied to his customers' needs or to his company's ideal image; no attempt to understand the rules and trends of the new electronic marketplace. He could build the site he wanted—he's a man who gets his way—but it would be money thrown into a black hole.

"So, seven million hits a month," he asked, "sound doable?"

"Sure," I said. "But I don't know what that means. *Playboy* probably gets seven million hits a day. So what? There are lots of ways to get eyeballs to your site, but, once they're there, there has to be something they want to do. Which would you rather have—seven million random swipes or thirty thousand motivated customers who come to do business? The Internet is just a bunch of connections unless you figure out what you want to do with it first."

"Right," he said. "So how many hits do you get a month?"

"Ten million. But it's not a number we pay much attention to. A hit could be a stray surfer searching for information on the Marshall Plan or movies starring Penny Marshall. What counts is that we get more than fifty thousand unique visitors each month, each clicking an average of twenty-five pages per visit.

"They come because we've designed our site to give them what they want the way they want it. That didn't happen by accident. A Web strategy won't work unless it's part of your larger design and mission and you have the organizational structure to support it."

"Right," he agreed. "But I don't have the time to talk about all that now. I just want to know what to do about the Internet."

In the end, I couldn't help him much. Although he's notoriously thick-skinned, no one wants to hear that his or her plans are 180 degrees off course. But a year or two down the road, when he's another million dollars in, he'll still be scrambling to catch up, chasing technology bells and whistles and wondering why the bonanza passed him by.

He won't be alone, either. Hundreds of thousands of businesses large and small will invest hundreds of millions of dollars in wiring themselves to the Internet over the next few years, as surging bandwidth makes usage take off. For some, like Marshall, the Net will become a transformative tool that will redefine their processes, reinvent their relationships, and build their brand. But many more will just waste their money—and watch, baffled, as customers desert them for more-effectively focused competitors.

They'll all make the same mistakes. They'll ask technology questions, unaware that a successful Web strategy is built around applications: it's the hole you need drilled, not the tool you're going to drill it with that's important. They'll chase on-line sales, not knowing that electronic commerce is just a by-product of the Net's more powerful capability, its ability to break down walls. And they'll think of the Net as somehow separate from their everyday people and processes, ignoring the fact that if it's not integrated into a larger vision of customer connection, they'll never discover its potential.

Five years ago, when we started www.marshall.com, my predictions that the Internet was the path to the future were dismissed as the overheated rantings of a novice CEO still too green to understand how the real world worked. "Too impractical," people said. "Too new. Too out there." Still, we saw early on that if we could wire Marshall to our suppliers and customers directly, we could dramatically improve everyone's performance. We envisioned using the Internet as a tool for both general public access and private, secure transactions. A new business channel was being created, driven by the global forces of change, with new rules and new opportunities: "The electronic marketspace," Kerry Young called it. At Marshall, we were convinced that the only way to discover what we could do with it was to be there.

We didn't set out to design a Web site, though, or even a Web strategy. Instead, we strove to solve people's problems by building on the foundation that our already-developed technology infrastructure could provide and leveraging our way up the learning curve in opportunistic, incremental steps.

Actually, we knew where we wanted to go before there was a way to get there. We'd been working toward customer alignment since undertaking our corporate redesign, dreaming of a seamless and frictionless connection with our business partners. For all of our changes, though, Marshall's work flow was still too inefficient to handle the pressures of shrinking product life cycles, shortened time to market, and build-to-order supply-chain management. There were still too many handoffs involved in moving products from our suppliers to our customers, too much wasted motion and expense. There had to be a way to use bandwidth to connect people through our junction box cheaper, better, and faster, but no one had yet figured out what to put at the end of the wires or how to make it go.

"It's coming," I'd promised Gordon Marshall back in 1992, on the day we abolished sales commissions. "Soon." Then bandwidth tripled, and tripled again, as new satellite, phone, and cable networks were built, spreading the global infrastructure. By 1994, Internet service providers such as The WELL and SeniorNet were being heralded as "virtual" communities, and the largest commercial player, CompuServe, was up to over 2 million subscribers. Then, late that spring, Kerry showed me a copy of Mosaic, the Web browser just introduced by an obscure startup called Netscape. Here, at last, was an easy way for our customers to connect with us. Thirty days later, Marshall debuted on-line, at 7:52 A.M. on July 27, 1994.

Our first homepage looks pretty simple by today's standards. It featured a new Marshall Connection logo, a few boxed links, each with a yellow lightning bolt, and a new motto: "It's about time." Despite the simplicity, there were real things to do there: users could look up data sheets, check prices, or click an order button that pushed a prompt to a Marshall salesman to phone back.

It wasn't perfect, but it was faster and easier than the old, thick paper catalogues that we issued quarterly and were instantly out of date. Of course, we hadn't expected perfect on day one. Getting the homepage up was just the beginning of its development: as with any technology application, the learning came after implementation. Once the page was on-line, we could start to explore other things that we could do with it, like enhancing and adding features and improving the navigation, and look for the next step, trying to leverage what we were learning.

Thirty days later we added PartnerNet, a secure extranet link inside the Marshall firewall that provided customers and suppliers with the same real-time access to QOBRA's transactional data, encrypted and customer tailored, along with all the client-server database applications we were developing: strategic forecasting, order planning, account profiling, and supply-chain management, all accessible at the click of a mouse.

Then, another thirty days after that, working with our European-based alliance partner, we brought a European server on-line. Now customers could connect in Dutch, German, Spanish, French, Italian, Norwegian, Finnish, or Danish, as well as English.

Another thirty days' time had us connecting our Lotus Notes intranet and adding a server and a data warehouse so that different technology platforms could all speak their own languages across the system.

Project cascaded upon project. What was next? How soon could we turn it on? Being early to the marketplace gave us the freedom to experiment, minus the pressure of expectations. Taking small steps allowed us to test new technologies without making big gambles, but still, each new feature was another chance to show our customers our commitment to innovation and mutual satisfaction.

We knew what the customer wanted: 100 percent share of mind, solutions to problems, free, perfect, and now. There was no way to know how the technology would evolve, but we didn't have to know. We were building applications to solve problems. That focus made choosing the tools a business decision, not a technology gamble, and balanced the strategic value of the application against the cost while considering speed, flexibility, and adaptability. Does it work? Is it fast and reliable? Is it intuitive to use? Does it make life easier?

I hadn't thought much at the start about selling through the new wires. Instead, I'd pictured some variant of an electronic data inter-change from computer to computer that would take steps out of our shared processes. But once we were actually connected, it was easy to imagine what would come as bandwidth grew: electronic com-merce and supply-chain management, data and voice, audio and video, cybercafes and on-line bookstores and travel agents. The challenge ahead was to design applications that customers would actually use, which meant first convincing them of the advantages of doing business a new way, selling the evolving power of the Internet itself rather than Marshall alone.

Engineers liked the interface from the start. They were already comfortable with PCs, and it was easier and faster to pull down a data sheet than it was to make a phone call and ask for a fax back. How else could we make their lives better? What would make the Marshall interface more perfect for them? What if we could teach them to use parts better, too, without having to take time to listen to another suit in another stuffy conference room? That would solve a problem for our suppliers, too, who needed a more-efficient way to teach the market about new products.

The answer was our live-broadcast NetSeminars and a spin-off company, ENEN, (Education, News, and Entertainment Network). But what if you don't have the audio or video software to watch or listen? No problem. We'll put it right on the Web site, ready to download, along with a text version for anyone who would rather read the material. Have a question? We'll add an interactive Q&A and global chat. Too busy for the seminar now? We'll keep it archived so that you can watch it from any place and at any time you choose.

What's next? What if we could cut an engineer's product-development time, too? How? The answer was Marshall's elec-tronic-design center, which offers software that simulates chip performance and thus cuts from six days to forty-eight hours the time it takes to get a sample burned in, debugged, and delivered.

Where can customers go today at www.marshall.com? Anywhere they want. Every service we provide in the real world we duplicate in the virtual one, twenty-four hours a day, seven days a week, from twenty-four different linked sites in twenty-four different languages, including Hebrew and Chinese.

Customers can search through 250,000 parts from 150 major suppliers by part number, manufacturer, or product parametrics, then pull up the data sheet or real-time inventory and pricing information. They can order in twenty-four different currencies, pay by cybercash, credit card, or purchase order, then track the order through our warehouse to their loading dock, expediting through a hot button to their freight forwarder. They can watch our robotic warehouse in action on our live-action Web cam; they can go to a product seminar or the design studio, follow the headlines through our daily broadcast of industry news, subscribe to an individually customized briefing service, or create their own digital Web programming for us to broadcast on ENEN. And if they have a problem, they can find a real human being from Marshall on-line in our live help chat room.

Take a look at our homepage and see for yourself. Someone will be there, around the clock.

It's not our homepage that makes Marshall on the Internet succeed, though. Anyone could copy anything we've done on the site, although they might find it difficult to execute. What makes our site so effective—as I tried to explain to my friend, the Silicon Valley CEO—is the structure behind it, the larger system that aligns Marshall's people, methods, material, environment, and technology around the definition of quality that we'd been building since the Deming seminar.

The Internet isn't separate from Marshall; it is part of the daily fabric of our corporate life. Our strategy promises customer service anytime, anyplace, and via any method. The Net is just another method of access, a more-perfect interface. We don't have a separate Internet business unit, a separate Internet sales process, fulfillment system, or warehouse. We don't have a separate Web sales team, either. The key to our success is that every marketing person has responsibility for the site, and hundreds of people contribute to its design and development.

Could we have harnessed that creativity if we hadn't changed

Marshall's pay policies? Probably not. Internet commerce is good for the customer and good for Marshall, but it could take dollars out of a commissioned salesperson's pocket. How enthusiastically would our salespeople have supported the growth of our Net business if it cost them income? That's why the first question you have to ask before you invest a dime is whether your structure and system are aligned with your goals.

We don't try to quantify the success (or failure) of our activity on the Web conventionally, either. Although we spend $2 million annually on research and development, we've never looked at the Internet as a cost center. Like the phone system, it's a strategically critical part of our enterprise infrastructure. We don't try to calculate the Internet return on investment, either, any more than we try to calculate the ROI on a long-distance phone call.

I'm not trying to be flippant. Like every manager, I prefer hard figures when I can get them. But sometimes in business, as Dr. Deming said, "the most important numbers are unknown and unknowable." When you're investing in innovation, it may be impossible at the outset to predict an exact future return. Don't let that be paralyzing. If you're trying to help shape a new marketplace, you can't let finance by itself dictate the initial terms. Let marketing and sales, tied to your mission and strategy, lead the way, and the financial models will follow.

The Internet was Marshall's breakthrough, the unpredictable opportunity we had been preparing for through all the headaches and fear of our enterprise redesign. We weren't just moving boxes anymore; we were moving information, helping our business partners manage increasingly complex supply chains. We had been looking for new ways to add value, and the Net gave us a rapidly expanding range of tools to do that—better, more efficient ways to service the demands of our customers and create demand for our suppliers, all of which won share of mind as well as share of market. We had been looking for differentiation, and the Net gave us ideas. It has become our most powerful marketing voice, a new system for delivering the company's brand message clearly and consistently. We had been looking for visibility, and it provided that, too. Being named the number-one business-to-business Web site in the world for two consecutive years by *Advertising Age's Netmarketing* magazine—followed, in order, by Dell, Cisco, FedEx, and IBM—gave us a turn in the national spotlight unprecedented for a distributor.

Marshall's Internet capabilities today are as close to state of the art as imagination and the limits of our budget can create. But the *Netmarketing* award wasn't a tribute to our technology, or even to our strategy and design. It was a tribute to Marshall's employees. They were the ones who convinced our initially skeptical customers and suppliers to give the new tool a try. Like any new technology, the Internet expands power geometrically for every new user. The more we learn and teach about its potential and test new ways it can serve our business partners day by day, the more real virtual distribution can become.

From "Anyplace" to "Your Place"

You can smell the anxiety in the air when distributors gather to talk about the future of our industry. Even the diehards admit that a change is coming, but no one knows what that change will be or how fast it will come, and few seem eager to embrace it.

I feel that anxiety, too. Remember the "time bomb" at the end of chapter 2, the J curve that climbed slowly at first, then shot up like a rocket? That's what's happening with Internet use today. After five years of gradually increasing interest, America's consumers and businesses seem finally on the verge of accepting the "information superhighway" en masse. That's a seismic shift, but no one can predict what it means—except that it will bring even more change faster.

In 1994, there were only a handful of Web sites and about a million people on-line worldwide. Today, in 1998, there are millions of sites and over 100 million users. Five years ago, Internet sales didn't exist. But last year, they reached $6.1 billion. Next year, they're expected to exceed $11 billion. And that's just on the "surf" side, where access is open to anyone on the World Wide Web. Sales inside the firewall, where access is by password, are already far larger.

On top of that, more than half of the American public has Internet access at work, school, or home, and half of those people are frequent users who log on at least every other day, according to a study by the University of California–Santa Barbara's Bruce Bimber. Those numbers should increase exponentially as faster connections, greater bandwidth, and more intuitive navigation systems come online in response to market growth and user demand. Already traffic is doubling every hundred days. Every killer app has followed the same pattern: more users mean that entrepreneurs and programmers try to design more and easier functions in a chase to capture the growing market, which brings in still more users. This never-ending spiral eventually turns a complex technology into as familiar a tool as the spreadsheet, the fax machine, or the overnight letter.

For today, though, the Net is still a wide-open Wild West. There are new ground rules and protocols being hammered out, new questions about security and privacy, taxes, and regulation. The traditional planning model—picture an endgame, three to five years out, then figure how to get there—doesn't work. No one knows what the Net will look like next year, let alone three to five years from now. Technology development is too unpredictable, and applications don't evolve in a straight line.

The growth of the Net creates new management issues for Marshall, too. In the mid-1990s, it was easy to stand out amid thousands of sites, but how do we differentiate ourselves among millions? How can you build trust and create personality? It was easy to lead when we were the only distributor in the on-line market, but now everyone has at least a homepage. We can do virtually anything we want, within the constraints of time and money, but so can anyone else, anywhere in the world. What can we do to stay ahead?

We don't have all the answers to those questions. No one does, and there are more new questions every day. The best we can do is position ourselves to look for answers. But, just for the moment, let's put aside the issue of how powerful the Net might become and first look at the Web as we would look at any new market. The future may not be clear, but at least we can see what's driving the trends.

Business is still business, even at the speed of light. You still have to serve customers; you still have to deal with suppliers, prices, and margins. You still have to follow the same basic selling process: research, market, prospect, qualify, present, close, and follow up. Technology is just another enabler that makes some processes harder and some easier. The marketing dynamics, however, would look familiar to any storefront retailer: you have to draw people in, you have to have stuff they are looking for once they get there, and you have to keep them coming back. The Internet may let you move faster than you could in any conventional market, but that just means you can crash and burn faster, too. It's not necessary to have goods in hand or bricks and mortar, but in their absence, focus and execution become more important than ever.

With bricks and mortar no longer necessary, small upstarts can leapfrog established market leaders. Barnes and Noble, for example, would never have had to worry about Amazon.com, had the on-line bookseller needed to build warehouses to store its inventory. But that very flexibility, coupled with the speed of technology innovation, makes every market advantage gained through the Web temporary. Today, Amazon.com has to worry about Acses.com, an on-line bookseller with a new feature for customers: a smart agent that scours all of the other Web booksellers and reports back on who has the best price for the title you want.

In electronic commerce, the conventional barriers to market entry and growth don't apply. Anyone with a phone and a better idea for how to broker airline space could compete with FedEx tomorrow. You could open anywhere in the world for pennies, without having to worry about local laws, taxes, or employees (although you'd still have to understand the local market to succeed there). And if all competitive advantage is temporary, the rules of success are different, too. Rather than trying to maximize the long-term return of any innovation, you have to try to hasten its obsolescence, by looking for the next step forward.

The Internet ideal states that information should flow freely and instantly to anyone, anywhere, anytime. Value is added by serving that standard, not by slowing it down. That certainly is new, and it presents problems for most conventionally structured organizations. How freely can you move information if you still have hierarchy, bureaucracy, and command and control? How can you embrace an open-architecture model if there are parts of your operation that you can't let people see?

The Internet hasn't changed what customers want; it's just given them more freedom to find it. They'll buy Volvo brake pads from Norway, software code from India, and shipbuilding equipment from Poland, because they can, and because it's cheaper or faster or closer to exactly what they're looking for. They want control of the process, instant service and total accessibility, individual solutions to individual problems, 100 percent share of mind. They want it now, not seven clicks away, and if they can't find what they need, they'll go elsewhere, instantly. Price isn't the main leverage point anymore; speed is almost invariably more important than cost. To a customer competing in a global build-to-order, rush-to-market, supply-chain world, taking steps out of the processes translates into competitive advantage and financial result. It's all about doing more work in less time.

As the Internet has changed customer relations, so has it altered the nature of what and who customers are.

Marshall's definition of a customer changed as soon as we went on-line. We weren't doing business with this division of IBM or that department at Hewlett-Packard anymore. Instead, we were dealing with individuals, often engineers, sitting before a screen, exploring for ideas. Decisions weren't being made for them by corporate governance any longer, either, and access to information wasn't limited by the chain of command. Now, Jack in purchasing needed inventory details, Sonya at the plant needed order status, and David, a hobbyist from Nevada, was looking for tips on sale parts. Our homepage had to make them all feel welcome, and give them what they came for.

Although we wanted to know who came and why, we never made anyone register in order to visit the site—the Internet ideal said that people should be free to come and go as they pleased. We never tried to retrieve data about them surreptitiously, either. That's invasion of privacy, if not theft. So we try to get them to volunteer information for our database, encouraging them to sign up for a free seminar, for example, or to subscribe to the electronics-industry headline-news service. But if none of this appeals, they can push their shopping cart through our virtual warehouse and pick parts without anyone's asking their names until they're ready to check out.

Just like in the real world, no one ever asks for a salesperson. They come for information. They may not want to buy anything, and they certainly don't want to be pressured by a manipulative sales pitch. For most transactions, in fact, they prefer to serve themselves, as long as they can find what they need easily. And this is not unique to Marshall's customers: in 1998, according to Carter Lusher, vice president and information-technology research director of the Gartner Group, 30 percent of all customer transactions will be electronic and self-served. Like the ATM, which customers grew to prefer over walk-up tellers because of its twenty-four-hour convenience, people like the Web because it lets them keep control.

Customers have always wanted individual attention. Net technology enables you to deliver that and serve a demographic of one, no matter how large your market. With dynamic Web-page loading and similar preference software, you can start to anticipate tastes and wants, much as Amazon.com can show each shopper titles related to the books he or she picks. Because you can capture in database-management libraries every click of every transaction, your ability to read the market is robust and immediate: you know when people come, where they go, how long they stay, and what they look at. More important, if a customer says he or she wants a different experience, you can change their experience of your site in an instant by individualizing the connection.

That capability drove the first of two Internet-driven shifts in Marshall's focus. Our strategy had said that we would serve you anyplace and anytime. Internet technology enabled us to move closer to perfect: with it, we could serve you at your place and on your time.

A customized interface brought us new sales and new customers, but that was a happy offshoot, not the foundation of what we were trying to design. We had been looking for a way to work more closely with our business partners by marrying people and technology in a system aligned with customer needs. Using the Web as a common networking standard let us turn Marshall into a virtual collaborator, because it took down the walls between our organization and theirs by providing faster order processing, improved inventory tracking and management, more-accurate order fulfillment, and support for just-in-time manufacturing, all of which helps them manage their competitive battles better—just as our mission and strategy mandated.

The Internet ideal has never been focused primarily on selling. It's more about connections, the free flow of information, and bringing people together. Look at the early Web successes, from The WELL, the discussion group that flourished in the early 1990s, to The Motley Fool, the financial-advice site that was the first big hit on AOL. Each succeeded because it created a place in cyberspace where people could connect with others like themselves, creating a virtual community of shared interest. That's why chat groups were instantly popular, too: they used an electronic medium to make human contact.

Our sites serve those same ends, through access to the database systems, Net seminars, and broadcast services, or connection to the chat groups that gather spontaneously on our always-open live help line. It's less like an electronic mall than a town-hall meeting center for our customers and suppliers. The shared interest is their business, and the community is a supply-chain community, gathered to look for solutions to problems. Connectivity has to come before commerce.

Thanks to extranet technology, we can even customize that community for you by connecting whomever you choose to Marshall through a system that reflects how you decide your business needs to work. Secure behind the Marshall firewall, your Boston office can talk with your Boulder office about a contract in Beijing, each of you tapped into the same real-time transactional data from QOBRA as if it were part of your own plumbing. So, technology let Marshall build private communities within the public one, a new capability that we would leverage into the second shift of Marshall's strategic focus.

From "Your Place" to "Our Place"

Like all of Marshall's evolving technologies, our Internet applications had their roots in the Pearl Harbor Day redesign of our old mainframe operating system. By the end of 1993, a year after QOBRA came on-line, the expected productivity bonus was kicking in. Sales were up, as were profits, and Wall Street anaylsts were starting to notice the payoff from our computer prowess.

After so many hard knocks, the compliments were nice, but, more important, our success made us realize that even a fifty-plus-year-old distributor could turn technology into a strategic weapon. QOBRA hadn't just improved our data processing; it had given us a steadily expanding knowledge base. Was there some way, then, that we could leverage what we were learning?

QOBRA had been focused on eliminating inefficiencies inside Marshall. What if now we looked outward and focused on the processes that we shared with our customers and suppliers? Could we use our technology to make our partners more competitive, too?

These weren't idle questions. Reengineering was newly in vogue, and consultants were preaching "disintermediation": take out wasted middle steps and tighten up the system. That was a scary thought to a middleman like Marshall, unless, somehow, we could find a way to take out the steps ourselves first—and prove our worth while doing so. To pursue this, I held a series of meetings with Kerry and his team through that winter and into the spring of 1994, looking at distribution from a macro perspective, then breaking it down process by process, searching for transactions we could reduce or eliminate.

I started by drawing pictures on the whiteboard, each a different snapshot of the electronics business: suppliers on one side, customers on the other, with all the relationships and dependencies in between. In the first, of the old Marshall, we were a tiny dot on the periphery, one more undifferentiated franchisee/vendor. In the second, depicting Marshall after QOBRA, we were still small, but we were at the center: we functioned as the junction box between the two sides, thanks to new capabilities such as our relational database-management systems. Now we had to create a third picture, with Marshall still at the center, but bigger, with skills and expertise that would bring us closer to the heart of our partners' businesses.

When we analyzed the system, it was easy to see wasted motion. Most of electronics distribution hadn't changed since Gordon Marshall sold his first potentiometer after World War II. Still, even though we saw the inefficiencies, we didn't know how to get our technology solutions into someone else's infrastructure. A software package on floppies? Some variant of a local-area network?

I was staggered when Kerry showed me the Mosaic browser in the spring of 1994. There wasn't much to see, really; a list of upcoming concerts by the Rolling Stones, a primitive version of the search engine Lycos, and a handful of other sites, but I couldn't stop pacing back and forth, staring at the screen. The fact that you could connect one computer to another was unbelievable to me, and the potential was instantly apparent. For the next month, until we actually got Marshall on-line, I was a crazy man. I was sure that every distributor everywhere would see what I'd seen, if they hadn't already seen it. "It's a race," I told Kerry. "We can't come in second."

I was wrong about Marshall's competitors, it turned out. It was a full year before any of them launched even a bare-bones homepage, giving us a head start no one has been able to overcome so far.

I was wrong also about how fast our customers and suppliers would adopt the new tools. From the start, we thought that the Net presented unprecedented opportunities, but it still would take us years to convince them that it was more than a high-tech gimmick, a waste of time and money that Marshall could ill afford. There are skeptics even today.

Our first problem was finding a name for what we envisioned, something that said "new" without being too threatening. We chose "e-trade" initially, "e" for "electronics," but after we'd registered the domain and created a marketing package, our lawyer found a tiny Palo Alto securities company called "E*trade." So, rather than get into a court fight—our domain name versus their corporate name—we switched to "v-trade," the "v" for "virtual."

That, however, didn't last long either. Too esoteric, we decided. Not many people in 1994 knew what "virtual" meant. So we settled on "Marshall on the Internet," although we kept the "v-trade" domain, along with scores of others we registered to use when the time seemed right, such as "@ONCE" and "spot market." And "E*trade," meanwhile, went on to become an electronic stock-trading company powerhouse handling 325,000 accounts.

Getting on-line was easy. Getting people to notice was hard. I thought that "MARSHALL FIRST ON THE INTERNET!" would be headline news, at least in the industry trade paper, but the story was buried in the back pages. We did some advertising, but the Net was too new for conventional marketing, and anything we could have said would sound self-serving. So we tried to build word of mouth, talking up the Internet every chance we got.

The Net was a non-event at that fall's Comdex, our industry's biannual exhibition of what's new and what's hot. Row after row of booths filled the cavernous Las Vegas convention center, but we didn't see a single Internet display or product among them. There were acres of terminals, though, many with Web access, so the Marshall contingent prowled through the aisles and called up our homepage on as many screens as we could, until you couldn't miss Marshall no matter where you turned.

The show's high point for us came on the last day. Walking by the Digital Equipment booth, we saw a small sign inviting people to "MEET NETSCAPE'S MARC ANDREESSEN, 2:00 P.M." There he sat, five feet away, in sneakers and jeans, eating a sandwich, totally unnoticed.

I introduced myself and told him how staggered I'd been the first time I'd seen Mosaic. Would he be willing to take a look at our site?

"Hey," he said, clicking on. "Cool."

Cool. But back in the real world of warehouses and parts, people's eyes were starting to glaze over. Caught up in the enthusiasm occasioned by our cascade of new applications, we kept trying to explain the benefits of the new ways to work in every conversation and on every sales call. Anytime a customer asked what made Marshall different, our answer was always "the Internet."

Our competitors had a field day. Marshall, they said, had gone over the edge, banking everything on another half-baked idea.

To our suppliers, who depend on Marshall to get them to market, it seemed as if we were squandering resources. We work in a tight-money world and critical calls came in almost every day. "Internet, Internet, Internet," one supplier groused. "Is that the only strategy you've got?"

Even the most skeptical was willing to let Marshall put its product on our Web site, though. Why not? It didn't cost them anything. For many suppliers, we would provide their only presence on the Net for years, a relationship that turned to our competitive advantage once they saw Net usage begin to climb and wanted sites of their own. We got to help them set up their sites and set their standards, directing them to Adobe Acrobat for data sheets, for example, or Oracle for the database. Through this involvement, we were automatically integrated into their Web pages, which meant an easier flow of information and easier access to our site and theirs for our customers.

Today, virtually all of our suppliers swear by the Net. Texas Instruments, in fact, told *Fast Company* magazine that Marshall was the inspiration for its entire Web strategy. There are still people who don't get it, though. They think the Net is whiz-bang technology or marketing and public relations, not a new way to connect to a new market. "Hey, Captain Internet," one supplier laughed when I came to his office last winter. "What new toy do you have to show me today?"

That really frosted me, I'll admit. We wouldn't invest nearly $1 million a year in hardware, software, and personnel for a toy. Besides, I did have something new to show him. We'd taken another step up the learning curve by leveraging three different technologies to create a whole new capability for our business partners and a new role for Marshall.

For this, too, we had started with a problem to solve. This time, however, the problem lay at the heart of our customers' most critical issue: how to compete in a world of constantly accelerating global time-to-market pressure.

Years ago, it was easy for an electronics manufacturer to get a product built. Concept, engineering, marketing, forecasting, and production were all in the same building. Today, they aren't necessarily in the same company, or, often, even in the same country; they're outsourced around the world.

Outsourcing is a competitive necessity, the only way manufacturers can improve their capabilities overnight. But it's a mixed blessing. Relinquishing control of any part of the process increases unpredictability and dependency.

Think of your own supply chain. How long is the list of people you depend on to get to market? How much wasted motion is there, how many "should haves," "could haves," and "sorrys" are there?

It's even worse for our customers, who may outsource everything but their initial concepts. Remember the children's game of telephone? Electronics manufacturers play that game all the time, but they play it over three times zones and in four languages, with fifty or sixty people. An engineer's finished prototype may include a hundred different pieces from fifty different suppliers, each of whom is constantly upgrading and enhancing his or her own products, and all of whom have to be coordinated.

No one competes company versus company anymore. Companies today compete supply chain versus supply chain. Speed matters most, for product life cycles keep shrinking. The first to market establishes the standard and earns a bottom-line premium. However, with so many different supply-chain partners, it's often the Tower of Babel all over again. How can anyone build anything? Each different supplier has a different computer system and a different orientation to true north. Every transaction, handoff, and data conversion slows them down.

Marshall's answer was the virtual integration of our customers' supply chain via the Internet, using three different tools, a series of intranets, our data warehouse, and an "inference engine," a piece of software called "middleware" that tells other software how to perform. With an intranet, we can connect anyone a customer chooses to a private supply-chain community, and with our data warehouse, we enable all of the different systems and platforms to talk to one another. And with an inference engine we can create "rules of engagement," a set of instructions that can be coded to make things happen automatically.

It's all about time and work. Time, as we've seen, is today's currency, unrenewable and irreplaceable, the critical component in a supply-chain-versus-supply-chain world. And work takes time. Whether you use activity-based costing or economic value-added analysis to measure productivity, the faster the work is done the faster the supply chain can compete.

Manufacturing efficiencies in the electronics industry, as in many other industries, have improved throughout the last decade, achieving very high quality standards. Progress will continue, but is unlikely to yield further dramatic reductions in the supply chain's time to market. But what about work in progress (WIP)? Not just factory work, but all work—phone calls, faxes, voice mails, travel, meetings, and so forth? The less work, the shorter the necessary lead time.

Work makes work. Communication, coordination, and measurement all take time. But if you can create a common understanding of processes and procedures, and provide valid and reliable measuring systems, people and technology working together can root out the inefficiencies, moving, reducing, and eliminating the unnecessary work while improving quality and productivity and thereby maximize each tick of the clock.

The more we automate non-value-added tasks, the faster our supply chain moves. A company's focus, therefore, has to be on speed, transactional efficiency, communication, and connectivity. The objective should not be just to move expenses, but to reduce and eliminate expenses and transactions while increasing the efficacy of every channel partner's processes.

This starts at the design stage, with a system view of the supply chain, a platform from which to analyze the processes and identify the inefficiencies in the work flow. By creating a three-step process—identification and planning, technology introduction, and assessment—systems can be designed to codify the rules of engagement in automatic process instructions for each participant. Supply-chain managers, working as a steering committee, can decide what those rules should be. Once the rules are set, intranets, extranets, and a data warehouse can provide seamless information transfers in and out of each supply-chain member's database engine. Simple intranets can use work-flow processes themselves to enable transactions and to make sure the management rules are followed. "Expert" middleware can manage and monitor exceptions and improvements.

We call our system MACRO.link. ("MACRO" is an acronym for "Marshall's agreement to coordinate resources and organizations.") A macro view looks at the big picture, like the system perspective we first learned from Dr. Deming. And a macro in computerspeak is an algorithm, a formula that when initiated tells a software program how to perform.

Let me give you a simplified example of how it works. A rule might say that for any part under one dollar, if supplier A, B, or C comes up with an improved version with the same fit, form, and function, manufacturing specs should be confirmed to the improved version automatically, without requiring anyone to sign off on the change; and news of the change be sent instantly to the suppliers responsible for forecasting, purchasing, manufacturing, and finance, without any other steps in between. The design mandate behind such a macro is to take out the inefficiencies, remove the barriers between everyone in the chain in the same way that Marshall had taken down the walls with our own suppliers. The more partners and the more macro rules of engagement you add, the faster the system becomes.

Conventional wisdom holds that the only way to control suppliers completely would be to buy them and stamp on your logo, principles, and systems. But that can't work, even if you could afford it— you would stamp out the very entrepreneurial spirit that made the supplier valuable in the first place. A system like MACRO, though, frees you to collaborate by combining an off-the-balance-sheet asset with control of the system, all of it accessible through a simple point-and-click screen, secure and customized. It doesn't limit the value of anyone's skill and creativity; rather, it frees everyone from the asses-and-elbows mechanical work. You can't build a supply chain by throwing vendors a dinner and giving out trophies, or even by inviting your alliance partners into your strategic-planning meetings. Long-term competitiveness is created by design, by developing a system that takes down the walls between your place and my place, to create an "our place" that is virtually integrated to compete in a supply-chain-versus-supply-chain world.

"Why should I bother to worry about someone else's inefficiencies?" skeptics ask. "By outsourcing, I've already moved those costs off my balance sheet."

"That's fine," I'll agree. "But if your competitor not only moves those costs but reduces—or even eliminates—them, no matter where they occur in the system, who will win the supply-chain battle?"

"How much is this going to cost me?"

"All you need is a PC and twenty dollars a month for Internet access. The question you should ask is how much money it could save you."

MACRO is one path to Marshall's future, and like the others, it's rooted in all we've learned from five years of pushing the frontier of electronic commerce. There is no way to predict how it will evolve; every day, we're working to enhance it and find the new breakthroughs it might enable. But it's already fundamentally changed Marshall's role in the marketplace. The old middleman is dead, just as we had hoped. We've disintermediated ourselves and become an invisible but integral part of our customers' and suppliers' plumbing. But we've also "reintermediated" ourselves with a new value proposition: we don't just move boxes and deliver parts; we manage supply chains through the power of connectivity and our expertise in virtual collaboration.

That's the Marshall of the future that I sketched on the whiteboard five years ago, when we first started exploring what the Internet would enable us to do. I didn't know how to describe it then, and we didn't have the tools or knowledge to build it, but I saw the potential from the start, much as a sculptor can imagine the finished work in an untouched piece of marble.

The hard part, then as now, has been getting other people to see it too.

What's Next? How Soon?

People say that I'm enamored with the Internet, but that's not true. I'm awed by what the technology makes possible. I feel the same way when I watch a 400-ton Boeing 747 lift from the runway. People can explain to me how and why it flies, but the power is in what it changes as it leaves conventional time and space behind.

I'll admit that I'm threatened by the Net, too. We've got forty-five years of blood equity in the bricks and mortar of Marshall, but that doesn't protect us from on-line competitors established yesterday. It may even slow us down. Anyone who comes up with a better way to move a box or a byte could be our rival tomorrow. We've got five years of experience on the Internet. So what? I'm sure that I'm not the only one who's drawing circles on the board, trying to imagine how to reintermediate in a world of disintermediation. The Internet may give us an infinite number of opportunities, but it also means that there are an infinite number of people who could come along and eat my lunch.

People ask me all the time, but I don't know what the Net will look like in three to five years. I do know that a voice-based interface is coming, finally, after years of development missteps: ease of use makes it inevitable. I also see push technology continuing to surge: it's a more-effective use of the network because it maximizes the potential of bandwidth, and it's better for customers, as it gives them information automatically tailored to their preferences. Smart agents, software that can search the Net automatically, will make competing on price alone an even riskier proposition.

Beyond that, though, I can't predict. The Internet has never developed in a straight line. Will we be wearing our computers, like John Sculley predicted fifteen years ago? Will there be software that performs surgery, artificial intelligence that plots strategy, smart houses, or smarter cars? That kind of blue-skying makes people roll their eyes, but its building blocks are here already, in research labs and startups. All around the world, people are pushing the limits of bandwidth and chip technology, wrestling with programming, memory, storage, security, and privacy. The ones who can figure out how to solve the problems will change the way we live and work. The only thing that I can say with certainty is that the next generation will be able to navigate effortlessly through a totally wired world. Telecomunications, computers, and the Internet will converge, and new chip designs and software applications will make our old store-and-download model seem as quaint as a rotary phone. The Internet will be virtually free and virtually now and literally everywhere. Only the competitive battle will stay the same as it is today: find new ways to get closer to perfect.

I know—you've heard all this before. But don't take my word for it. Look at what eleven- and twelve-year-old kids are doing on the Internet every day. When they become our employees, colleagues, bosses, and customers, will they be willing to do things our old way? Will they stand for manually typing, copying, and filing hard documents, working the phones, sitting in progress meetings, and sending salespeople on the road? Or will they expect to just point and click?

The Internet forces all of us to ask the same question, no matter what our level or organization: What will my strategic value be in the future? If bandwidth is expanding exponentially and my job today is to take a piece of paper and read it, sign it, or hand it off, will I have a role tomorrow? If I'm in sales, my customers are just a point and click away from price, delivery, and solution. How can I add value to the process? If I'm in leadership and the old management models and metrics don't work anymore, how can I fulfill my responsibility? Should I be learning something new or trying something different?

You don't have to be a dinosaur. If you can see the world changing, you can try to change with it.

You don't need executive approval to invite innovation into your life. Even if you work in the most neolithic bureaucracy, you can still try to discover how bandwidth can help you do your job cheaper, faster, or better. The power of the Net is that it slices through barriers, giving all of us equal access to a world of opportunities, solutions, and learning. But the only way to find out what you can do there is to go.

Manager's Workbook

Planet implodes! Everything is changed! Few notice!

— STEWARD BRAND

What Measurements Matter?

Hits count. But they don't count for much. They tell you the volume of requests your server has to handle, which is useful from a technology-capacity standpoint. Yet when a user clicks on a page, each individual element there—the text, the photo, the fancy logo—registers as a hit. So hits don't give you an accurate measure of the number of people coming to your site. For that, you need a count of unique visitors. Still, though, unique-visitors statistics only tell you how many people are looking, not what they are looking for.

Technology gives you the power to monitor everything everyone does from the moment they come to your site to the moment they exit. You can track daily visit trends, the number of requests per visit, or who's using what browser. So what? No one needs more data in their life. What you want is news you can use.

The Net can be a powerful interactive tool that enables you to respond to the voice of the customer and redesign your site to fit his or her needs in an instant. Your measuring system should be a way to listen to that voice. There are four key areas to monitor:

- *Transactions*. What are people actually *doing* on your site? Buying? Checking your inventory or price? Checking order status? How often? What are they requesting most? If they aren't doing what you thought they'd be doing, you may have a design flaw—or you may have a new opportunity to consider.

• *Behavior.* Do users click through the site the way you set it up for them, or do they bail after three clicks? Tracking the paths users trace through your site can help you figure out how effective your design is. If you're running a special product-marketing campaign, for example, testing multiple versions in the early stages lets you see which one best connects with the customer so that you can make the necessary course corrections before full rollout.

• *Identity.* Who are your users? Even if customers don't fill out a form or register on your site, you can often see what companies they work for. You can always see what site they came from, which might tell you if they have common interests that you should note. If a lot of your users click to your page from, for example, an on-line computer magazine, that might suggest a different way to spend your advertising dollars.

• *Opinion.* The softest information may also be the most telling. What do people think of your site? Is it easy to use? Could they find what they wanted? A general feedback button will let you gather soft data on opinions, and give you a way to react to problems and complaints immediately.

The key word with each metric is the same: *React.* Your customers will tell you what they want from your site, if you'll learn to listen. But if you don't respond to what you hear, you might as well be throwing points on a chart.

The Global Connection

You can see tomorrow's global economy being created today. People and technologies are connecting and communicating across borders and time zones in a seamless and frictionless collaboration, moving information, services, and products digitally.

These new virtual partnerships work anytime, because the world is awake twenty-four hours a day. They reach anyplace, because the

People and Technology.
Connecting across borders and time zones.

Global Connection

entire world is competing. And they happen by any method, because Internet connections can be infinitely customized.

How to Get to How-to

How-to should be the last question you ask when you're building an Internet presence. You can't choose the right technology for the job until you know what that job will be. You have to first look at your site as part of your enterprise design and make sure that it can be integrated into your larger strategic purpose.

Start with these four basic questions:

Who is your audience? Do your customers use the Web today? If they aren't part of the demographic on-line, and you don't think they will be, don't bother going on-line either.

What will you do with the site that will *complement* your business, not just reproduce it, on-line? Is it faster than doing business traditionally? Is it better? Is it more convenient? What are you trying to accomplish? Saving money? Gaining customer base?

Why will customers use your site? Calling an 800 number to order a product is incredibly easy. You have to give customers a compelling reason to change to what may be an initially intimidating interface.

Where does it make sense for your company to be in the technology-adoption cycle? Is there real value in being the first with the most bells and whistles? Or can you afford to wait until a technology is tested and refined? Some companies have to be out on the bleeding edge to beat the competition. Others can wait without losing much, and end up spending less.

TrendWatch

It's not enough anymore just to have something to sell on-line. There are thousands of Web sites competing today, selling everything from grocery delivery and swimsuits to construction equipment and financial services. Purchasers are getting more sophisticated and demanding more services, more features, and more convenience when they shop the Net.

Your customers will tell you exactly what they want—eventually. By then, though, they may well have found it somewhere else. Therefore, it's not enough to monitor your own site's performance, or to keep an eye on what your competitors are doing on-line: you need to watch the trends in the larger electronic marketplace, looking at the innovators in other industries who are exploring new capabilities. What are they doing for their customers that you could adapt?

Four key areas of development have moved into the mainstream over the last year:

Help yourself: Customer self-service
Think about the automated teller machine. It took off because people preferred twenty-four-hour convenience and control over personal attention from a teller.

The same goes for Web sites. If you can give your customers the means to find technical support, get product information, or place and track orders on-line, they'll flock to your site. It saves them time while it saves you money.

Cisco Systems (www.cisco.com), celebrated for its networking hardware and software, is one of the undisputed kings of customer self-service. Their site has more than 80,000 registered users and accounts for 40 percent of the company's sales—about $3 billion worth of orders in 1998.

Cisco customers can help themselves to real-time information on price, availability, configuration requirements, ordering, invoice status, and validation as well as shipping. They can forward procurement information to their own employees for modification and approval, download software patches and tools, and register to receive bug alerts, too.

It takes as little as fifteen minutes, and never more than an hour, for an order to come from a customer, get processed, and then be forwarded to Cisco's back-end systems for production. Before the Web site was launched, the process often took weeks and involved several sales- and support-staff people. The system saves Cisco money, too, for it takes some $270 million per year in support and service costs out of the expense column.

Rolling out the red carpet: Building relationships

The most successful Web sites build relationships. Some track preference information that can be of value to customers, the digital equivalent of the sales clerk who remembers what size blazer you wear. Others create a sense of community, like the diner you frequent because you know all the regulars.

Amazon.com (www.amazon.com), arguably America's best-known on-line merchant, has built their book business by tracking customers' purchase information. The site, which has more than 2.5 million titles available, makes recommendations based on your buying history. If you've purchased three hardback thrillers off the bestseller list, for example, the site will alert you next time you log on that the new Stephen King book is out. The site also tracks buyer patterns in aggregate, so when you purchase, it shows you what other books were selected by the people who bought your same selection.

The market is impressed. As of the summer of 1998, Barnes and Noble, a physical bookstore that came late to the virtual game, owned 11 million square feet of retail space and had a market cap of $2.4 billion. Amazon.com owned *zero* square feet of retail space and had a market cap of $4 billion.

Tripod (www.tripod.com) is an on-line community for twenty-somethings. Often called "training wheels for life," it caters to college students or recent grads, offering advice, products, and community connection. Users can set up their own homepages, chat with other members, or get help with a résumé. The key to the site's success is that it creates an environment where its audience of 300,000 users feels a sense of belonging.

Stocking up: Linking the supply chain
One of the most-powerful trends in e-commerce is one that customers can't see when visiting a Web site, though they'll feel its effects. Internet technology allows companies to link the sales process to suppliers through an extranet (a secure extension of an intranet that only authorized companies or people can visit). Extranets create faster order processing, improved inventory tracking and management, more-accurate order fulfillment, support for just-in-time manufacturing, and improved customer service.

Herman Miller SQA, a division of the office-furniture company of the same name based in Holland, Michigan, sends customer orders through an extranet directly to its suppliers, who then determine how to batch orders most efficiently. As a result, SQA needs to keep just two hours' worth of parts on hand for assembly, and turns its inventory about two hundred times per year. For customers, that means all orders are filled within ten days, 75 percent faster than the industry standard.

Get smart! Using intelligent agents
A year or two ago, people fantasized about being able to send a digital Rover into the Net to retrieve the information they wanted—

just like a live Rover might fetch your newspaper. Today, it is commonplace. Intelligent agents (also called "robots," "bots," or "spiders") are sophisticated search programs that sort information or perform specified functions on groups of data.

Several of the more popular search engines on the Web (such as Digital's AltaVista) use smart agents to index and sort Web content for users. A spider, for example, might be sent to collect all the Web pages—out of the millions out there—that use the word "Shakespeare." So when you come to the search site and look for the Bard, you search a database that the spider has built of all the appropriate pages.

One of the most successful applications of this technology is Deja News, a site that archives Internet discussion groups for its users. The site is constantly adding to its store of information, which includes on-line discussions dating back to 1979. Three times a day, an intelligent agent is sent out with instructions to gather all the newest conversations and add them to the site's database. The result is an incredibly rich (and large—more than 180 gigabytes) resource for almost any topic. The site is one of the most active in the world, drawing more than 3.5 million unique users per month.

What do smart agents mean for you? Most obviously, they mean that if you sell on price, your competitive challenge has increased exponentially. Look at Amazon's upstart competitor, Acses.com, for example: using smart agents, they can scour the entire on-line book market, then report back to customers with who has the best price on any given title.

Smart agents create an opportunity, too, though, no matter what you sell. What would your customer like to be able to find on the Web? Could you add new value if you gave them a way to find it from your site?

10
The Upside
of Perfect:
Creating an Innovative Culture

Whose Name on the Door?

Ask novices to name the most important piece on the chess board, and most will say the queen, for she is the most mobile and potentially the most powerful. A few might choose the king, because losing him means losing the game. But the correct answer, a grand master will tell you, is more subtle: Any piece can be critical—it depends on where you are in the game.

That's equally true in business, most managers agree, although it is usually honored more in word than in deed. Every morning in meetings across America, would-be leaders stand up and announce that "People are this company's most important asset," then retreat behind closed doors, sending out decisions by decree. They talk about "teamwork," "empowerment," and "innovation," then walk away without giving those words a way to come to life.

It's no wonder that many old-line managers dismiss corporate culture as unimportant, easily dismissed "soft stuff." They think it's just pumping up the volume with a pep rally or saying thank you by sponsoring a company picnic. They'll send out a steady stream of photocopied magazine articles with the latest buzzword marked in yellow highlighter, and talk up every flavor of the month—then leave human relations to the human-resources department, signing off on this proposal or that initiative without considering how, or even whether, it advances their larger strategic purpose.

Creating a more-competitive workplace is the critical responsibility of leadership from the CEO on down to a newly promoted team captain. But no one can do it alone. Everyone has to play a role—if anyone's job isn't important enough to, why is that person there? The more people understand and buy in to your objectives, the more they'll be able to contribute, whether you're trying to lead eight people or 80,000. You can't teach that by sitting in your office. You have to get out and show it, and the more that people believe you understand the problems of the front line, the closer they'll listen to what you say.

You can never know everything you'd like to know as you face the future. The world is too complex for that. Your job is to keep learning and to engage all the people around you in helping you learn. If they feel like pawns to your king, you'll lose all your leverage. If you don't respect their role in the game, why should they?

You can't create a competitive corporate culture with a halftime pitch. Passion and celebration have their place, of course, but they don't build lasting performance unless they are directed toward a larger ambition than generating enthusiasm. A culture has to be designed like any other strategic weapon, with a clearly defined target, a method by which to reach that target, and a way to measure your result. It has to be developed in context, responsive to people and trends, and grounded in cost, content, coverage, capability, connectivity, and commitment, the competitive universe we sketched out in the Manager's Workbook in chapter 6. Everything has to be aligned: departments, teams, and individuals; mission, strategy, and management style; metrics, compensation, promotion, and training. All must be focused on the same purpose: agile response to change.

Virtual distribution, as I've described, wasn't my creation. I supplied the initial system perspective and the vision of a seamless and frictionless customer connection, but the reality was invented over five years by all of Marshall's employees working together, taking the mission statement off the wall every day and putting it into practice. Everyone asked the same question—"How can I serve the customer better?"—then we built our company around the answers we heard.

A culture that can ask that question, one on one, customer after customer, and colleague after colleague, then act on what it learns, doesn't just happen. It requires a common understanding of the why of change, a collective sense of urgency and purpose, and processes and leadership to promote individual responsibility. It depends on shared values, too: integrity, the humility to admit all that we don't know, and the courage to face our fears about the future.

In our situation, we needed everyone to act as if it were his or her name, not Gordon Marshall's, on our company door. So, we designed our systems to treat them as if that were the case. We broke down the barriers between them and their customers, dismantled the bureaucracy and jettisoned the old, narrow performance targets. Our new system was designed to connect people to their customers' needs more directly, to promote learning and teaching, and to build awareness of our internal mutual interdependence. The employee performance-evaluation system that we developed when we abolished management by objectives, as well as the Marshall Process we developed when we dropped commissions, gave people the hands-on tools that they needed to achieve those goals.

The process we used to design our new system was just as important as any of the processes that came out of it. Remember the problem Dick and I faced when we came back from the Deming seminar? We knew that Marshall had to change, but we didn't know what it had to change into. All we had were questions: What is the voice of the customer saying? How can we differentiate ourselves? Where can we add value?

We found the answers by helping our employees learn to ask those questions for themselves. Starting with the why of change, we invented the how-to as an organization, leveraging our human capital up the learning curve in incremental steps.

That's how we want our culture to work today, too: as a joint learning experiment, driven by questions.

For all our changes, the issues we face have stayed the same. Surmounting the challenges of disintermediation, supply-chain inefficiencies, time to market, mass customization, and globalization has become even more critical. The pace of marketplace change constantly accelerates, so we will have to learn to change faster, too, or risk losing everything we've built. Survival is not mandated for any of us, individually or collectively: we have to earn it. Where can we connect with our future? What are the barriers to free, perfect, and now? How can we get past them?

What has changed is the way in which we help people ask those questions as our expanding information-technology infrastructure continues to enhance our system-design capabilities. Internet and intranet technologies enable us to deliver our message more clearly and directly than ever. In combination with our database-management systems, they have turned employee performance reviews into Marshall's foremost teaching process, thanks to two new tools: the performance matrix and the company dictionary that lies behind it. In tandem, these two tools focus us on the development of a complex mix of skills rather than on the performance in a few simple activities, and create a curriculum for dynamic career-long learning custom-designed for each employee. And employees who are always learning give us a better way to chase the "continuous improvement, innovation, and mutual satisfaction" our mission prescribes.

Dr. Deming used to say that business performance depends 94 percent on the system and just 6 percent on people. That may be, but it is the final 6 percent that makes everything else possible. People have to want to be part of the organization, as Rita Megling, Marshall's vice president of global marketing communications, keeps reminding us. They have to support the vision and programs. Key to that is understanding—the better everyone understands what we're up against, the better we can decide what to do next.

You can't change an organizational environment overnight. Culture is based in processes described by a series of *"-ing"* words: learn*ing,* teach*ing,* grow*ing,* invent*ing,* refin*ing,* enhanc*ing.* Trying to shortcut past necessary steps is like trying to lose ten pounds in ten days with a fad diet: you may lose the weight, but your body always pays a price and the pounds never stay off long.

It takes time for people to trust you, to know you mean what you say about wanting to hear what they think. Your actions have to be consistent, and consistently explained, as you embrace the constancy of customer-driven change as a value as critical as trust, respect, or integrity. You have to teach the same simple themes consistently, day in and day out, until people can internalize them, rearticulate them, and act upon them for themselves. I, for example, still tell the familiar stories about hamburger restaurants, marathon runners, and the statistical lessons of the daily commute that I told when we launched Marshall's initial system redesign. But I have some new themes, too, including the name on the door, what makes a professional, and could you sell a rock?

Soft stuff? In part, perhaps. But that soft stuff pushed people to cut thousands of small costs and inefficencies out of our work flow, develop our 24/7 service, become Internet pioneers, and build a network of global alliances. Creating a culture isn't about building a kinder, gentler workplace: it's about building a more competitive team. The more curiosity we bring to the world and the better we learn to listen to problems, the more innovative solutions we can develop—and innovation, we had agreed, represents our only hope for a future.

Every conversation I have about work begins the same way, with our need to respond to the accelerating demands of the marketplace. Every conversation ends the same way, too, with some variant of the same critical questions: Are you in or out? Can you commit to helping us move this company into the future? What could we do better? What's in the way of doing it?

"How would you feel about work if it were your name on the company door?" I'll ask. "If your name were on the door, you'd want to know as much as you could about your customers' competitive issues and the emerging market trends. You'd worry about paper clips and travel expenses and new technology and whether the company was treating people right. You'd be pushing, pulling, sweating, worrying, walking on water, if that's what it took.

"You'd connect with customers and suppliers differently, too. You'd be confident that you had the full muscle of the organization behind you. You'd know that if you saw a problem, you'd have the authority to make sure that it got fixed.

"That's how you should feel. Work is where you spend your days and build your career, and where the marketplace assesses your value.

"There is no 'they' at Marshall. No memo has ever gone out signed the Management. There are the three of us—Dick and Henry and me. You can call any of us anytime.

"If you see something that doesn't work, you don't have to be a victim. Either you can talk about it in the hallways and the cafeteria, or you can help us try to fix it.

"It's not enough just to be a manager, salesperson, or technology expert anymore. You have to be a professional, a businessperson with a speciality, practicing your skills as a doctor practices medicine or a lawyer practices law.

"Practice means accepting that you don't have all of the answers, and that no single answer applies to all situations. Professionals look at each problem individually, up close. To them every new customer, like every new patient, presents a whole new series of challenges to be solved.

"Think of Marshall's mission as your own version of the Hippocratic oath. It doesn't tell you what to do every day or how to do it—it tells you who you are and what you're committing to. Think of the Marshall Process as a diagnostic tool. It helps you ask the right questions to work out individually customized solutions.

"Professionals don't stop with their initial prescription, though. Maintenance implies action and continual effort. Professionals monitor the patient's response continuously, focusing on long-term health, and search the journals for new treatments. That's how we have to connect with our customers as well, questioning, probing, learning, looking for the breakthrough solutions that create new marketplace value."

Nobody Likes Eddie Haskell

There is no place to hide at Marshall. Everyone answers his or her own phone; our office walls are glass. All our doors are open, by policy, all the time. There are no barriers between departments or divisions, no bureaucracy to obstruct anyone's good idea, no secret policies or hidden management agendas.

The role of leadership at every level is to serve, to give those on the front line the coaching, resources, and support that they need to add more value for their customers. Leadership cannot nag, nitpick, or second-guess; it takes the same concern for health and long-range growth as parenting, the same discipline and consistency. A leader must balance patience and urgency, humility and strength, and know which one will work best in any given situation.

A decade or two ago, it was good enough to bark out orders: take the hill, hit the number, do or die, or else. But that old command model is obsolete, killed by, among other things, the connectivity of the Internet, the speed of the chip, and the need for flexibility, adaptability, and the urgency they create. Leadership's responsibility today is to articulate and monitor the organization's critical values, to choose what's right over what's popular or easy. The need to change in response to marketplace change is today's one great constant, but the only thing you can change by decree is your own behavior. If you want people to act as if their names were on the door, you have to demonstrate why and how to act that way, and hope that your example inspires others to emulate you.

That was Harry Truman's strength. In tears at Franklin Roosevelt's death, he went on national radio to ask for everyone's help and prayers. Then he put the famous sign on his desk—"THE BUCK STOPS HERE"—and went to work. He admitted that he couldn't do it alone, asked for assistance, and then took ultimate responsibility for whatever happened.

It can be humbling to admit that you don't have all the answers.

But if you think that your job is to know everything, you're defeated before you start. You can't learn about the front line's obstacles without listening to the front line. You don't have to agree with their perspective, or act on it, but you have to seek it out if you want to hear the truth. I guarantee you that every person who reports to you has gone home at least once muttering something to the effect of, "If management only knew what we know, they'd do things differently."

They may be right. You'll never know if you don't ask.

You can't fool people. They watch you in action and will quickly see if you are serious about what you say or promise. But trust is built with little things, too, like a public thank-you note for a job well done, or a handwritten private note. Answering my own phone and giving my home number to employees feels like a little thing, but most of my fellow CEOs think it is nuts. Nuts or not, though, it sends a message. The fact is, most people will never call my home number. Making the option available, however, tells everyone that I think they're important: "Call anytime, direct. I want to hear what you have to say."

"The truth shall make you free," the Bible says, but truth can be hard to find in a business setting, especially for people in authority. Nothing is more critical than an accurate read of how the marketplace is responding to your strategies, systems, and tactics, particularly if they're flawed. But how often do people ask you, "Can I tell you the truth?" (What do they expect you to reply—"No, thank you"?) How often do people volunteer it, even if invited to?

I often wonder how a company as brilliant as Coca-Cola, the best-known brand in the world, goofed so badly with New Coke. After all the research was done, did someone in authority just say, "Hey, let's do it," and everyone agreed? Did no one see the risk, or were they just afraid to speak out?

Nobody likes Eddie Haskell. "What a good idea, Mrs. Cleaver," he'd say, then when her back was turned snicker and go back to tormenting the Beaver. But do you ever walk away from a meeting and wonder just how sincere the support you heard really was? Have *you* ever Eddie Haskelled your boss?

The truth is that the truth often hurts. Think about how often the messenger gets shot for delivering bad news or the critic gets lambasted for pointing out flaws in the book, the play, the movie. Think about how often people sandbag their projections or manipulate procedures so that they'll hit a required number. According to a survey of 40,000 Americans reported by *Fast Company* in 1997, 93 percent admitted to lying on the job. Who can blame them? Fear, and the self-protective mechanism it triggers, may be the most rational way to respond to an irrational system.

Nothing will poison trust faster than fear of speaking the truth. The leader's job is to help people confront and overcome that fear.

Don't misunderstand me. I can see the wisdom in Andy Grove's *Only the Paranoid Survive.* Rational anxieties form the basis of Marshall's strategy and mission; they're what make people pick up the phone at the end of a twelve-hour day for one more customer call, or keep them up at night, worrying about the consequences of changing technology. What I want to eliminate are the irrational fears that make people feel like victims of the organization, powerless to change their situations, take risks, speak their minds, or challenge leaders' decisions.

I can't remove anxiety about change from people's lives. But I can try to take some of the anxiety out of their workplace, if my design is consistent with my goals. Everything has to align: little policies, such as answering my own phone and keeping my door open, larger structures like our compensation system and performance evaluations, and my own personal commitment to remember that I still put my pants on one leg at a time.

It's not enough to be open to criticism, for the higher you rise in leadership, the harder it is for people to challenge your point of view. So you have to actively invite challenge. Imagine me being so color-blind that I couldn't pick a tie to match my suit. Who, except my wife, would tell me whether today's choices clashed? I'm the CEO. Who would want to risk bruising my ego? If I actually asked my colleagues, "Is this tie OK?," a few might say, "Not great." But if I asked everyone, all the time, people would start to believe that I really wanted their input.

I'm not color-blind, fortunately enough. But I may be blind to a slippage in a process or ignorant of a change in what the market wants. I don't know what I don't know. Only someone outside a system can see its deepest flaws, Dr. Deming said. I heard much the same thing from my parents growing up. "Oh, what a godly gift," they'd say, "to see ourselves as others see us." That's what practicing business like a professional means, too—having the courage to ask hard questions, relentlessly, of yourself and others, then finding better solutions with what you learn.

"Look," I'll reassure people, "I suspect that my list of things that are wrong with our company is longer than your list. I may be the harshest critic here. But I really need to know what you see going on, what you think and want."

People respond tentatively at first, of course. Building trust is a process, taught and learned together over time. But if you invite it, there will always be criticism—no one can design a perfect system. Access to leadership gives Marshall's people a channel for complaint, if they choose to take it, and the responsibility to speak out if they see some barrier to our mission. It helps keep other managers consistent with Marshall's values, too: if someone comes to them with a problem, they're more likely to try to fix it because they know that everyone has access to executive leadership as a final recourse.

It was easier for me to talk to people one on one when Marshall was smaller. Today, for all my best efforts to manage by walking around, I'm still just a figure behind a podium or a voice on a conference call to some people. To address this, once every two or three weeks I schedule a "Marshall Live" lunch, a chance to talk over pizza and salad with a group of twenty-five or so—the headquarters' credit department, for example, or the Silicon Valley warehouse team—about what we could do better.

Marshall Live is for the front line. Their managers aren't invited. I want to hear the criticisms unvarnished. My commitment, in return, is to take some kind of action—even if it's just a short verbal response—within two weeks on anything anyone brings up. I may say, "We'll tackle that next year," or "No, we can't do that, and here's why," or "Why don't you help me put together a team to work on it?" But they'll get a response, and if there's a performance barrier, we'll remove it.

I'm not naive enough to think that because I joke about my tie and put myself on the hot seat, I can make everyone instantly candid. But if I listen and follow up, and hold another lunch, and another, over the years, people will start to recognize that I'm serious about wanting their help. In any group, there's always at least one outspoken person who's fearless enough to come right at me; that draws other people in. By the end of two hours, we'll always have a dozen or more projects to think about.

It can get uncomfortable hearing all of the things that people think our company should do better, from earthquake drills and parking policy to credit, staffing, and sales procedures. Employees find problems faster than leaders can solve them. But that discomfort is where learning begins, with a chance to ask questions together. What's the real problem here? What result are we trying to achieve? What's in the way? How could we fix it?

Hundreds of new ideas, large and small, have come out of Marshall Live lunches, including "Food for Thought," the informal education program discussed in this chapter's Manager's Workbook. But the process is as important as any result, because asking the same apparently open-ended questions has always driven Marshall's redesign. Sometimes the suggestions are legally or economically impossible, or just plain wrongheaded, but good idea or bad, each is another chance to draw people in to management by method, to teach them a hands-on lesson in putting their names on the door.

It's important for employees to understand that there are a zillion problems facing us, and that they can't all be solved at once. Our approach has been to take on the big ones first, just as we did when we first began Marshall's redesign. My job in the process is to help people see their individual problems in the context of our larger competitive needs—the why of change that comes before the how-to—then give them the support, authority, and resources to solve them.

How do you create teamwork? Give the team work. How do you empower people? Teach them the perspective, humility, and courage that transforms power into leadership—then provide them with a method to turn those lessons into action, and get out of their way.

Participatory problem solving, over time, creates its own legacy. When people on the front line talk to one another later about how they changed this invoicing policy or that security system, they send a message about Marshall's values to the rest of the organization that is far more powerful than anything I could say. They become the champions of change, allies in our ongoing attempt to pull the organization into the future.

Soft stuff? I'm sure I have employees who'll read all this and think that it's just hot air. "Big deal—lunch. I went to one and it didn't solve my problems."

"It's not just one lunch," I'd respond. "Don't look at the snapshot; watch the movie. The lunch is part of a larger system designed with just one purpose, to make our company more competitive by getting everyone involved.

"If I fell short in my execution, I apologize; I'll try to do better. But you've got to take your responsibility, too. If the system isn't working, your job is to keep asking why not, and push us to fix it. Are you in or are you out?"

From Acceptable to Desirable

With all due respect to celebrity coaches such as Pat Riley and Bill Parcells, I've always thought it risky to compare business to sports. There is no beginning or end to the business contest, no schedule of opponents, no final score, no off-season, and no referees. But there is one lesson that managers could learn from sports teams, and that is how to evaluate and develop talent.

Great coaches know that they can't win with just great runners. A football team, for instance, needs great blockers, punt-return specialists, and middle linebackers, along with great trainers and locker-room personnel. Talented athletes aren't enough. Intangibles, such as knowledge of the sport, attitude in the locker room, and competitive zeal, count as well. Players are tracked against a complex set of performance measures and trained to reach their maximum potentials. Individual stats, by themselves, aren't important: what matters most is each player's ability to perform inside the team's system against the next competitor. That's what wins games.

Although most businesses need a far broader range of skills and behaviors to succeed than does a sports team, businesses' performance-evaluation systems are usually much simpler, focusing primarily on individual numbers, not on contribution to team success. Everyone is judged against the same narrow range of criteria, given an acceptable minimum target such as a sales quota or a profit-and-loss (P&L) forecast to hit, then ranked and advanced accordingly. Such practices nurture the Peter Principle.

That's not how organizational competitiveness is created, however. No two or three skills suffice to lead an organization forward. What's acceptable and what's desirable are not the same, and "good enough" isn't. Acceptable is static, but customers today are moving targets. An effective performance-review system helps people see those targets better and improves their aim.

We had seen firsthand at the old Marshall the folly of trying to manage by numerical objectives. It focused people on personal performance and thus pitted branch against branch and division against division. People almost always hit their projections, even if they had to hide inventory and bury costs to make it happen, but the result was frustration all around, and lagging corporate quality and service.

Under such a system, planning was impossible. Every day, the tech staff would wheel a three-foot stack of data into our offices, but there was no way to know what the numbers meant or which ones to react to. Which were "real" results? Which came from someone manipulating the system?

Management by method was an attempt to solve those problems, a corporate initiative to design from the why of change to the how-to, from goals to strategy to operational definitions. Once we agreed on the results we wanted, we could try to create a method to achieve them.

We created our employee performance-management matrix the same way.

It's the system, we agreed, that most defines what an organization can accomplish. No matter their abilities, no one can be better than the tools and resources they're given. So we wanted our review process to provide a way to manage and improve system effectiveness first. Then we could address the individual's growth in the system, using the review process as another way to spread our values and principles, and build perspective, trust, and buy-in through participatory problem solving.

Once again, we started with a question: What makes people succeed in our culture? Our answer was accountability and responsibility. If it were their names on the door, they'd have to understand our services, technologies, methods, and mission. They'd need communication skills to explain those aspects of the business and the leadership skills to ensure that they were acted upon. Accordingly, those professional requirements became the six categories down the side of our matrix: business skills, customer knowledge, supplier and product knowledge, system knowledge, personal development, and leadership skills.

Across the top we put the Marshall Process (see chapter 7), the necessary steps to serving the marketplace, from market research and marketing to prospecting, qualifying, presenting, commitment, and follow-up. Working together, the two axes define Marshall's competitive playing field and offer a guide to the complex blend of skills and qualities professionals need to excel at every stage of the customer relationship, whether they are professional warehouse personnel, professional salespeople, or professional managers. An example of it appears in the Manager's Workbook at the end of this chapter.

Merely instructing people to "practice like a professional" serves no purpose by itself, however; it has to be tied to a common understanding of how the best professionals actually practice their arts. That's where the Marshall dictionary comes in.

Our dictionary is a database built around Marshall's years of activity and a means to grant all of our people access to corporate knowledge and capability to leverage the organization's accumulated learning. It starts with basics—what does "follow-up" mean at

Marshall? "Market research"?—then moves down through multiple levels of increasing detail and complexity, providing the operational definitions behind the strategy for every point in the matrix. It tells you the four business skills needed for prospecting, for example, and the two elements of supplier knowledge that you need at follow-up.

Have to know more? The dictionary contains details on each point, step by step. The second part of supplier knowledge at follow-up, for instance, is collecting data, it tells you. Then it shows how to use sales reports to analyze sales to budget, gross profit trends, customer base and market share, product mix, ranking in customers, year-to-year comparison, and design registrations.

Written in-house, championed by Les Jones, Rega Plaster, Rob Watson, and Nida, the definitions represent the best thinking of our top performers on how to execute our strategy. Yet although everyone works from the same matrix, no two people have the exact same dictionary. We identified thirty-six different job categories at Marshall, including six in sales alone, and wrote customized definitions for all of them. Those definitions, in turn, are individually customized to reflect each individual's customers and supplier lines. So, when an employee sits down with a manager to talk about performance, the two have a complex range of issues they can discuss, all tailored to a demographic of one.

Enhanced by technology, and the database that supports the dictionary, the matrix is a powerful tool for guided learning. Need to understand your customer's chip market better? Click on that box in the grid for a market profile for a detailed analysis of suppliers, customers, and competitors, as well as opportunities, trends, and projections, tailored specifically for your current project. Need more? Delve into each competitor's market strategy and customer base, competitive weaknesses and strengths, and Marshall's plan to address them. Still want more? Click further to see each supplier's products, technologies, current numbers, and demand projections, all updated in real time. Drill even deeper to expose the details of each suppliers' daily activity, customer by customer, down to the last phone call made or fax sent.

Working together, uniting people and technology, the matrix and dictionary become a curriculum for the future and one more way to leverage our human capital and create a shared understanding of the challenges we face. Disciplined by process, they change as the world changes, mandating constant learning. Careers develop as individuals learn, and contribute to, the knowledge we share. And Marshall grows as a result.

Sound complicated? The execution, in fact, is easy.

Imagine that you're an account manager and I'm your sales manager. Presumably, we talk often about your specific customer and performance issues, and work together on project strategy and tactics. The review is a more structured meeting than these day-to-days.

A week or so before we're scheduled to sit down together, I'll ask you to make up two short lists. On the first, jot down three areas in the company as a whole that you think could be improved. Don't think only about your individual area—look at the whole company, as if your name were on the door. What could work better, large or small? With the second list, indicate three categories from the matrix that you'd like to address for your own growth: what would help you practice business more like a professional?

As the manager, I'd choose three items from the matrix, too, areas to focus on that I think would help you improve on the job. Those nine points will constitute the agenda of our meeting.

Given human nature, there's no way to take all the anxiety out of a performance review. But our process has been designed to start us out on an equal footing, concentrating together on whether the system works for us and how we can improve it. Our conversation is driven by familiar questions: What are we trying to accomplish here? What's in the way? We're not looking back in a rearview mirror, rehashing the last six months; we're looking forward. And we're not talking money, either—that's a negotiation about market value, for another time. We're talking about improving personal and organizational competitiveness.

At the end of our meeting, our nine points become an agenda for the future. Whose responsibility is it to follow it? Should I arrange for you to take some classes in our Marshall Business Academy

(MBA) program? Should you spend more time studying industry trends? What's the time frame?

Repeated every six months, the review is an effective way to make sure that managers and the front line share a common understanding of each other's needs. It teaches them to work as partners, committed to continuous improvement and mutual satisfaction, as our mission dictates.

The matrix, too, may well be the culmination of the process that we started when we flipped over the old conventional chart. Our intention was to break down the obsolete command-and-control structures, to redesign the manner in which we related to one another and our customers so as to better align our company with the real-world imperatives for collaborative partnership, flexibility, and speed. The matrix is one more tool to advance that ideal, because rather than ranking people on acceptable performance of a few basic activities, it helps us recognize and promote a wide range of necessary skills and through that build fluid project teams based on each individual's abilities and ambitions. It abolished the Peter Principle by replacing the single ladder up the organization with a number of routes to advancement.

No one has a "job" anymore at Marshall, at least in any conventional sense. Assembling the matrix showed us how unrealistic it is to put anyone into so static a slot. Instead, we give people assignments, shorter-term projects matching their talents to our changing marketplace needs. "I'd like you to help us develop a training program for six months," I might say, or "I want you to run this branch for the next two years." People are more likely to buy in when you can show them how their abilities match the company's needs, and, as our needs change, knowing employees' skills enables us to create new assignments and projects without having to reorganize our internal structure every six months.

We know what has to be done for the company to be competitive today, or at least we think we do, but we don't know what may be important tomorrow. An assignment-based organizational structure that harnesses employee capabilities—no matter what the employee's position is in the hierarchy—reflects that truth.

From Shoelaces to Velcro

How do you nurture innovation? It's easy to say "Go hire a bunch of Ph.D.s and you can get some bang for your buck." However, the future isn't invented with a single lightning bolt: it depends on a sustained flow of new ideas, large and small, with everyone in the organization looking for better ways to add value, searching for what we call "the upside of perfect."

Most managers define "perfect" in the negative: no mistakes. To achieve that goal, they focus their energy on continual improvement of the processes they have, developing ever more sophisticated quality-control campaigns in a quest for statistically error-free work. But that's not a route to innovation. Incremental improvement, as necessary as it is, eventually becomes a dead end. The real opportunities lie on perfect's upside, with the creation of better solutions to your customers' problems, new features and benefits that enhance their experience of your partnership.

A perfect meal isn't a meal without a fly in the soup, after all. No flies is merely a zero-defect meal. The perfect meal, on the other hand, encompasses an evening's total experience: food, company, music, atmosphere, wine, conversation. The more it exceeds expectations—what Tom Peters calls "the WOW! Factor"—the closer to perfect it gets.

Innovation comes from asking the right questions and focusing on the benefit you can deliver to your customers, not the process you perform to deliver it. If we could do anything we wanted, what would we do? What would this look like if we were inventing it from scratch? You can't get from shoelaces to Velcro on sneakers by looking for better ways to make a shoelace. You get there by looking for better ways to help people keep their shoes on.

Consider, for example, our decision to run the company twenty-four hours a day. The catalyst was a customer-service problem: How can we make sure that phone calls coming in overnight are answered in the morning? Technology would have been the conventional solution—add more voice-mail boxes and better answering machines, or aiming for service that is defect-free. But we found a better opportunity by looking for the upside of perfect and asking what customers wanted when they called. They didn't care how good the voice-mail system was. Most people hate voice mail. They wanted somebody to talk to.

There is no software program that can identify those nonlinear opportunities. It takes an educated eye to see the connections to innovation and build on trained customer understanding, marketplace experience, and perspective on change. We can't make the lightbulb come on in anyone's head. But we *can* give everyone a system that develops the necessary talent, knowledge, and raw materials in his or her daily activities; that drives out the fear of trying new ideas; and that mandates continuous focused customer qualification through all our methods, processes, and organizational culture. The better everything works together to teach people to explore their customer's point of view as they envision, feel, and ponder each new problem, the more likely people are to come up with innovative solutions. That's "management by method."

Technology, through our dictionary, enhances that capability by making the collective experience and wisdom of the whole company available to anyone, in accessible, digestible form. It's a way to keep track of what we're learning and leverage off of it, like the maps the Portuguese explorers made as they pushed their way around the coast of Africa, each one going a few hundred miles further into the unknown. But you can't have leverage without first designing an aligned system. There's just too much friction when any two parts of the organization operate at cross-purposes, too many opportunities for missed handoffs and misdirected communication.

Our dictionary is an early-warning system, too. It instantly highlights little things like a competitor in New York's Hudson Valley changing pricing structure or a customer in Park City, Utah, wanting different specs on a specific part. Such little things often signal the birth of market-shifting trends. As you recognize them, and the problems that drive them, you can mass-customize your solutions, thereby spreading the reach of anyone's better idea.

Management by method has one other benefit as well: It improves the quality of our strategic intelligence at the same time that it improves our performance. Because everyone practices the same processes and measures the same things the same way, we gain richer and more reliable data.

The only way to predict tomorrow's performance is to study today's results, as inexact a science as that may be. It usually means pulling up the latest summary P&L reports, then trying to deconstruct them into their thousands of different components. But none of those necessarily tell you anything about how the world in which you operate is changing.

At Marshall, technology gives us the ability to hook sensors into all our databases to create a virtual dashboard displaying the real-time results of all of the focused questions that our people and processes ask customers every day. No one can monitor everything—you'd drown in data—but thanks to management by method, we don't have to. We know our numbers derive from a consistent companywide system, not someone's manipulation of a flawed system. So we have to watch only the data that deviates from the norm, "special-cause variations," in statistical terms. That lets us filter out the noise and recognize the important signals. That, in turn, adds management by exception to our toolbox.

Built into the organizational telemetry, management by exception can be a powerful route to innovation. In such a scenario, I might, for example, say to the system, "Let me know if you see a plus or minus 10 percent change in the booking level at these five customers in the Bay area, if you see any lead time stretching out by more than 5 percent on these five major commodity drivers, or if you see a 5 percent rise in productivity of our top fifteen customers with their top five lines anywhere nationwide." Those are all exceptions, and, if alerted to them, I can react.

Technology can't tell me what those exceptions mean, of course, or how their effect might reverberate through sales, inventory, or margins. That takes wisdom. But technology does tell me what I should pay attention to, and gives me a better way to train an educated eye on the changing marketplace.

Once again, it's all about work and time, one more step in the evolution from management by doing to management by directing, management by objective, management by method, and, now, management by exception. The right technology equips you to enhance and monitor your processes simultaneously, so, rather than trying to corral the collective knowledge of the organization by sifting through infinite amounts of data, you can design a system that will report on itself, with rules to trigger an automatic response like pushing an e-mail message or action item to anyone who needs to know or respond to a special-cause variation. Rules can monitor the system for exceptions, with metarules—rules about rules—to "watch" the "work."

Once again, too, success depends on alignment. Implementing poor rules to watch poor processes on top of a poor system gives you poor data and disastrous results. But if the organization is consistent by design, with people and technology working together to ride, not fight, the trends of change, work can be streamlined to maximize each tick of the clock.

Could You Sell a Rock?

Want a simple test of your own competitiveness? Take out one of your business cards and tear off the corner with the logo. Then take a pen and cross out your title.

Now, take a look at what's left.

If you walked into a customer's office without the power, assets, and infrastructure of your organization behind you, what would you have to sell? How well do you know your marketplace? How developed are your professional skills? How educated is your eye? Could you sell a rock?

It's easy to get comfortable, to confuse your title with your competitive value. Survival, though, isn't a given for any of us: it has to be earned. If you were applying for your job, would you get it? If you had to bill for your hours, would anybody pay you? If your job were outsourced, would you get the work? How much could you charge?

When the answer to these questions is no, it's easy to blame things you can't control: your boss or your board, "management's" policy, or your colleagues. Yet whoever "they" are, they aren't ultimately responsible for your competitiveness. You are. You have to open your eyes to everything and everyone, acknowledge the forces of change, admit all you don't know, and start to invite in learning.

Too often, people sit in their offices writing memos and taking conference calls and confuse that with management. Management's job, however, is to manage, out in front of its multiple constituencies, one on one. That's the only way to know if you're trying to sell a square peg for a round hole. You have to lead the charge and set the example by listening to customers and suppliers in the marketplace as well as to employees at all levels in the organization. How else can you learn what you need to know?

Don't talk. Listen. Don't fall in love with your own story—fall in love with the other person's story. It breaks down expectations and leads to better solutions. It's hard, I know, to find the time. But if you believe that customers' definitions of value keep changing, that organizational structures are crumbling, and that the future belongs to a demographic of one, what choice do you have?

The truth is out there, but you have to seek it actively every day. You may have grown up in the organization, as I did at Marshall, but if you haven't done a job in the last two years, you don't know what it takes anymore. If you haven't talked to a frustrated employee without someone from human resources at your side in the last two months or taken an angry customer complaint that wasn't screened and soothed by your secretary in the last two weeks, you can't know what's happening on the front line now.

If you don't know what it's like, why should anyone buy what you say?

Creating a more-competitive organization is the critical responsibility of leadership. But the way there and the values that guide you have to be demonstrated, not delegated. You can't just tell people that you think it's important to listen and learn: they'll only believe that you mean it when they see you do it—for about a week. Then they forget, and they've got to see it again.

Manager's Workbook

What I hear I forget. What I see I remember. What I do I understand.
— CHINESE PROVERB

Marshall's employees are evaluated and developed using our performance matrix, a grid that incorporates the seven steps necessary to get to market with the six key skills integral to performing professionally. On-line, behind each box lies a definition of excellence drawn from our corporate dictionary, customized for each user.

The truth is that no manager sits on top of an organization responding to a well-ordered world. Instead, our days are a series of disjointed yet interconnected moments and events, phone calls and meetings, customer problems and employee issues, tax laws, financial standards, human resources, sales, marketing, and operations. The Marshall matrix is an attempt to create a system that acknowledges that complexity.

Managing people by objectives pretends that the world is black and white. Managing people with a matrix, in contrast, encourages

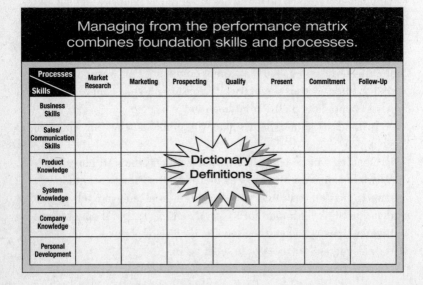

Managing from the performance matrix combines foundation skills and processes.

Processes / Skills	Market Research	Marketing	Prospecting	Qualify	Present	Commitment	Follow-Up
Business Skills							
Sales/ Communication Skills							
Product Knowledge			Dictionary Definitions				
System Knowledge							
Company Knowledge							
Personal Development							

you to look at all of reality's changing shades of grey. Management-by-objective systems give you just one measure, good or bad, and just one performance knob, volume. The matrix, however, recognizes that that's not good enough anymore, and provides a means with which to align the organization with the fluid challenges of competitive differentiation, giving everyone a common understanding of management's expectations and the marketplace performance imperatives. It's a learning tool, constantly adapting to the changing environmental context.

Nerf Balls, Dollar Bills, and the Free Lunch

Communication is the key to instituting change. But you've got to wake people up before they can grasp anything.

Flipping a series of black-and-white charts onto an overhead projector in front of a thousand people in a dark room may not be the best way to get their attention. Who would sit through that kind of meeting by choice? They're too long, too boring, and the chairs get too hard.

A new idea should be exciting, and its introduction visual, accessible, and memorable. You need a delivery system that accentuates your message.

Toss them the ball

Want to show your people what wasted motion looks like? Let them experience your service from the customer's perspective.

Put all of your top decision makers in a room and give each of them a table tent with a "job" written on it: salesperson, chief financial officer, inside sales, CEO, and so forth, on through every function in the company. Then, take a Nerf ball and toss it to the salesperson. "This is a question about price and delivery. Show me what you do with it." He or she will toss the ball to someone else—say the inside-sales person—who will toss it to the product manager, who will toss it to the credit manager, and so on.

After the first ball is tossed a few times, toss in another, with a different question. "This is a request to expedite." Then another. "This is a service complaint." And another. By the time you have seven or eight Nerf balls whizzing through the air, the room will be in an uproar. People will be laughing, teasing bad catches or sloppy throws, arguing "I get the ball next!"

Then the lightbulbs will start to go on: those aren't Nerf balls bouncing off the walls. They're customers with a problem, and we aren't exactly giving them free, perfect, and now.

Try it yourself. The Nerf-ball game shows you your system inefficiencies, it pinpoints command-and-control bottlenecks, and it's more fun than another consultant's interactivity flowchart.

Show them the money

How often have you stood in front of your people and exhorted them to watch the little things, the unnecessary photocopying and the personal long-distance calls, and gotten nothing but blank stares?

I know how that feels. Marshall grosses over $120 million a month. That's an inconceivable sum to many people, and hence they can't imagine what we do with it all. Terms like "cost of sales," "SG&A," and "operating expenses" are meaningless words. What difference do a couple of long-distance calls make?

Marshall's dictionary defines all those terms, and puts them in perspective. We don't just say what the words mean; we illustrate it with a dollar's worth of change.

"Our cost for the products we sell is eighty-five cents," I'll say, putting down three quarters and a dime. "Our salaries are our next biggest thing, about eight cents." And I'll put down a nickel and three pennies. "Our computer and phones and Xerox machines are two cents. Then we pay taxes. And at the end of all that, for every dollar we started with, here's what's left." Then I'll hold up my four remaining pennies.

It's a lesson we repeat quarterly with profit sharing. We pass out a copy of a dollar bill with a pie chart showing where all one hundred pennies go. Afterward, I'll hear about it for weeks. "How come we leave the lights on in the conference room all day?" someone will ask, or "Could we save money if we brought our own coffee cups instead of using paper?"

Buy lunch

Structured education programs like our MBA (Marshall Business Academy) aren't the only way for our people to learn. We sponsor a less-structured program, too, which was initially created out of a complaint voiced at one of my Marshall Live lunches.

"You say we have to prepare for the information age," someone challenged me. "So why don't you give us training on the company's PCs?"

I thought it was a great idea, and offered to sponsor employee-led classes with a free lunch for anyone who wanted to attend. "Food for Thought," we called the program. Today, three years later, there are not only classes for PC users, but also regular classes in health and nutrition, public speaking, and foreign languages. (Technology classes remain the most popular.) It opens Marshall to learning beyond our narrow specialties or disciplines, and we feel that any kind of learning is a net gain for the organization. Also, anyone with expertise can teach, and learn something about teaching in the process.

Teacher's Notes

The measure of a great teacher is his or her ability to create new perspectives, to ask the questions that help open people's eyes. I've had several during my career. But the most important one throughout Marshall's ongoing experiment has been Nida Backaitis.

Nida is a scholar, grounded in theories of systems, learning, psychology, and statistics, but she also has an extraordinary ability to see inside an organization in the real world at the same time, a radar system for disconnects. While consistently empathetic, she can simultaneously be as confrontational as a prosecuting attorney, probing everything you say, pushing you to consider all the unforseen ripples of what you're thinking about doing.

Nida has shown me many things, but two lessons particularly reverberate through my day-to-day at Marshall.

"You teach what you need to learn," she says. That's a reminder that the teacher's job is to look for better answers—to be a student as well as a teacher, to invite in knowledge and criticism.

"The teacher arrives when the student is ready," she says: When you admit how much you need to learn, you can start to see all the teachers around you, and then learn and teach one another.

11
Millennium
Rules:

What's Next?

My Year of Living Dangerously

There is nothing magical about Marshall. We're all-too-fallible flesh-and-blood men and women prone to the missteps and uncertainty of any ambitious enterprise. For the last six years, we've been trying to design a system that would align us with the forces of change in our marketplace and the needs of our customers, trying to utilize people and technology to find new ways to work together internally as well as with our suppliers and customers. Nevertheless, the fact is that for all the work we've done, we have yet to find the answers that guarantee survival in the value-added future.

I never thought that I'd write a book. I'm not Andy Grove or Bill Gates, moving markets and technologies with my decisions. Like most American managers, I just try as best I can to find my way through a world of dizzying uncertainties—and that's precisely why I wanted to tell Marshall's story. Most of us will never testify before Congress or be named *Time*'s Man of the Year; most of us are most of us. But, as Marshall's story shows, any of us can change.

Back in 1992, Marshall felt stuck in place. We didn't have deep pockets or unique resources; we didn't sell anything that customers couldn't buy from two hundred other sources. And we didn't have any way to slow the competitive day-to-day operation while we figured out a plan to get us unstuck. All we had was a shared understanding of the market peril and a willingness to ask hard questions, then act on what we learned.

For all our new technology and organizational change, that willingness remains our greatest asset today. The questions we have been wrestling with for the last six years—design and differentiation, interface and attention, disintermediation and supply-chain efficiency—have only become more critical. What do we need to create today in order to survive tomorrow? How can we increase customer satisfaction and loyalty? Where are the new competitors, new technologies, and new models of organization and design that could take our market away?

These are dangerous times for electronics distributors. Margins have been going down for the last decade, but the decrease keeps accelerating: ten percentage points over the last ten years, five points over the last three years, and two points in 1997. In 1998, Intel's volume has started to slow, and that trickles down through everyone's performance, while the financial crisis in Asia has depressed sales globally. There's less business for more people to compete for, and earnings have dropped throughout the industry.

"It's just a cycle," one of my competitors told me optimistically last summer. "We've seen them before and we'll see them again."

That may be—but I don't want to stake my future on it. In fact, I believe that we're going through an unprecedented shift in how customers—driven by the pressures of bandwidth, globalization, and demographic change, shrinking time to market, mass customization, and supply-chain-versus-supply-chain competition—define marketplace value.

Such pressures are not unique to the electronics industry; the same seismic forces confront booksellers and furniture makers, consultants, car dealers, and stockbrokers. You may be selling the same things you've always sold, but the context, customers, and competitors are new—and change faster. Technology is altering how content can be created and delivered, and changing what customers will pay for. Our organizations have to be redesigned to adapt to and enhance those changes; we must create new ways to leverage our human and financial capital.

The world has gotten riskier. Like American foreign-policy makers after the fall of the Soviet Union, we can no longer predict where the threats will come from, or even whether they will show up on our radar screen before it is too late.

The forty-hour week and fifty-week year is obsolete. The world competes twenty-four hours a day, every day. Thus, we have to find new ways to maximize every tick of the clock.

Business is no longer conducted company to company, two organizations meeting as buyer and seller. Bandwidth lets us connect and communicate individual to individual, and so we need new ways to get attention and new interfaces to keep it. To find them, we borrow the ideas and techniques of consumer-product and media companies.

Customer and supplier partnerships are no longer just two hands shaking. Today, they depend on the many hands that turn a network of complex processes, technologies, and people that have to be designed and wired to work as one. You can't coordinate those multiple collaborative relationships by focusing on the results of each one. That's why so many business plans fail. We need new ways to focus everyone and everything in the system on the unchanging center of the universe, the customer who pays the bills.

As a young man, I studied karate for several years, and one lesson stays with me: You can't fight force with force. Likewise, in business, no one, even a giant, is immune from marketplace change. Look back at the great brand-name successes of five years ago: Greyhound, Nike, McDonald's, Polaroid, GTE, AT&T. Great companies with great talent and well-developed infrastructures, all of them. But if they can get hit—and they have been—anyone can. But look, too, at companies like IBM, Continental Airlines, and Sears—resurrected because courageous leadership opened their eyes to the marketplace and invited in change.

I don't know what Marshall's numbers will be by the time this book appears on the shelves. While they're critical to us, a year's results don't measure how far we've traveled, because the real bottom line is more stark. If we hadn't changed our company, drastically and totally, we might not exist at all today. Six years ago, our story was simple and undifferentiated: we sell stuff, and we care. Today, we're redefining the role of the middleman, adding new capabilities that enable us to create new solutions, working to earn the right to serve tomorrow's marketplace.

As it drives for free, perfect, and now, the market keeps pushing for consolidation. So, in 1998, Marshall made its first acquisition since 1982: Sterling Electronics, a $400 million Houston-based distributor with a similiar supplier line card but different customer base.

In addition, customers and suppliers want to do global business faster and more efficiently. In response to that, in 1998 we also added alliances in Israel and Southeast Asia to our existing partnerships in continental Europe, Scandinavia, and the United Kingdom. Then we created a uniform brand, The Global Connection: six different companies with facilities in thirty-six different countries, all sharing the same logo and mission, all wired together in a seamless $3 billion Y2K-designed technology infrastructure that blankets the planet.

Acquisitions are easy financially. Everybody knows his or her role: the lawyers do their work, then you sign the contract and put it in a file. It was relatively simple to switch Sterling to Marshall's information-technology (IT) infrastructure, too, given our experience in changing Marshall's own operating system. We cut over in a day, the day after we signed the deal. The hard part was creating the cultural connection, adding Marshall's system strengths to Sterling's operation without crushing the entrepreneurial drive and individual commitment to performance that made them so attractive in the first place.

Alliances are harder to orchestrate than acquisitions, particularly when they stretch across several different languages and cultures.

While everybody wants to do a deal, the challenge is finding entre-preneurial partners who understand our larger purpose, share our standards, and can add their own energy and local marketplace per-spective to our common search for global customer solutions.

The initial contracts specifying how an alliance's joint operations will work are far more detailed and complex than any buy/sell agreement. But, as soon as the terms are worked out, the rules of engagement can be put directly into the shared technology infra-structure—and managed by exception. What's hard, once again, is finding a cultural connection beyond financial investment and mu-tual board representation. The answer, in our case, was the Marshall mission, now shared throughout our alliance: "Serve our business partners by adding value with a commitment to continuous im-provement, innovation, and mutual satisfaction."

The day that we launched The Global Connection was one of the most emotional in my career. There were some twenty of us, con-vened on a sunny spring day in Seville, Spain, each with a different homeland and background. One by one, we all got up and trans-lated the mission statement into our native tongues, then explained what it meant professionally and personally. Sharing the mission added a critical human connection to our IT integration; it tied us together as if it were a rope we could all keep hold of to stay aligned, no matter what might come.

The Global Connection pointed us toward the future, too, and another learning curve that we will have to climb. As competition continues to accelerate, our growth will increasingly depend on our ability to reach outside Marshall itself and collaborate with new al-lies and partners as we seek new ways to take time and work out of the supply chain. We'll need new skills in coordination, standardiza-tion, and compromise in order to leverage our existing human and technology strengths, whether through short-term joint ventures or long-term partnerships, acquisitions, or alliances. Eventually, the future of every discipline involved in getting products to market—demand creation, design, engineering, forecasting, production, marketing, sales, distribution, and customer service—may be tied less to individual companies than to a group of companies, a consortium working together to speed communication and develop standards and protocols.

That future is already coming to the electronics industry, with organizations like RosettaNet, which concentrates on developing common IT operating standards, and CommerceNet, which focuses on making electronic commerce easy, trusted, and ubiquitous. Traditional trade organizations like the National Electronics Distributors Association (NEDA) will always have their place, but their membership is exclusive: with NEDA, for example, suppliers, freight forwarders, or Internet companies cannot apply. Consortiums, on the other hand, are inclusive. RosettaNet, for one, links Marshall to twenty-seven other partners, including manufacturers, distributors, resellers, financiers, suppliers, software publishers, and end users, all focused on a similar system perspective: looking to tear down performance barriers in the larger global processes.

Consortiums are an industry response to an industry problem, however. There is another, more dramatic change just around the corner that will reach far beyond our industry, with consequences that no one can predict.

Remember all those stories about the house of the future, the one with smart appliances in the kitchen and smart cars in the garage, each with its own powerful embedded chip, all networked together? "Ubiquitous computing," the forecasters called it, and predicted its arrival for sometime around 2015.

Well, the forecasters were wrong. The first signs of ubiquitous computing will show up beneath Christmas trees on December 25, 1999, in the form of cell phones, PC peripherals, digital cameras, and digital TV, all capable of communicating with each other via the Web using Jini, a new software platform based on Sun Microsystems's Java programming language.

The specific consumer products really don't matter much, except to the thirty different manufacturers involved. Most will be obsolete in months, replaced by a second and third generation that is cheaper, more powerful, and easier to use. Nor does Jini necessarily herald the imminent demise of the Windows desktop operating system—

although Microsoft, just to be sure, is working on its own platform, which they call Millennium.

What matters is what Jini and Millennium and their ilk represent. Computing technology is about to take its third evolutionary step, away from the self-sufficient individual machine with its own operating system, memory, programs, and processing power, toward distributed computing, in which everything is housed in the network, waiting until it is needed. When that happens, the world in which we live and work will never be the same.

Technologies evolve to meet changing organizational needs, but as they change, they change our organizations, too. Mainframes reflected and supported the post–World War II military-style hierarchy: one giant machine with many users. Then, as business became faster and more complex, mainframes couldn't keep up. So, in the mid-1980s, primacy passed to the PC: one person to one computer.

PCs reflected how businesses were reorganizing in that they supported a flatter, decentralized structure and pushed that decentralization forward. Today, though, as the Internet emerges as technology's driving force, connectivity is becoming more important than computing itself. Primacy is passing to the network, to one person, many computers. In this third era, computers will cooperate without a main host, exchanging messages and data without any central master. The network itself will become a metacomputer of sorts, dividing tasks into many small parts, with millions of small programs each executed by different machines, putting the processing power of a supercomputer in the hands of anyone who needs it.

What might the world of distributed computing look like?

Imagine all of our time bombs exploding together.

Today, there are millions of Web pages, hundreds of thousands of hosts, hundreds of millions of users, all screaming out for attention. What will the next generation bring, when all those thousands and millions can communicate directly? How will we grab and focus our customers' attention then? Will marketing eclipse finance as the driving engine of strategy?

Think about how difficult it is to coordinate our outsourced organizations today, what with employees telecommuting and suppliers and partners scattered around the globe. What will our organizations look like in three years, with everything connected seamlessly and bandwidth tripling every year? Will managers still work at a desk in an office? Will salespeople still knock on doors and wait in lobbies? What if those doors and lobbies don't exist anymore? What kind of connections will we need, and how will we coordinate them? What kind of organizational structures will we need to support those new connections?

Information is already becoming our world's most highly prized asset. In the future, will our old bricks and mortar have any value at all? When customers can take just what they need from the network and distribute it as they choose, will they be willing to pay for our infrastructure and overhead? Can we survive by fighting the network's capabilities, or will we have to redesign our businesses to augment and enhance them?

Organizational value will still lie in organizational values, just as it does today. But everything else will be up for grabs. Tomorrow will be even more demanding, exciting, frustrating, and risk-filled than today is. We will have to be leaner and more nimble, flexible, responsive, and courageous. There will be no rules for survival in the new millennium, except to keep your eyes open and embrace what's next.

Even as I contemplated all of this change, I'd always assumed that there would be one constant: no matter what the future might bring, we could always steer our course by the customer imperative we have targeted from the start of our six-year experiment in change: free, perfect, and now. Then a customer who was visiting Marshall pulled me up short.

"You don't get it yet, Rob," he insisted. "It's free and perfect, but . . ." Then he crossed out "now" and wrote in "yesterday."

He was joking—sort of. But he reminded me of the great truth of business, whether yesterday, today, or tomorrow. No matter what we do, our customers will always want more. There is no security in this emerging interconnected and ultracompetitive universe except our own creativity and resourcefulness. We will either find new ways to meet our customers' individual demands, or we will lose them to competitors who can.

That's why I still lie awake at night, worrying that someone could come along and eat my lunch.

There is still no pill that we can take to stay ahead of the curve, not in this book, and not in this world. The minimum requirements for survival keep growing. There will always be more to learn. Alignment with the needs of the marketplace is a journey, not a destination, and our path will be changed by forces we can't control in ways we can't predict.

Some journey, right? I lie awake worrying in the first chapter and I lie awake worrying in the last chapter.

But I don't worry about the same things that I worried about six years ago. Today, while we can't predict the future at Marshall, we can prepare for it by responding to the new and knowing that Marshall's systems won't hold us back. Our old performance barriers are gone; our infrastructure is flexible and fluid. Our culture and technology are open, collaborative, and innovative, and we're learning to listen to the market, to look around corners and question what we see, then leverage what we're learning. We are becoming our customers' connection with tomorrow, connecting people to people, people to technology, and products to market. We provide answers to questions, solutions to problems, and order to chaos. By any method. From anyplace. At any time. Because that is what the world demands.

Acknowledgments

This book, like everything else involving our ongoing experiment in change at Marshall Industries, has drawn on the creativity, dedication, and enthusiasm of the entire Marshall team. Without their collective efforts, there would be no story to tell. Special thanks are due to Jacob Kuryan, for his insights into our changing industry and market; Les Jones, who helped shape Marshall's culture of curiosity; Kerry Young, who continues to stretch our sense of technological possibility; and Henry Chin and Rita Megling, for their leadership, hard work, and commitment. Thanks to Michael Tveite, who first told me that "data is like garbage." I am also deeply grateful to Lorraine Robles, who brings order to my day; Frank Clemente, who made the El Monte–to-Boston connection work smoothly; and Barrett Duff, who keeps me connected to the world. Particular thanks are due additionally to the late Dr. Deming, whose insights live in our company today. I would also like to thank my parents, brother, the Obot family, and my friends for their ever-present support.

Fred Hills, who championed the project from the start, has been the kind of editor most writers only dream of. Supportive and insightful, patient and demanding, he brought rigor and clarity to the project. Thanks, too, go to Carolyn Reidy, president of Simon & Schuster's trade division, for her early and ongoing support, as well as to David Rosenthal, publisher; Annik LaFarge, associate publisher; Lawrence Norton, director of sales; and Victoria Meyer, director of publicity.

We owe a particular debt of gratitude to E. J. Kahn III, who first suggested the collaborative pairing that led to this book, and to Bill Taylor and Alan Webber, founding editors of *Fast Company*, who assigned the article that led to the initial proposal. Cheryl Dahle, along with Claire Greene and Randi Purchia, provided extraordinary research help. Terry Moran fact-checked the initial manuscript, while Pat Wright did the copyediting. Ron Sweet did the illustrations for the graphics. And special thanks are due to Anne Hartman, CEO of Career Investment Strategies, for her patience and encouragement during the months of early mornings and working weekends while this book was being written.